W9-BMH-779

The KidChat Series

KidChat
KidChat Too!
KidChat Gone Wild!
KidChat Oh, the Places to Go!

The Question Guys™

Kid Chat
Gone Wild!

**202 Creative Questions
to Unleash the Imagination**

Bret Nicholaus and Paul Lowrie

A Deborah Brodie Book   ROARING BROOK PRESS * New York

To Grant and Luke
Love, Dad

Text copyright © 2007 Bret Nicholaus and Paul Lowrie

A Deborah Brodie Book
Published by Roaring Brook Press
Roaring Brook Press is a division of Holtzbrinck Publishing Holdings Limited Partnership
175 Fifth Avenue, New York, NY 10010

Distributed in Canada by H. B. Fenn and Company, Ltd.

Library of Congress Cataloging-in-Publication Data

Nicholaus, Bret.
Kidchat gone wild! : 202 creative questions to unleash the imagination / Bret Nicholaus and Paul Lowrie,
The Question Guys. — 1st ed.
   p.   cm.
"A Deborah Brodie Book."
ISBN-13: 978-1-59643-316-8
ISBN-10: 1-59643-316-7
1. Children's questions and answers. 2. Animals—Juvenile literature.
3. Curiosities and wonders—Juvenile literature. 4. Creative thinking in children.
I. Lowrie, Paul. II. Title.
AG195.N533 2007
031.02—dc22
2007010984

10 9 8 7 6 5 4 3 2 1

Roaring Brook Press books are available for special promotions and premiums.
For details, contact: Director of Special Markets, Holtzbrinck Publishers.

Book design by Míkael Vilhjálmsson
Printed in the United States of America
First edition October 2007

welcome again!

Hello again, and welcome to another exciting collection of
KidChat questions, written to get kids thinking creatively and
talking enthusiastically. This time around we have focused on a
specific topic that kids love to talk about—animals! From Africa
to Antarctica, dinosaurs to dogs, sea creatures to land animals,
these "wild" questions cover it all! In addition, we've introduced
a brand-new element to this book: trivia. Many of the questions
in this book begin with a fascinating animal fact, and the question
itself ties into that particular piece of trivia. As a result, kids not
only learn how to think, talk, and write more creatively, they also
learn about the animal kingdom along the way.

Since there is no specific order to the questions, kids can open
the book to any one of the 200-plus questions and start right
there. Sometimes they might go through three or four questions
in a few minutes; at other times one question will lead to a
15-minute dialogue. There is no way to predict where these
thought-provoking, fun questions will lead; in fact, a question
might be answered one way today and completely differently
tomorrow!

Regardless of whether this book is used in the car, in the classroom, or while sitting on the couch with friends or family members, kids will have a blast providing their own unique answers to these entertaining questions. And as for all of you adults out there, don't be surprised if you end up enjoying the book as much as kids do—after all, the thrill and freedom of creativity knows no age limit!

Happy answering!

Bret Nicholaus and Paul Lowrie, The Question Guys™

SPECIAL NOTE

Every 15 questions or so, kids will notice a heading that says "IMAGINATION IGNITER." These words indicate that the question below it is specially designed to stimulate very creative thinking and the full-blown use of their imaginations.

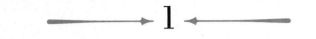

1

Talk about large crowds! Every year roughly 2 million wildebeest, zebras, gazelles, and other hoofed animals gather together on Africa's famous Serengeti plains at the start of their annual migration.

WHAT IS THE largest crowd you've ever been a part of? Did you feel comfortable in such a large group? Why or why not?

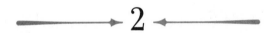

2

IF YOU HAD TO choose between having spots or stripes, which pattern would you choose? Why?

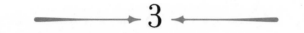

3

While hunting for food, cheetahs have been known to run 70 miles per hour over short distances.

IF YOU HAD THE super speed of a cheetah, how could you use it to help yourself and others?

4

IF YOU WERE AN animal, would you rather be small but very fast or large but very slow? Why?

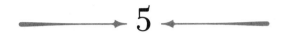

5

Each species of butterfly has its own unique wing pattern.

IF YOU COULD design the wing pattern for a new species of butterfly, what would it look like (colors, pattern, size, etc.)?

6

Some animals live in trees, some live underground, some live in the water.

IF YOU COULD live in anything at all besides a house or an apartment, what would you want to live in?

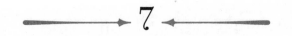

7

A pregnant female polar bear can go without eating for up to 8 months, staying alive on her body's built-up fat.

HOW LONG DO YOU think you could go without eating any food? What is the longest you can remember going without eating anything?

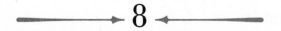

8

IF YOU COULD have the tail of any animal in the world, which one would you want? Why?

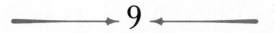

9

Koalas sleep 18 hours a day! (When they're not sleeping, they're eating eucalyptus leaves up in the trees.)

WHAT IS THE longest you've ever slept at one time?

DO YOU THINK IT would be fun to sleep 18 hours a day? Why or why not?

Every type of perching bird (a bird with feet that can wrap around something) in the world has its own unique song.

IF YOU HAD TO pick one song to sing that would be your very own song, which one would it be?

SUPPOSE YOU could have a live bird sit outside your window each morning and wake you with its unique sound. Which of the following 7 birds would you choose as your real live alarm clock: crow, duck, mourning dove, owl, rooster, seagull, or woodpecker?

The hedgehog whistles nonstop while searching for food.

WHAT ARE SOME of your unusual eating habits?

IMAGINATION IGNITER

→ 14 ←

More animals live in the ocean than in any other habitat in the world—after all, water covers about 70 percent of Earth's surface.

IF YOU COULD BE a marine biologist and spend your life studying one type of marine animal, which one would you choose? Why?

15

Dromedary camels have 1 hump; Bactrian camels have 2 humps. (It's easy to remember which is which: A D turned on its side looks like one hump; a B turned on its side looks like two humps.)

IF YOU WERE A camel, would you rather have one hump or two humps? Why?

16

IF YOU COULD DO anything at all to a typical zoo to make it more fun and exciting to visit, what changes would you make?

17

The longest earthworm on record was 11 feet long (21 feet when its body was stretched out)!

WHAT IS THE most unusual-looking or strangest creature that you've ever discovered on your own?

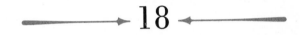 18

IF YOU COULD teach a monkey to do any trick at all, what would you teach the playful primate to do?

 19

Of all the foods they devour, raccoons are especially fond of sweet corn.

Which vegetable is your favorite to eat?

→ 20 ←

IF YOU COULD create a brand-new animal, what would it look like, what would it do, and what would you name it?

→ 21 ←

A healthy dairy cow produces 30,000 glasses of milk per year.

IF a KID DrInKS 4 glasses of milk each day, how many kids would get their fill of milk in one year from one cow?

22

IF YOU HAD TO create an alarm clock that used the sound of a farm animal to wake people in the morning, what sound would you choose?

23

After leaping out of the water, the spinner dolphin can spin up to 7 times in midair! (That's how it gets its name.)

IF YOU COULD teach a dolphin to do any unusual trick, what would it be?

24

IF YOU WERE ABLE to swim with a dolphin, would you do it? Why or why not?

25

At just 1 inch long and weighing only 2 grams, the bumblebee bat is one of the world's smallest mammals.

IF YOU WERE ONLY 1 inch tall, what are some things you would want to do and places you would want to explore?

26

IF YOU WERE A zookeeper, what animal would you most want to take care of?

27

A male lion can eat about 65 pounds of meat in one meal.

CAN YOU FIGURE out how many quarter-pound hamburgers this would equal?

28

WHAT ANIMAL would you like to know the most about?

Imagination Igniter

Groups of Adélie penguins waddle more than 300 miles across the Antarctic ice every year to reach their nesting grounds (that's where they lay and hatch their eggs and raise their young).

IF YOU HAD TO GO on a 300-mile walk, which two people would you invite to keep you company on your long journey and why? (No fair taking your parents along.)

—→ 30 ←—

WOULD YOU rather be an animal that flies or an animal that swims? Why?

—→ 31 ←—

Rhinos have very poor eyesight, but they have excellent hearing.

In your opinion, would it be more difficult for you to go through life with very poor eyesight or very poor hearing? Why?

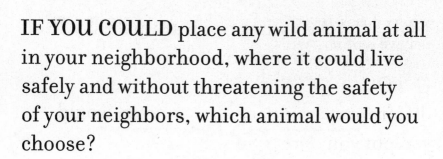

32

IF YOU COULD place any wild animal at all in your neighborhood, where it could live safely and without threatening the safety of your neighbors, which animal would you choose?

33

The warthog has to be one of the ugliest animals on Earth.

IN YOUR OPINION, which is the ugliest animal of all?

34

WHICH DO YOU think is the most beautiful animal?

35

Where does a long-horned grasshopper have its ears? Believe it or not, on its legs!

IF YOU COULD move your ears to a different part of your body, where would you put your ears and why?

36

IT'S ALWAYS FUN to try and make the sounds of different animals. What animal sound do you think you can imitate best of all?

Vets recommend that dogs be given a bath in tomato juice . . . if they've been sprayed by a skunk!

IF YOU COULD take a bath in any liquid other than water just for fun, which one would you choose?

IF YOU COULD take a skunk's bad-smelling spray and make it smell like something that most people like, what would you choose as the spray's new scent?

39

With its two coats of thick wool and outer layer of thick hair, the Arctic musk ox can survive in temperatures that approach −100 degrees Fahrenheit!

IF YOU HAD TO choose between two extremes, would you rather live where it's very cold (like the Arctic) or very hot (like the Sahara Desert)? Why?

40

IF YOU COULD take a 10-minute ride on any animal—and be safe during the entire ride—which animal would you choose?

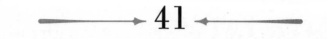

41

Like all reptiles, alligators and crocodiles are cold-blooded. This means that they can't regulate their own body temperature and have to lie still and soak in the warmth of the sun. Without this heat, they couldn't move or hunt, and they would die.

IF YOU COULD BE fully energized by doing one particular thing, what would you want to do?

42

THINK ABOUT ALL of the professional football teams that are named after animals (you'll be amazed at how many there are!).

If you were in charge of choosing an animal name for a new football team in your town, which one would you pick?

 43

In the wild, lemurs live only on the island of Madagascar, which is about 250 miles from the African mainland.

IF YOU HAD TO live on an island for the rest of your life, where would you want this island to be located? If you could give the island a name, what would you call it?

IMAGINATION IGNITER

→ 44 ←

IF YOU HaD TO take the head of one animal, the legs of another, the body of a third, and the tail of a fourth, which four animals would you combine to make your new creature?

45

A tiger will roam as far as 30 miles in one day to search for its food!

WHAT IS YOUR favorite restaurant, and how far would you be willing to travel to eat there?

46

WHEN IT COMES to naming a continent associated with wild animals, many kids and adults think of Africa. But suppose you had to study the wildlife of one of the other six continents (Antarctica, Asia, Australia, Europe, North America, South America). Which continent would you choose?

47

The rhinoceros beetle can carry an object that's 850 times its own weight, which is like a person carrying a 50-ton army tank!

IF YOU WERE ABLE to carry something that is 850 times your weight, what would you like to carry?

48

There are more than one million species of insects that have been identified.

IF YOU HAD TO BE an insect for one day, which insect would you be and why?

49

Dolphins "talk" to one another through high-pitched whistles and clicks called phonations.

IF YOU COULD talk with your friends using a form of communication that did not require words, how would you want to communicate?

50

IF YOU COULD add wings to any ocean-dwelling animal, what sea creature would you want to watch fly through the air?

Around the year 1800, as many as 70 million bison roamed the Great Plains of the United States. Primarily due to hunting, that number was reduced to fewer than 1,000 by the year 1900!

IMAGINE THAT you were a pioneer. How would you have felt or reacted as your covered wagon rumbled over a hill and you suddenly saw thousands and thousands of bison in front of you?

→ 52 ←

Each year, the Arctic tern migrates farther than any other bird: it flies more than 20,000 miles from the Arctic to the Antarctic and then back again!

IF YOU HAD TO fly back and forth between two spots every year (spending half of the year in one location and half in another), which two places would you choose?

→ 53 ←

IF YOU COULD have wings like a bird for just one day, what do you think would be the most awesome thing to fly over?

54

A giraffe is the tallest animal in the world: it can grow to a height of 20 feet!

IF YOU COULD BE 20 feet tall for one week, what are some activities you would want to try while you had this incredible height?

55

WHAT IF A COW had stripes and a zebra had spots? What if an elephant had colorful feathers and a parrot had rough, wrinkly gray skin? If you could take the coats or coverings of any two animals in the world and switch them, which two would you choose?

A sloth's fur grows in the opposite direction to that of most animals. Why? Remember that a sloth spends most of its life hanging upside down. With fur that grows from the stomach to the back, the water will run off the sloth's body when it rains!

IF YOU DIDN'T have to worry about getting dizzy, do you think it would be fun to go through life hanging upside down? Why or why not?

57

In your opinion, what animal lives the most boring life of all? Which animal do you think has the most exciting or adventurous life?

58

Most spiders have 8 eyes (although, ironically, they have very poor eyesight).

IF YOU COULD have 8 of any one of the following, which would you choose: ear, eye, mouth, or nose? Why?

Imagination Igniter

WHAT IF DOGS oinked or lions quacked? What if parrots meowed or giraffes mooed? If you could give the sound that one animal makes to a different type of animal, what animal sound would you switch?

— 60 —

The black coloration around a raccoon's eyes looks just like a mask!

IF YOU HAD TO wear a mask every day, what would you want your mask to look like?

— 61 —

IF YOU HAD TO choose an animal that best describes your personality, which animal would you choose?

62

Hyenas are known for making a noise that sounds as though they are laughing!

OF ALL THE people you know, both adults and kids, who has the funniest-sounding laugh?

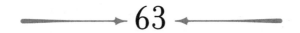

63

IF YOU WERE IN charge of writing a children's story with an animal as the main character, what animal would you choose, what would you name the animal, and what would you title your book?

— 64 —

For an animal that can weigh more than 10,000 pounds, elephants are extremely good swimmers: they have been observed swimming more than 6 miles without stopping!

WHAT IS ONE talent you have that few people know about, or something you can do that might surprise others?

— 65 —

IF SOMEONE GAVE you an elephant as a pet, what would you name it?

— → 66 ← —

Unlike most other fish, sharks have skeletons made up of rubbery cartilage rather than bones.

IF YOU DIDN'T have any bones in your body—and so didn't have to worry about breaking any of them—what activity or stunt would you try that you otherwise wouldn't?

— → 67 ← —

IF YOU WERE A fish, what type of bait would a fisherman want to use to get you to swim over and nibble on the line?

68

Anteaters have no teeth, so they must rely on their long tongues to lap up food such as termites.

IF YOU COULDN'T chew anything because you had no teeth, what type of food would you most want to eat that only requires the use of your tongue?

69

IF YOU COULD BE famous for doing or achieving something that relates to animals, what would you want to be known for?

Cats have an unusual ability—they can jump off very high objects and land safely on their 4 feet.

IF YOU COULD jump off any extremely high object knowing that you would land safely, what would you want to jump off?

WHAT IS YOUR all-time-favorite animal-themed movie?

Young burrowing owls keep away predators by doing a great job of pretending. When it is threatened, an owlet will make a hissing sound that fools its enemy into believing that there is a dangerous rattlesnake inside the burrow.

WHICH PErson DO you like to pretend to be? What is your favorite thing of all to pretend when you are playing?

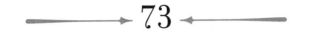

73

Animals live and thrive in all sorts of different habitats.

IF YOU HAD TO choose one of these habitats to live in—cave, desert, forest, jungle, mountain, ocean, or swamp—which one would you pick and why?

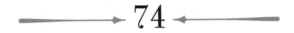

74

Beavers build their homes from twigs; bees build their homes from beeswax.

IF YOU COULD build a house for yourself out of any unusual materials, which would you use?

IMAGINATION IGNITER

→ 75 ←

Animals do not need to be taught how to do most things; they know how to do them instinctively. For example, a bird is born knowing how to build a nest; a fish is born knowing how to swim; a spider is born knowing how to spin a web.

IF YOU COULD have been born knowing how to do one particular thing, and do it really well right from the start, what would it be?

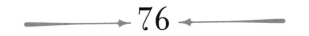

In wintertime, when they have their thick coats of hair, moose actually feel hot if the temperature reaches a whopping 20 degrees Fahrenheit!

HOW HIGH DOES the temperature have to be before you start to feel hot? What are your favorite things to do in hot weather? What are your favorite things to do in cold weather?

IN YOUR OPINION, which U.S. state has the most interesting wild animal?

78

About 1,000 bees must work their entire lives to produce just 1 pound of honey!

WHAT IS ONE thing that you work really hard to be good at? Do you think that when you're older you'll look back and think that all of that hard work was worth it? Why or why not?

79

IF YOU HAD THE ability to do something that only animals can do (for example, be able to change the color of your body like a chameleon), what animal "skill" would you want to have?

Rats can be really good at solving problems. They have been known to kick traps around until the traps are sprung so that they can safely grab the bait and nibble away.

WHAT IS THE biggest problem you've ever solved? What was the key to solving it?

81

Did you know that Mickey Mouse, the most famous mouse in the world, was almost named Mortimer? (Thank goodness Walt Disney took his wife's advice about changing the name!)

IF YOU HAD TO think up the name for a brand-new animated animal character that would be the star of a new movie, what name would you choose?

82

A camel can go for months at a time without drinking one drop of water. When it finally does take a drink, a camel can easily drink more than 30 gallons of water in just a few minutes!

IF YOU COULD drink 30 gallons of something at one time knowing that you would not get sick from it, what would you want to drink?

→ 83 ←

WHAT IS YOUR all-time-favorite animal joke?

→ 84 ←

Parrots can mimic human voices—and have been known to have vocabularies of more than 300 words!

IF YOU GOT a parrot for a pet, what are 10 words that you would be sure to teach it to say?

→ 85 ←

IF YOU COULD have any bird in the world as a pet, which one would you want?

→ 86 ←

A walrus's tusk, which is actually a tooth, can be as long as 3 feet and weigh 12 pounds!

IF YOU COULD bring the tooth of any animal in the world to a show-and-tell, which animal's tooth would you bring?

87

IF YOU WERE A dentist, which animal's teeth would you definitely not look forward to cleaning?

88

Most experts agree that hippos are Africa's most dangerous animals. Each year, hippos kill more people than lions or crocodiles.

IN YOUR OPINION, what is the scariest animal in the world?

IMAGINATION IGNITER

→ 89 ←

WHAT ANIMAL DO you think best symbolizes peace? Happiness? Frustration? Anger?

Bad news for a honeybee: when it stings someone and tries to pull its stinger out of the person's flesh, the stinger is torn out of the honeybee's body and the bee dies.

OF ALL THE things that you own, which would be the hardest to give away or lose forever?

WHAT IS YOUR all-time-favorite song about an animal?

92

The orangutan absolutely loves to eat: it can spend half a day just sitting in a fruit tree eating.

IF YOU COULD plant any fruit tree in your yard, and you could eat from it whenever you wanted, what type of tree would you plant?

93

IF A TOY COMPANY asked you what type of stuffed animal it should make to give away to thousands of needy children, what animal would you ask the company to use as its model for the stuffed toys?

94

The name *koala* means "no drink;" the name *elephant* means "ivory."

DO YOU KNOW what your name means? If you could make up the meaning of your name, what would you want it to mean?

95

IF YOU ASKED 20 people what their favorite wild animal was, which animal do you think would be the most popular? Now, why don't you really ask 20 people and find out? And don't forget to ask them why that particular animal is their favorite!

Domestic cattle don't sleep very long—only 8 minutes at a time, and they never sleep more than 60 minutes total over a 24-hour period.

IF YOU COULD DO your sleeping only 8 minutes at a time (rather than for 8 hours at a time), do you think you would rather do it that way? Why or why not?

The silo on a farm is most often used to store food that will be used to feed the farm's animals.

IF YOU COULD have your very own silo so that you could keep a HUGE supply of any one thing you wanted, what would you store in it?

 98

Fireflies, or lightning bugs, make two special chemicals in their bodies which, when mixed with oxygen, create the yellowish light that we see at night.

IF YOU COULD change a firefly's light from yellow to a different color, which color do you think would be really cool to see a firefly make?

SOME ZOOS HAVE little trains that take visitors throughout the zoo to see many of the animals without having to walk all around. If a new zoo asked you to come up with a name for the zoo train, what name would you choose?

An octopus has 3 hearts, but that's still 5 fewer than the number of arms it has—8!

IF YOU HAD 8 arms and could do up to 8 different things at the same time,

what types of things would you most enjoy doing all at once? (Keep in mind that you may need 2 arms to do certain things, so you may be able to choose fewer than 8 things total!)

—→ 101 ←—

IF YOU COULD open a brand-new aquarium or aquatic park, what would you do to make it the most unusual and fun place ever built?

An impala can jump more than 8 feet high and 30 feet long in a single leap!

HOW MANY jumps would it take an impala to go from one end of a football field to the other? (Remember that an official football field is 100 yards long.)

IF YOU HAD A choice, would you rather hop as fast as a kangaroo (which can jump up to 40 miles per hour and leap more than 25 feet) or swim as fast as a swordfish (which can swim up to 60 miles per hour)? Why?

IMAGINATION IGNITER

→ 104 ←

The nine-banded armadillo always gives birth to four identical offspring (babies that look exactly alike) at a time.

IN YOUR OPINION, what would be the best part of having three identical siblings? What would be the worst part?

105

After baby chickadees hatch, the parent bird may make as many as 40 trips a day per baby to bring them food!

HOW many different things can you think of that your parents do for you because they love you?

106

IF YOU HAD TO spend an entire year in a U.S. national park observing and researching one of the animals that lives there, which national park and which of its animal inhabitants would you choose?

107

Elephants can live to be more than 60 years old!

WHAT DO YOU imagine you will be doing when you are that old? What do you think you will look like at that age?

108

IF YOU HAD TO come up with a new circus act that involved animals, what would it be?

109

Adult gorillas sleep in a new nest every night.

IF YOU COULD sleep in a different location each night for a week, what seven places would you choose? (The locations can be anywhere, no matter how far apart they are.)

110

IF YOU COULD PUT any four types of animals in the world on one small island, knowing that they would live peacefully together, what four animals would you choose?

About 30 years ago there were so few American alligators that the species was placed on the endangered species list. (This is a list of the animal species that are in danger of disappearing from the earth forever.) Being on this list meant that it was illegal for alligators to be hunted. Now there are so many alligators in parts of the South that some hunting is allowed in order to control their numbers.

IF YOU COULD guarantee that any one animal would never, ever become endangered, which one would you pick?

112

IF YOU COULD make one change in your favorite animal, what would it be? (For example, if your favorite animal is a lion, you could decide to give it an all-white mane.)

113

The duck-billed platypus and the spiny anteater are unique among the 4,250 or so known species of mammals: they are the only two warm-blooded animals that do not give birth to live young. These two mammals lay eggs instead!

WHAT IS something you do that makes you very unique among all of your friends and family members?

— → 114 ←

IF YOU COULD invite an animal expert to come to your school and talk to everybody, what type of animal expert would you invite? What question would you be sure to ask that person at the end of the presentation?

— → 115 ←

Hippos spend most of their time in water—about 19 hours a day. (When they're out of the water, their skin dries out quickly and begins to crack.)

IF YOU HAD TO spend most of your time in water, where would you want to be?

— 116 —

IF YOU COULD tame (and potty train!) any wild animal and keep it as a pet in your house, which animal would you choose?

— 117 —

Talk about extremes: the bee hummingbird is the smallest bird in the world—it's just 2 inches long, including its bill. The ostrich is the world's biggest bird—a male ostrich can grow up to 9 feet tall and weigh about 280 pounds!

IF YOU COULD have either the bee hummingbird or the ostrich as a pet, which bird would you choose? Why?

imagination igniter

---→ 118 ←---

IF YOU COULD plan an animal Olympics, where various animals representing different countries would get together and compete, where would you hold it, what events would you include, and which animals would you choose as competitors?

→ 119 ←

Blue whales are the heaviest animals in the world;
the heaviest one on record weighed about 190 tons
(380,000 pounds!).

HOW MUCH DO you weigh? How many of
you would it take to equal the weight of that
190-ton blue whale?

→ 120 ←

WHAT IS THE largest animal you have
ever seen in the wild (that is, not in a zoo
or an animal park)? What is the most
dangerous animal you have ever seen in its
natural habitat?

Black bears love honey—so much so that they are willing to endure lots of bee stings to get at it!

WHAT ARE SOME things in your own life that require pain, practice, or perseverance but are worth it to you because of the rewards they reap? (For example, getting good at a sport often requires some pain and perseverance; doing well on tests may require that you persevere and study hard; and excelling at a musical instrument requires practice and perseverance.)

122

IF YOU HAD TO spend the next 12 months observing the animals native to one of the 50 states, in which state would you want to live?

123

When diving through the air to catch prey, a peregrine falcon can reach a speed of 220 miles per hour!

AT THAT SPEED, how many miles would the peregrine falcon dive in just 60 seconds?

124

IF YOU HAD TO pick an animal other than

the eagle to appear on the back of a quarter as a symbol of the United States, which one would you choose? Why?

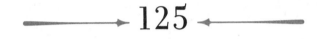

125

An adult elephant eats approximately 75 tons of vegetation each year!

HOW many pounds of vegetation does this mean an adult elephant eats every day? (To get your answer, find out how many pounds there are in a ton, multiply that number by 75, and divide that by the total number of days in a year.)

126

Many zoo animals have a favorite toy in their exhibit—and they often play with it throughout their entire life.

IF YOU COULD have just one toy to play with for the rest of your life, which one would you choose? (It can be a toy that you own now or one that you'd like to have.)

127

The termites that live in Africa build huge, rock-hard mounds made from soil and saliva that can be 19 feet high—you might call it a termite skyscraper!

IF YOU COULD build a real skyscraper, what would you do to make it really stand out from all the other buildings?

 128

IF YOU COULD choose any animal in the world to lead a parade in your hometown, which animal would be at the front of this parade?

129

Sometimes a little grain of sand gets inside the shell of an oyster and rubs against the oyster's soft body. To stop this annoying rubbing, the oyster wraps the sand in layer after layer of a shiny coating. Eventually the grain of sand is wrapped in so many layers that a little ball forms. That ball is a pearl!

WHAT IS ONE thing that really annoys you? What are some things that you do that other people might find annoying?

130

HOW WELL DO YOU really know the animal kingdom? Ask a friend to time you for 5 minutes and see how many different

types of animals you can write down on a piece of paper. (It's okay to list different members of the same animal family, such as a black bear and a grizzly bear.)

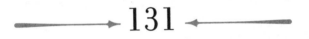 131

Very few types of animals have both miniature and full-sized versions of themselves, but the hippo is an exception. A full-grown Nile hippo can stand 5½ feet tall and weigh up to 8,000 pounds, while a full-grown pygmy hippo is only 2 to 3 feet tall and weighs no more than 550 pounds!

IF YOU COULD create a miniature version of any full-sized animal in the world, which one would you pick?

IMAGINATION IGNITER

→ 132 ←

IF YOU WERE AN animal, would you rather be someone's pet or live in the wild, where you would be totally free? What would be the advantages and disadvantages of each situation?

133

Brown County, Wisconsin, has 76 cows per square mile—more cows per square mile than any other county in the United States!

IF YOUR COUNTY had more of something than any other place in the United States, what would you want it to be? (For example, more playgrounds than anywhere else.)

134

IF YOU LIVED ON A farm and could have one farm animal as a pet, which one would you choose?

→ 135 ←

SOME ZOOS HOST birthday parties for their popular or long-living animals. If you had to organize a birthday party for a zoo animal, which one would be the most fun to plan a party for? What things would you do to make the day memorable for both that animal and the visitors who attend the party?

→ 136 ←

IF YOU WERE invited to a bear's birthday bash, what would you bring along as a gift? (Have fun, be creative—and think of something besides honey to bring!)

— 137 —

After the female emu lays her eggs, the male emu sits on the softball-sized eggs for about 2 months straight until they hatch.

IF YOU HAD TO SIT in one location for 2 months, where would you want to sit and what one thing would you want with you to pass the time?

— 138 —

WHAT WAS YOUR most interesting experience with a wild animal?

→ 139 ←

A baby kangaroo, called a joey, spends the first 6 or more months of its life safely riding around in its mother's pouch.

IF YOU COULD spend the next 6 months being carried around in something or riding on something, how would you want to travel?

→ 140 ←

IF YOU COULD float above any animal habitat in the world in a hot-air balloon, which one would you most want to observe (for example, an African savanna, the

Alaskan coastline, the Amazon River, the Arctic tundra, to name a few)?

 141

Humpback whales can weigh more than 70,000 pounds, yet they can leap out of the water, or breach, several times in a row. (The record holder is a humpback whale that was seen to breach more than 130 times in a row!)

WHAT IS YOUR favorite thing to do over and over and over again?

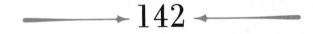 142

IN YOUR OPINION, what animal makes the most awesome sound?

→ 143 ←

A worker bee makes an average of 10 trips from its hive in one day, and on each trip it can visit as many as 800 flowers!

IF YOU WERE A BEE, what would be your favorite type of flower to visit? Why?

→ 144 ←

How can you get three animals to join you for breakfast? Simple. Just have eggs (hen), a glass of milk (cow), and a little honey (bee) on your toast!

IF YOU INVITED A bunch of friends over for the best breakfast ever (and didn't have to do the cooking and cleaning up), what would you serve them?

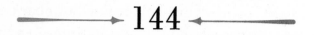

Elephants have the largest brains of any land animal, so it isn't surprising that they are very intelligent and have great memories.

WHAT IS YOUR best subject in school? Do you have any idea why you are smart in this subject?

IMAGINATION IGNITER

→ 146 ←

IT'S GREAT FOR kids to have role models—people they look up to and want to be like. If you had to choose an animal as a role model (presumably because of certain qualities it is known for), which animal would it be? Why?

147

Contrary to popular belief, wolves do not howl because the moon is full; wolves howl as a part of their daily social behavior and to communicate with other wolves.

WHAT are OTHer animal "myths" that some people believe are true?

148

IF YOU WErE a barber, which animal's hair would you definitely not look forward to cutting?

During the American Civil War (1861–1865), the 8th Regiment of the Wisconsin Volunteer Infantry had a most unusual mascot: a bald eagle named Old Abe. During battles, he soared high above the fighting. Although he received at least one battle wound, he survived the war and went on to live 15 more years in the state capitol.

IF YOU COULD pick any animal as a mascot (or a new mascot) for your school, which one would you choose? What would you name it?

CAN YOU THINK of some events in American history in which an animal played an important role?

Many animals are not only extremely large when they are born, but they can walk almost immediately afterward. For instance, giraffes weigh about 150 pounds and are nearly 6 feet tall when they are born, and they can walk on their own within 1 hour of their birth!

HOW MUCH DID you weigh when you were born? How long were you? How old were you when you started walking on your own? (If you aren't sure, ask a parent.)

→ 152 ←

IF YOU OPENED A new ice-cream parlor in your town and all the names of the ice-cream treats related to animals, what would 1— or 2, or 3—of the desserts be called? What would they be made of? (For example, Squirrel Swirl would have different types of nuts swirled into vanilla ice cream.)

→ 153 ←

When a salmon is ready to spawn (lay its eggs), it swims back to the same stream where it was born many years earlier. Swimming against the current and sometimes leaping waterfalls as high as 12 feet, the salmon can travel 1,000 miles or more to get from the ocean back to the place where its life began.

WHEN YOU ARE AN adult, do you think
you will still want to live where you do now?
Why or why not? If you end up living far
away from the place where you were born or
raised, do you think you will want to return
to visit? If so, what spots would you like to
see again?

— 154 —

WHICH ANIMAL would you pick if you
had to create a cartoon animal-monster for
a TV show?

The smallest newborn mammal in the world is the mouse opossum: it's the size of a grain of rice! Some things in this world can be right in front of us yet are so tiny that their details can be seen only through a microscope. On the other hand, things in outer space are extremely large but are so far away that they require a telescope in order to be seen.

IF YOU HAD YOUR choice, would you rather spend time looking at small things under a microscope or at big things through a telescope? Why?

156

REGARDLESS OF what it looks like when it's an adult, which animal do you think is the absolute cutest as a baby?

157

Like hornets and yellow jackets, paper wasps build nests from a paperlike material. How do they get it? They make it by chewing tiny pieces of wood and mixing it with their spit!

WHAT TWO things do you think would be really fun to mix together just to see what the combination would create?

158

IF YOU WERE ASKED to design an entire vacation resort centered around an animal theme (such as Walt Disney World has done with its Animal Kingdom Lodge), what would the theme be, and what specific details and activities would the resort feature to carry out this theme?

159

Meerkats dig and live in their own little "towns," called warrens. Some of the more complex warren systems can have 90 or so separate entrances!

IF YOU COULD HAVE the key to any door in the world—and whatever was beyond that door—which door key would you choose?

imagination igniter

Lions in a pride (a group of lions) tend to get along with one another quite well—except at mealtime! The social order says that males eat first, then cubs, and then females. But huge fights can break out over a good piece of meat, and cubs are more than willing to defend their portions of the meal against much bigger and stronger adults.

CAN YOU THINK of specific times when it's sometimes hard to get along with your siblings, your parents, and your friends? In each of these situations, why do you think you can't get along as well as you do at other times?

161

Many people have dogs as pets, but they do not allow them to jump up on the bed or the sofa, or to beg for food when the family is eating.

WHAT IS ONE thing that your parents don't allow you to do but you wish they would? Do you understand their reason for not allowing you to do it?

162

IF YOU WERE IN charge of planning a new animal-themed exhibit for a large natural-history museum, what type of exhibit would it be, and what type of educational activities

would it feature? (Remember, it's a natural-history museum, so no living animals are allowed!)

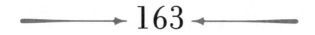 163

Trees are no obstacles for the gibbons of Southeast Asia: gibbons, a type of ape with extremely long arms, can swing between 2 trees that are 30 feet apart!

IF YOU HAD TO create a fun obstacle course for yourself and your friends, what types of challenges and obstacles would you be sure to include?

—— 164 ——

The sailfish is the fastest fish in the entire ocean—it can move through the water at speeds of more than 68 miles per hour!

IF YOU HAD A choice, what would you want to be the fastest at?

—— 165 ——

ANIMAL CRACKERS are among the most popular cookies for kids. If you could choose 8 animal shapes to use in boxes of animal crackers from now on, which animals would you pick?

Although elephants have a thick skin, the skin is actually very sensitive. To protect itself from insects, sunburn, and skin disease, elephants often roll around in mud—which dries into a thick coat of "armor."

IF YOU COULD ROLL around in anything at all just for fun, which substance would you choose?

SUPPOSE YOU WERE hired to write a fun animated animal movie featuring a boa constrictor, butterfly, giraffe, hippo, porcupine, and sloth and it was your job to give each of them a personality, voice, and name. What would the personality, voice, and name of each animal be?

— 168 —

Dogs wag their tails when they're happy.

WHAT IS something you usually do when you're feeling happy?

— 169 —

Many animal trainers use "positive reinforcement training": when the animal follows the command of its trainer, it receives a pat on the head, a rub, or a food treat of some kind; but when it ignores or disobeys a command, it is not rewarded at all.

IF YOU WERE rewarded every time you did what you were told to do, what would you want your reward to be?

The toucan is known for its huge beak. You may think the beak is heavy, but it's actually hollow and very light— the outside is made of keratin, just like your fingernails; and the inside is made of a rigid foam. Amazingly, no one seems to know for certain why the toucan's beak is so huge.

IF YOU COULD solve any mystery at all, which one would you choose?

A TRIP DOWN THE Amazon River and through the South American rain forest might give you a chance to see animals such as anacondas, crocodiles, jaguars, monkeys, piranhas, tapirs, and toucans. If you had to rank these rain forest animals from 1 to 7, with 1 being the animal you would most want to see and 7 being the animal you would least care about seeing on the trip, how would you rank them?

The American kangaroo rat is a desert animal. It may go its entire life without taking a drink of water because it gets all the moisture it needs from the food it eats and from recycling its own breath!

EVEN THOUGH you may change your mind as you grow older, what is one thing you can think of right now that you are almost certain you will never do in your lifetime?

IF YOU COULD donate $1,000 to a cause that helps animals in some way, how would you want the money to be used?

Due to the shape of their jawlines, bottle-nosed dolphins always look as if they're smiling. It's quite appropriate that they have permanent "smiles" since these dolphins really are very friendly: they often swim near boats, and they work very well with people or trainers.

WHAT CAN PUT a smile on your face faster than anything else?

IMAGINATION IGNITER

→ 175 ←

IF YOU WERE A dog and got a human as a pet, what would you name your person-pet?

If conditions are bad (for example, if it's too cold or too dry), a snail can seal the opening of its shell and hibernate (go into a resting state) until conditions improve!

IF YOU COULD GO to sleep tonight and wake up at some point in the future, what age would you want to be when you wake up? Why?

SUPPOSE YOU were a newspaper reporter and you just found out that your city's zoo will be getting a new animal: a polar bear. What would the headline announcing this news to the public be?

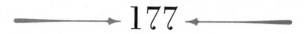

Cleaning up after large animals is probably not a zookeeper's favorite part of the job—one full-grown elephant alone can produce 88,000 or more pounds of poop (known as dung) a year!

WHAT ARE A FEW jobs that you think would be fun to have when you grow up? What are some parts of these jobs that probably wouldn't be much fun?

IF YOU COULD change the stripes on a zebra from black and white to 2 different colors, which colors would you choose?

→ 180 ←

The aardvark, an animal known for its long nose and gigantic claws, can shovel dirt as fast as a mechanical digger when it is looking for a meal or is making a home.

IF YOU WERE ABLE to do one thing that only a machine could, what would you like to be able to do?

→ 181 ←

Have you ever heard of Buffalo, Kentucky? How about Possum Kingdom, Texas; Eagle River, Wisconsin; Elk City, Idaho; or White Bear Lake, Minnesota? These are just a few of the many towns in the United States that have an animal in their name!

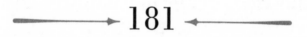

IF YOU HAD TO come up with a town name that had an animal in it, what would you call the new town?

 182

The Major Mitchell's cockatoo, which many people consider to be the most beautiful parrot in the world, was named for Sir Thomas Mitchell, an early explorer of Australia.

IF an animal were named for you, which animal would you want it to be? Would you want to use your first name or last name for the name?

→ 183 ←

IF a HEN LAID AN egg for you every morning that had something inside the shell besides an egg yolk, what would you want your special egg to contain? (For example, it could have a piece of your favorite candy.)

→ 184 ←

One way that male chimpanzees establish their status and rank is by seeing which one can make the most noise!

WHAT IS THE loudest sound you've ever heard? What is the most annoying sound you can think of? What is your favorite sound?

IN A TYPICAL national park in Africa
you can see many of that continent's most
famous animals. If you were on an African
safari in one of the national parks and were
able to see crocodiles, elephants, giraffes,
hippos, rhinos, lions, and zebras, in what
order would you rank these animals, going
from the most exciting to the least exciting
one to see?

186

Nearly 600 years ago, in 1414, China became the first country to receive a giraffe as a political gift when the African kingdom of Malindi presented the awe-inspiring animal to the emperor of China.

IF YOU HAD TO give a gift from the United States to a small, remote country far away, what would you bring that country as a gift? (No, the gift does not have to be an animal.)

187

IF YOU COULD paint or wallpaper your bedroom walls in the design of the coat or skin of a wild animal, what animal's pattern would cover your walls?

188

A giraffe's legs are so long that each walking stride is 15 feet long!

HOW LONG IS each of your strides when you walk? How many strides would it take you to equal one giraffe stride?

In Africa, many different kinds of animals gather together at bodies of water called watering holes to drink, bathe, and frolic in the water.

WHAT IS YOUR favorite spot to get together with a bunch of friends? If all of you could get together in any place in the world, where would you like everyone to meet?

IMAGINATION IGNITER

→ 190 ←

A chameleon has eyes that can move independently of each other and swivel in all directions. As a result, the chameleon can look both forward and backward at the same time!

WOULD IT BE a great help if you were able to see forward and backward at once? In what situations would this be most helpful? Why?

IF YOU COULD bring one type of dinosaur back to life, which would you choose? (Sorry, you can't pick *T. rex*!)

There are 2 basic types of elephants in the world: African elephants and Asian elephants. Here's a really easy way to tell them apart: an African elephant's ears just happen to be the same shape as Africa!

WHAT ARE SOME tricks you use in school or at home to help you remember things?

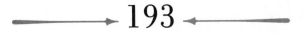 193

If a starfish is cut into 4 pieces right down the middle, each piece will eventually grow into a whole starfish!

IF YOU COULD break or cut something you own into many pieces and get whole new things, what would you most want to multiply? (For example, if you broke a toy truck into 10 pieces, you would get 10 brand-new toy trucks out of the original truck.)

194

KIDS WHO LIVE on farms usually have to help take care of the farm animals. If you lived on a farm, which animal-related chore would you absolutely not want to do?

195

How loud is a lion's roar? Loud enough so that it can sometimes be heard 10 miles away!

WHAT LANDMARK is roughly 10 miles away from your house?

WHAT ANIMAL mentioned in this book would you love to know more about?

Baby blue whales weigh roughly 4,400 pounds at birth and gain weight at an astounding rate: during the first 6 months or so of its life, a baby blue whale gains about 200 pounds per day!

AT THIS RATE, how many pounds does the whale gain each hour? How many pounds would the whale gain every month for the first 6 months?

198

Believe it or not, people in some parts of the world tie praying mantises to their beds to catch harmful and pesky insects!

IF YOU COULD have a large glass container in your bedroom to house any type of insect you wanted, which insect would you choose?

199

Hibernating animals wake themselves up from their long "sleep" by shivering violently, which makes their muscles move and gets their bodies going!

IF YOU HAD TO wake up each morning by some means other than an alarm, what creative way can you think of to get yourself moving?

————→ 200 ←————

IF YOU WERE given a square mile of land to develop or use however you wanted as long as it involved animals, what would you do with the land? (Don't worry! You'd also get as much money as you needed to fulfill your plans.)

TRY AND FIGURE out the answer to this animal riddle:

I'm 25 feet long,
and I like to hang from trees.
My name begins with an A,
and I really like to squeeze!

(The answer to this riddle can be found in question 171.)

Now it's your turn! Write a 4-line rhyming riddle about an animal (but make sure you check your facts first!).

IF YOU COULD add a fun animal question of your own to this book, what would it be?

Got a question of your own that you'd like to send us? How about giving us your answer to one or more of the questions in this book? We'd love to hear from you. Write us a letter, put it in the mail, and we'll be sure to get it . . . as long as you address it as follows:

Bret and Paul, The Question Guys™
P.O. BOX 340, YANKTON, SD 57078

ABOUT THE AUTHORS

Bret Nicholaus and Paul Lowrie have coauthored twenty books, including the national best-selling question books *The Conversation Piece* and *The Christmas Conversation Piece*. To date, the authors have written more than 3,500 questions designed to ignite creativity in adults and children. Articles about their works have appeared in numerous publications, including *Family Circle*, *Publishers Weekly*, the *Chicago Tribune*, and the *New York Post*. Their books have also been featured on *The View* and *Boy Meets World*. Bret and Paul are graduates of Bethel University, St. Paul, Minnesota, with degrees in communication and marketing, respectively. Nicholaus and his family live in the Chicago area; Lowrie resides in South Dakota. For more information about the authors or their books, please visit their Web site at www.questmarc.com.

Praise for *Things We Have in Common*

"[A] perfectly orchestrated girl-who-cried-wolf thriller.... Kavanagh's second-person narration...reveals the very thin line that separates garden-variety teenage agita from dangerous delusion.... [T]he artfulness with which [Kavanagh] deceives and manipulates is so downright creepy that one periodically finds oneself in the discomfiting posture of cheering on the bullies and the mean girls."

—*The New York Times Book Review*

"[W]ildly clever...spectacular... The conclusion underscore[s] the author's searing insight into teenage behavior and the desperation for connection."

—*Publishers Weekly*

"An unreliable narrator in the most intriguing way.... A quick, thoroughly enjoyable read."

—*Booklist*

"Kavanagh does orchestrate some successful plot twists that are reminiscent of other psychological thrillers—classics by Ruth Rendell, for example, or more recent hits like *Gone Girl*."

—*Kirkus Reviews*

"A pitch-black comedy thriller. This is a novel you read half covering your eyes, willing it not to venture where you fear it might. But of course it does, with great panache."

—*The Guardian*

"A tale of loneliness and teenage obsession which could be the next *Gone Girl* success story."

—*Independent*

"With a dark and suspenseful plot that keeps the reader guessing until the final pages...an assured debut narrated by an alarming and original voice."

—*The Irish Times*

"A striking and highly enjoyable debut."

—Sophie Hannah, *New York Times* bestselling author

"Tasha Kavanagh's Yasmin is as complex and believable a narrator as you will find. Her honesty drives the novel to its unflinching, brilliant conclusion and is why *Things We Have in Common* is so disturbing...so impossible to set aside."

—Travis Mulhauser, author of *Sweetgirl*

THINGS
WE HAVE IN
COMMON

TASHA
KAVANAGH

Kavanagh

PARK
ROW
BOOKS

Recycling programs
for this product may
not exist in your area.

ISBN-13: 978-0-7783-3033-2

Things We Have in Common

Printed in U.S.A.

$15.99
2/27/18
N.K

114285083

for my mum

THINGS

WE HAVE IN

COMMON

CHOCOLATE HOBNOBS

THE FIRST TIME I saw you, you were standing at the far end of the playing field near the bit of fence that's trampled down, where the kids who come to school along the wooded path cut across.

You were looking down at your little brown straggly dog that had its face stuck in the grass, but then you looked up in the direction of the tennis court, your mouth going slack as your eyes clocked her. Even if I hadn't followed your gaze, I'd have known you were watching Alice Taylor because she had that effect on me, too. I used to catch myself gazing at the back of her head in class, at her silky fair hair swaying between her shoulder blades as she looked from her book to the teacher or said something to Katy Ellis next to her.

At that moment she was turning to walk backward, saying something to the girls who were following her, the sketchbook she took everywhere tucked under her arm. She looked so light and easy, it was like she created space around her:

not space in the normal sense but something else I can't explain. Even in our green school uniform it was obvious she was special.

If you'd glanced just once across the field, you'd have seen me standing in the middle on my own, looking straight at you, and you'd have gone back through the trees to the path quick, tugging your dog after you. You'd have known you'd given yourself away, even if only to me.

But you didn't. You only had eyes for Alice.

I looked around to see who else had spotted you. There were loads of kids on the field, but they were all busy with each other, footballs or their phones.

I looked back at the windows of the school building. I thought I'd see a teacher behind one of them, fixed on you, like *I know* your *game, sunshine.* I saw Mr. Matthews walk past the History window reading from a piece of paper and Miss Wilcox one floor down in the staff room talking to Mrs. Henderson.

Then the bell went.

I didn't see your reaction because Robert pushed Dan into me, shouting, "He wants you, Doner—don't deny him," then staggered backward, laughing as Dan swore at him and tried to get him in a headlock.

I caught a glimpse of your blue jacket disappearing between the branches, though. The saying *Saved by the bell* came into my head because Dad always used to say it, and as I walked back across the field, I whispered the words slowly—"Saved by the bell, saved by the bell," even though I knew that you weren't saved by anything, that you'd be back.

★ ★ ★

My name's not really Doner. It's Yasmin. It's just Doner at school—which is hilarious by the way because it's short for *Doner Kebab* and as well as being overweight. I'm half Turkish. It used to be plain "Fatty" at junior school, then "Blubber-butt" when I came to Ashfield, or "Lesbo" till Mel Raynor and Natalie Simms started publicly making out, making lesbianism à la mode, whatever that means.

Anyway, I didn't see you at school the following day, even though I watched for you. At break and lunch I sat against the games hut where all the PE stuff such as nets and balls and bibs is kept. I could see the whole of the fence that runs alongside the wooded path from there. I ate the chocolate Hobnobs I buy every morning on the way to school, chewing slowly and trying to ignore the fact that my bum was going numb from the concrete, scanning the trees for a bit of your jacket and listening for the kind of bark your little dog might make. I was *vigilant*, and I wouldn't have missed you because of being distracted by friends, because I don't have any. People look at me and think the same as I thought when I saw you: freak. So I figured, as well as feeling compelled to stare at Alice Taylor, being freaks was something else we had in common.

English is the only classroom I go to that overlooks the playing field, so I looked out for you there, too. I have to sit in the third row from the window, but I could just about see the fence at the bottom of the field if I sat up, except that it was difficult to look without being obvious about it—which I was, because Robert threw a screwed-up piece of paper that hit my ear, and because a few minutes later Miss Frances, my English teacher who's really a Borg, said "*Yasmin*" in that sarcastic tone teachers use just to waste everyone's time because they know you're not listening and won't be able to answer whatever it was they asked.

I looked at her, rolling my biro in my fingers.

What she was telling me with her ice-blue eyes and black triangular eyebrows was, *I hate you, Yasmin Laksaris, and wish with all my frozen heart that you'd leave this school I have to teach in, but while you're still here don't think I won't make you pay for it*. What she said was: "Any ideas about why Robert Browning chooses to set his poem in a storm?"

I thought about what the weather had been like when you were watching Alice. Dull and gray and so still it was as if the world had been sucked into another dimension where everything moved in silent, super-slow motion.

"She doesn't know, miss," Robert said. "She's a kebab" (said like *shish a kebab*).

Miss Frances didn't laugh, even though I'm sure she found it quite amusing. She didn't want Robert stealing her spotlight. She folded her arms till she had everyone's attention again, then said, "Do you have any opinions about *anything*, Yasmin?"

I stopped twirling my biro. It's chewed, the plastic split halfway to the tip, and the blue bit that fits in the end isn't there (I'm a chewer as well as a freak). I thought about giving my opinion that her drawn-on eyebrows make her look like she's a member of an enemy alien race that's managed to infiltrate the education system. Then I thought about giving my opinion about you—about how you were watching our school and had your sights set on Alice Taylor and that, if I was asked, I'd say one day pretty soon you might even take her.

I don't think I realized till that second that I *did* think you were going to take her. I knew it then, though. I knew the way you'd looked at her was never just looking. It was *wanting*. I bet it was wanting in a way you'd never wanted anything before. Like you'd never seen anything so lovely, never even dreamed about having anything quite that good—being able to touch her hair, slide your hands beneath her crisp white shirt.

Anyway, luckily for you I didn't say anything. No one would've believed me in any case. I'd probably have been sent to Miss Ward, the Head, who'd have said something like *I've told you about telling lies before, haven't I, Yasmin?* Which she has, several times. Instead, I looked around. Everyone was staring at me and I realized they were all waiting for me to answer Miss Frances's question about having opinions. Dan sniggered.

"No?" I said. It came out like a question, like I didn't know whether I had any opinions or not.

The whole class laughed then, and even though I couldn't care less, I felt my face burn. I probably looked at Alice without thinking, *instinctively*, to see if she was laughing with the rest of them.

She wasn't. She was the *only* one who wasn't. She was just looking at me over her shoulder, her green eyes sort of observing me. I thought maybe in some parallel universe or via telepathy she'd heard my opinion about what you were going to do and that she'd understood somehow that I was going to save her, so I smiled. A small, secret smile. And even though she frowned and wrinkled her nose up before she turned away, I knew she'd felt it, too—the connection.

I've kept Alice's steady green eyes in my head ever since. I still think of them even now—usually when I'm alone in the house, doing something ordinary like wiping the worktop or changing the sheets on the bed. They appear as suddenly as they did that day in English, and float about the house with me, watching me wherever I go, whatever I do.

Anyway, that day after school, I didn't know Alice's eyes would watch me forever, so I concentrated all my efforts on not losing them—on keeping them there in my head. It was like a self-induced trance. I didn't speak to anyone and ate dinner gazing somewhere beyond the television, ignoring Gary pointing his knife at my plate and having a go at Mum for putting too much mash on it, saying, "You're not doing her any favors, you know," and moving along the sofa without a word when Mum patted me to move up, all the while hearing things only like they were far away and seeing only Alice's green eyes watching me, watching me, watching...

When the six o'clock news came on, I went up to my room. Mum had closed the curtains and it was nice and cozy. I shut the door, switched on my giant lava lamp and took Alice's Box out of my bedside cabinet. It's square like a cube and gold and probably had chocolates in it to start with. For years it had my hair things in it, such as clips and scrunchies, but

I stopped wearing them when I went to senior school and threw them away.

The first thing I put in it—the thing that made it Alice's Box—was a piece of green foil that went around a snack she'd had at break. That was in Year Seven when we were all new. It was a nice green, sort of smoky. I'd watched her lay it on her French book and smooth it carefully outward from the middle with her fingertips. I don't know if she meant to leave it behind, but when everyone'd gone and I'd slid it carefully between the pages of my textbook, I imagined she had. I imagined it was a secret message—her way of telling me she'd be my friend if she could, if Katy would let her.

I started keeping other things of Alice's I found after that. Not any old thing. I didn't want her used tissues or empty chips packages out of the trash—just things that were nice, or personal to her. Apart from the green foil, which was special because it was the first thing, I loved the heart: Alice's heart. She drew it. If I try to describe it, it won't sound anywhere near as lovely as it was, so you'll have to imagine the black lines, finer than cat hairs, swirling in and out and around each other. She was amazing at art, better than anyone. It was the way she saw things, I think, like she wasn't just looking, but feeling them, too. The thing in Alice's Box that you'd probably think was the weirdest was one of her sweat socks. For a few days I wasn't sure myself if it should go in, but then because I liked holding it and smelling it, I decided it should. It didn't smell of feet, if that's what you think (even though she'd worn it)—just a soft cottony smell. I got a nice feeling when I looked at her things, when I held them. They made me feel calm. I'd whisper to start with—just words, her name, things I'd like to say to her—turning and touching whatever I was holding till I got so calm I stopped needing to whisper, stopped needing to breathe, even. Till everything floated away and it was just me and her.

After I put Alice's Box away, I took the Cadbury's Dairy Milk Turkish Delight out of my bedside drawer. I broke off a row, broke that in half, then put both bits in my mouth and lay back on the duvet. I let the chocolate melt slowly across the roof of my mouth and held my eyelids almost closed so I was looking through my lashes. That way, the galaxy that Gary painted on my ceiling before Mum and I moved in two years ago looked more convincing. I think he forgot I was thirteen and not eight when he did it, but I suppose it was nice of him. He didn't have to.

I thought about how it'd be when you took Alice—where I'd be when it happened. I imagined myself walking into English after lunch break (which would make it a Friday). I notice that Alice isn't at her desk. Everything's normal apart from that; everyone's messing around. Katy's the first to act any different, looking up at the clock that's saying it's two minutes past and calling across to Sophie, *Where's Alice?* Miss Frances comes in then. Everyone settles down and then *she* asks, *Where's Alice?* I look out the window but of course you're not there. Nobody's there. Katy says she was with Alice at lunch. *She went back to get her coat after the bell*, she says. *She left it by the tennis court.* Miss Frances starts the lesson, reading from a book. She's distracted, though, and ten minutes later she glances up at the clock and checks her watch. She tells us to carry on reading, that she'll be back in one minute, and leaves the room.

I thought about how you didn't know I even existed, which gave me a nice feeling, like that even though you thought you were the one in control of things, you weren't because I was. *I* was in charge. I could save Alice. I thought if I told anyone what you were going to do, they wouldn't believe me, but that if I found out more about you, I could tell the police when the time came…when you took her. I thought I might even catch you in the act, if you tried to take her while we were at school. I thought I wouldn't let her out of my sight.

Either way, whether I was there or not, I'd still be the one who saved her. I'd be a heroine—Alice's heroine—and afterward Alice and I would be bonded forever in the way people are after something traumatic. And even though Alice's parents would try to give me thousands of pounds in reward money, which Mum and Gary would be pleading with me to take, I'd say all I wanted for my reward was your dog. And in the papers there'd be a picture of me holding him and it'd say I was a heroine in the true sense of the word.

I went downstairs to get a drink then, being quiet because I didn't want Mum, or especially Gary, to come out of the living room and catch me with a glass of his secret Coke stash. Fizzy drinks are strictly forbidden on my diet plan (along with Cadbury's Dairy Milk Turkish Delight and chocolate Hobnobs, in case you were wondering). Apparently I should drink water instead. Dr. Bhatt says it's nice when you get used to it. In his Indian accent he goes, "And with a bit of lemon or lime squeezed in it's really something rather special," his eyebrows all high like he actually believes it! I love Dr. Bhatt. He's my dietitian. He's sort of spiritual in the way he says things. He's kind as well, even though he's got to deal with me, which must be frustrating because I'm bigger now than when I first started going to him a year ago.

Anyway, I managed to get the Coke out from behind the Pledge Furniture Polish and Mr Muscle Window & Glass Cleaner without making too much noise. Mum and Gary think I don't know he keeps it there under the sink, and even though, when he's having a go at me about my weight (like he's not pretty *rotund* himself), it'd give me great pleasure to be able to point out what a bloody hypocrite he is, I want to keep it that way. I poured myself a glass and drank it down quick, then had another one. It's not as nice when it's not cold but it was too risky to fool around getting ice out of the freezer. Then I rinsed the glass under the tap and filled the bottle up with water to the same level it was before, because Gary, I bet you anything, makes a mental mark on the bottle of *exactly* how much is left every time he's had some. That's the kind of person he is, which is why, normally, I buy my own drinks.

I heard Mum and Gary arguing, then—or rather Gary delivering one of his lectures, his voice raised. When I was going back down the hall, I heard him say, "It's a bit more than just puppy fat, Jen! I hate to say it, but it seems to me like she is growing *in*to it, not out."

I stopped outside the living-room door. I suppose you just do that, don't you, when someone's talking about you, even if you really don't want to hear? Even if you couldn't care less what they're going to say.

"She's been much better recently," Mum said. "She's definitely lost a few pounds. Let's just wait until she's been to the hospital."

"Okay, fine. But I think you're avoiding the issue. You're burying your head in the sand."

"And I think you expect too much."

"It's not about what I *expect*, Jen. I want her to be happy."

"She is happy."

"Have a normal teenage life," Gary went on. "You know— friends. *Boy*friends. I mean, come on! Who's going to want to date her like…like she is?"

"Well, we're dealing with it, aren't we?" Mum said, her voice raised as well now. "She's losing weight. Honestly, Gary, she's only fifteen. I don't really want her doing anything with boys."

There was another silence. Then Gary, wanting to have the last word like always, said, "Okay then. Let's just pretend she's losing weight and everything's hunky-dory, shall we?"

"Everything *is* hunky-dory, Gary. Let's just wait and see." I did a silent cheer for Mum for beating Gary to the final word and started up the stairs, but she wasn't finished. She said—the words clipped like she was accusing him—"You weren't there."

Yeah, I thought. You weren't there, Gary Thornton, Gary Thorn-in-my-bum. You weren't there.

School felt different the next day, and it wasn't anyone else. Everyone was the same—basically either ignoring me or calling me names.

I was different, though. And I knew why. It was because I had a purpose now, because I had to save Alice. It put a new angle on everything. It's like the perspective thing we did in art last year: far away = small, close up = big. It's obvious, I know, till you've got to draw it (unless you're Alice, of course, who could make even rotting fruit look lush). What I'm trying to say with the perspective thing is that I've always felt like *I'm* far away, like *I'm* the dot in the distance, and that everyone else is close up—big—living. But suddenly that day I didn't feel like the dot anymore. I felt like I was the one who was close up—the one who knew the score, who could see the big picture—and I walked around the place like *Bring it on!*

I didn't get much of a chance to look for you, other than out of the top corridor windows on the way to History. For one thing, it was raining all morning and I wasn't so desperate to see you I'd get wet for the privilege, then there was a GCSE Drama meeting at lunch. I'm not really any good at drama. I took it only because I thought it'd be easy. And because I knew Alice would take it. And because I knew none of the Klingons such as Katy or Sophie would choose it, meaning I could look at Alice without getting evils off them all the time. Anyway, when I walked into the drama studio, Alice was in there on her own, sitting at one end of the semicircle of chairs, drawing in her sketchbook.

Normally I'd have sat at the other end, or maybe in the middle somewhere. I'd definitely never have had the guts to sit next to her. But with my new perspective I just strolled over like it was the most normal thing in the world and plunked myself down beside her. "All right?" I said, like no big deal.

She said "Hi," but she was a bit surprised, I think. She closed her book and did that leg-crossing thing where if you cross them away from the person, it means you don't like them. (She crossed her legs away, if you were wondering, but I wasn't going to let a little thing like that stop my rocket.)

"That's *good*," I said, meaning her drawing. I wasn't just saying it either, although I'd caught only a glimpse, because everything Alice drew was incredible. "Can I see?"

She hesitated and I thought I'd gone too far then. I thought she'd get up and move away—sit over the other side. But she didn't. She put the book in my hand. *In my hand*—just like that! And I thought of that saying that Dad used to tell me: *If you don't ask, you don't get.*

Everyone else at school plasters their sketchbooks with things cut out of magazines, such as words and dismembered bits of models and any other stupid stuff they can find to stick on. Alice's cover was blank, though. Black—just how it was when Miss Trainer handed them out. I loved that. It was like she didn't need to impress anyone; like she was telling the world that all the good stuff's on the inside and it's up to you to find it, like it didn't matter to her if you did or you didn't.

I flicked through with my thumb, catching colors and sketches and words written in fine pencil lines, and the beautiful delicate flowers she'd drawn in the corners with the page number in the center of each—some in color, some in pencil, some just in black ink, depending on whatever she had in her hand I suppose. I wanted to stop on every single page, of course, and stare at it all at every line—but obviously I couldn't. Not with her there. I got to the drawing she'd been working on. It was a girl, like a Manga girl, who glared out at me from the paper with gleaming eyes beneath a thick black fringe. She was standing defiantly, like she should have a sword in her hand or something, though what she was actually holding was an apple.

Alice'd spent time on it, you could tell. The shading was brilliant—cross-hatched so it got darker and lighter just where she wanted it, like Miss Trainer's always trying to get me to do instead of smudging with my thumbs. And around the edges were hundreds of tiny, wispy lines that were like ghosts of the finished drawing, or expressions of it or something. I don't know. It was beautiful. It took my breath away. "It's amazing," I said.

I didn't look up, but I saw Alice out the corner of my eye twist her lips and give a little shrug, like maybe it was, maybe it wasn't. "Thanks," she said. Some of her hair fell forward. It was inches away, pale and gold, like a waterfall or something, even though I know that sounds corny. The point is, it was right there. I could've touched it.

That's all I could think of then: imagining how her hair would feel slipping through my fingers, pooling onto my palms—cool, like water. My chest felt like it had an owl in it trying to beat its way out and I wanted to tell her, suddenly, about Alice's Box—*her* box—and how it feels when I hold her things. I wanted to tell her about you as well, and how she should be really scared but at the same time not worry about any of it, because I was protecting her and because I wasn't going to let anything happen.

Robert came in with Max Bailey, though. I didn't think so at the time, but it was probably lucky, because otherwise I might not've just closed Alice's sketchbook and given it back. I might've flung my arms around her.

A couple of days after, when I was watching the path for you from the PE hut after lunch, I saw someone through the trees and hurried down to the fence with my bag. It wasn't you. It was two women in rain boots walking three big dogs.

I kicked the fence. I was annoyed. I knew you were planning to take Alice, so where were you? Why weren't you there? Then the bell rang and right after that—after I'd turned to go back across the field—I heard a dog bark.

It was high-pitched and quite far off, but it came from a small dog. It's yours, I thought. It's your dog. I walked along the fence to the cut-through, did a quick scan of the playing field to see if anyone was looking, then a few steps and I was on the path.

I stood under the canopy of trees and listened. A bird was rustling about in the undergrowth and I could just make out the engine hum of cars on Aldenham Road.

Then I heard the bark again. It came from the other way, toward Finch Lane. I walked as fast as I could, wishing I didn't have to haul my schoolbag with me. I can't run because I get wheezy, which is one of the "motivators" Dr. Bhatt wanted to put on my list, as if running is something I'd do all the time if I could because it's such a fun thing to do. I told him

I never even need to run. The only time I probably should is for the bus when I'm late for school, but then I wouldn't dream of actually doing it, because any time I don't have to spend at school is a bonus.

The end of the path was ahead of me—an archway of white light. When I got there, I stood in the brightness of Finch Lane squinting up and down it and panting, the insides of my thighs stinging from being rubbed together. (Dr. Bhatt doesn't know about my stinging thighs or he'd add them to the list.)

The lane was empty. There was nothing except a cat dozing on the windowsill of one of the terraced houses on the other side.

I took my inhaler out of my bag and had a few puffs, then stripped off my cardigan, tied it around my waist and started walking slowly back along the path. I thought about how the dog bark could've come from the other direction or a garden somewhere or from any small dog—there are enough of them around. I thought, I haven't even heard your dog bark. I just really wanted it to be your dog.

I'd never been on the wooded path in the middle of the day before. Once I'd calmed down a bit and got my breath back, it was like being in a fairy tale. The sun was sparkling through the leaves high above me, birds were fluttering about with twigs in their beaks and squirrels kept popping their heads around tree trunks or running across the path. I felt like Snow White as I stepped along, looking all around me and listening to the birdsong. I thought how Snow White would've started singing, so I sang a couple of notes, but then I stopped because I didn't sound anything like a Disney princess. I know I don't look like one either, but imagining how I look when I can't see myself is a lot easier than imagining I sound lovely when I can hear I don't.

Some fat people, such as the ones who sing in operas, have amazing voices, don't they? And they look really smug to be as massive as they are because they can do this special thing they wouldn't be able to do if they were thin. I don't have a good voice, though. I'm just fat. So I forgot about the singing and just looked at all the animals running and flying about and the sun spilling through the trees and enjoyed being on my own somewhere so nice.

When I got back to near the cut in the fence, I sat on a tree stump just off the path. I still had more than half an hour before the end of sixth period. I was missing History, which if you're going to skip class, is a good one because Mr. Caplin is so blind he never notices if people are missing. He didn't notice the bin Robert put halfway between the door and his desk either.

There was only one chocolate Hobnob left in my bag. I ate half of it, then crumbled the rest up and threw the bits on the path. None of the animals came, though, even after ages. I thought, they can probably see me sitting here—or maybe they're all on diet programs, too, only better at them. It was obviously "smokers' seat" I was on, because there were cigarette butts everywhere. I picked one out of the grass. It had candy-pink lipstick on it and had been mashed out so fiercely the tobacco was all splayed out like crazy hair. I sniffed it, then dug my fingernails into the filter and pulled it apart to look at the fluffy yellow stuff.

I don't smoke. I wondered if you did. I thought you probably did because you're old and most old people smoke, especially old people who are bad. Then a voice said, "Unlucky for you, Yasmin."

It was Mrs. Wilcox, the French teacher and probably the one person you don't want to get caught by. She made me walk the proper way to the Head's office: down the path to Aldenham Road, then along that to the main entrance. She stood watching me till I was out of sight. Then I suppose she must've called the school office because the secretary said, "In you go, Yasmin," when I got there.

Miss Ward didn't believe I was looking at squirrels. She gave me the usual spiel about smoking, the usual spiel about skipping class, then sent me home, saying that because I was already on report, I was suspended till Monday.

Whoopidoo, I thought, suspended for a whole day. Actually, it was a day and nearly two hours and I decided I was going to make the most of them. In my head I was already there on my bed with all five pillows (four behind me, one under my knees), a bowl of sweet 'n' salty popcorn in my arms and *Star Trek: The Next Generation* playing on my laptop. I let the first bus go past, though, because I remembered Gary. He might be there. He's a plumber, which is a pain in the bum because sometimes he goes home between jobs or finishes early, and if he was there, he'd say, *What're you doing home?* straight off without even looking at his watch, and then he'd give me the Spanish Inquisition (whatever that is), then phone school to check my story word for word against theirs. The pull of *The Next Generation* was too strong, though, even in the face of a possible Gary encounter, and I got the next bus.

I stared out the window and thought about how it'd be just my luck if you took Alice while I was suspended, and I sent you a message via telepathy telling you that you couldn't do it yet. I also told you that even though I was happy I was suspended, it was because of you that I'd got in trouble— that because of you, I'd have to explain myself to Mum and maybe even (please, God, no) Gary.

It's official now, I told you. *You owe me.*

Gary wasn't at home, but Mum was. I could hear her in the kitchen going "Mmm" into the phone and sighing every few seconds and when she didn't put her head around the door to wave at me like she usually does if she's on the phone, I knew she was talking to school. I thought the Head was probably giving her the same lecture she'd given me about smoking (as if no one else in the world's ever been told about the dangers of smoking and it's her duty, as the lone crusader, to spread the word). Then Mum said, "Well, we've been trying. We've done that." There was another long pause, another sigh, louder this time, like she was getting annoyed, then, "It isn't easy, you know."

I went into the living room and waited for her, watching a magpie stabbing a snail on the driveway with its beak. When she came in, she flopped into the chair, leaning her head back and closing her eyes like she was completely knackered. She's a mystery shopper, which means she has to push a supermarket cart around different supermarkets all day, pretending to shop when really she's spying on people who hand out those tiny bits of cookies or cubes of cheese on toothpicks to make sure they're doing their job and not playing on their phones. It's hard work, even though Gary's always making fun of it, going "And who's watching *you*? Who's making sure you're doing *your* job properly?"

"I wasn't smoking," I said.

She lifted her head and looked at me. "I don't know," she said.

I wanted to say, *You won't tell Gary, will you?* but it didn't seem like the right moment. I said, "What d'you mean?"

She sighed again and picked up the Pizza Hut take-out menu that was on the arm of the chair. "I'm just too tired," she said. She was looking at the menu, but I could tell she wasn't really looking. She wasn't reading it. I thought she probably didn't even know what it was. It was making me hungry, though.

I said, "I didn't have any lunch."

She shot me a look to tell me 1) that she knew that was probably a lie; and 2) that she also knew exactly what I was doing and that, in the circumstances, it wasn't really acceptable. Then she said, "We'll talk about it tomorrow, okay? I'm not letting it slide, though."

I nodded. I said, "Don't tell Gary."

She pursed her lips and gave me the look again, but I was pretty sure she wouldn't. I don't think she relished the thought of a Gary lecture either.

I went upstairs then. I didn't have to tell her to get me the Deep Pan Stuffed Crust Hawaiian with extra Garlic and

Herb Dip because that's my number one favorite thing to eat (along with Cadbury's Dairy Milk Turkish Delight and sweet 'n' salty popcorn). And because Gary wasn't home, it meant she'd probably order me one that was actually big enough to fill a hole.

One thing I love about Mum is that she never makes things into massive dramas like most people. She usually just shrugs and sighs or says "Ah well" or "Never mind." I suppose it's because of losing Dad. Once you've been through something like that, it puts things into perspective—things like your teenage daughter possibly smoking a cigarette on a tree stump when she should be fifty yards away listening to someone so old he can only mumble in monotone.

I typed *How to spot a pedophile* into Google on my laptop. About a billion sites came up. I took a quiz on one. It showed pictures of people (men mostly) and you had to click *Yes* for pedophile or *No* for not a pedophile. I got only half of them right, which technically means there was a 50 percent chance I was wrong about you. Except I knew I wasn't. Anyway, I thought, you weren't just a photo, you were real. You *are* real, and I deduced therefore that it's a lot easier to tell a pedophile in the flesh than from a picture. It's the same with television or pop stars, isn't it? They seem super-duper lovely on screen but then you hear they're really vile and treat the people who work for them like crap. Hanna Latham at school said her friend's cousin was a runner on this TV show and that there was a really horrible presenter who'd tip packets of mixed nuts all over his desk, then make her pick out the cashews because they were the only ones he liked. Hanna said you'd never know he was like that from watching him, all smiles and jokes and floppy fun-guy hair. I bet if you met him in real life, though, you could tell straight away he was mean.

This other site said to pay particular attention to the mouth, to look out for the pedo-*smile*: apparently pedophiles usually have thin lips and are often smiling especially if you're a child doing the looking. Obviously, you weren't smiling when I saw you because you were on your own and too busy, I expect, imagining what you'd do with Alice when you got her.

The website said to look out for props, too, meaning things that would interest kids and make them trust a person, such as bikes or scooters or kittens. It didn't mention dogs, but *obviously* dogs—especially one as scruffy and cute as yours.

The one thing all the sites did say was that predators like you are almost always known to their victims. I thought that bit didn't really fit unless you did know Alice—which is possible, I suppose, but you didn't look like you knew her. I mean, you weren't exactly ready to wave at her if she happened to notice you. You were holding your dog's lead with one hand and the other one was stuffed deep in the pocket of your jeans.

Mum brought me a tea at nine o'clock the next morning. She said, "You awake, love?" even though it was obvious I wasn't, or at least hadn't been, and sat on the bed. Because I was officially in trouble, I couldn't tell her to pee off, so I pushed myself up, took the mug from her and had a couple of slurps.

She believed me about not smoking, but I had to come up

with a reason for being on the path. Watching squirrels obviously wasn't good enough (even though it ended up being the truth) and I couldn't tell her about you, so I told her I was just feeling a bit down.

"Oh, love," she said. She leaned forward and tucked my hair behind my ear. "You've not had an easy time of it, have you?"

I was thinking, stop tucking my hair behind my ear, Mum, but I said it was no big deal and that everything was fine really, I just had my period coming. But the way she was looking at me all sympathetically made it impossible not to think about Dad, which made me get tearful. She patted my leg through the duvet. "Hey, c'mon," she said, "let's go to the shop and get something nice." I reminded her I had to see Dr. Bhatt in the afternoon, but she said she was sure he was going to be pleased with me. She didn't know about the family-size Cadbury's Dairy Milk Turkish Delight in my bedside table drawer or the other three in my suitcase on top of the wardrobe, or about the packet of chocolate Hobnobs I buy in the corner shop near school every day. She said, "One treat won't hurt." She said it was a treat for her, too, because she'd got the day off. She'd given the work to one of the other mystery shoppers.

She came out the co-op with a box of Maltesers. "Look," she said, making me hold it when she got back in the car, "they're so light they won't even show up on the scales." We ate them there, sitting outside the shop. She told me she'd go on a diet, too, but that Gary likes his ladies large. "Something to grab hold of." She chuckled, popping several Maltesers into her mouth at once with a naughty look in her eyes.

"Mu-um," I said, because I really didn't need to be hearing what Gary does or doesn't like.

Then she said sorry, because she knew she wasn't being very helpful, but that the point she wanted to make was that it's what's on the inside that counts.

She looked really happy inside and out.

Dr. Bhatt wasn't pleased with me. He never is because every time I go I'm heavier than the time before (and I'm not getting any taller), but even so I like going to see him. He's calm and patient and talks to me like he understands how it's really hard to lose weight. But I like going because of the hospital, too. I like the way it's all white and quiet, the nurses and doctors walking around in their long clean coats and squeaky shoes, carrying clipboards or wheeling machines.

Ever since Dad was ill and Marion came to the house to look after him, I thought I'd like to be a nurse. You get to be kind to people, or firm with them if they won't do what you tell them to, like taking their pills or eating their meals. I think I'd like looking after old people the most because they're nicer and easier to talk to—especially if they're lonely. And I'd listen to them. I wouldn't be like those people who just pretend to listen, by nodding and saying "Yeah" or "Oh dear," when it's obvious they're really thinking about how they can escape. I'd listen for real.

Marion was nice. She chatted a lot, but at the same time she got on with all the things she had to do. She used to unpin her nurse's watch from her pocket and let me take Dad's pulse. She showed me how to put the inflatable thing around his arm and read his blood pressure, too. Then, if I was at home, she'd call, "Time for stats, Nurse Yasmin," and I'd rush from wherever I was to do all the checks and write down the numbers on Dad's chart. I asked her once if she wished she was a doctor. She said, "Never." She said she'd always wanted to be just what she was. Marion went away as well when Dad died. I know it's obvious she would, but I hadn't thought about that. I thought I'd lose only Dad.

Dr. Bhatt didn't react as he watched the numbers on the scales settle on 219 pounds 12.472 ounces, but when he wrote it on the chart in my ring binder, I saw his eyebrows go down and his teeth pull on his top lip. I thought he was probably thinking what he could say to me this time, because he'd tried saying a lot of different things already that obviously hadn't worked because basically I was failing the program, as in *failing* the program. "Okay, Yasmin, take a seat," he said in his Indian accent.

I sat down next to Mum and he sat down the other side of his desk. He looked at her, then at me and said, "Well, you have put on some weight. Almost four pounds, in fact, which means your BMI will also have risen by around point five."

I tried not to notice Mum wilt in her seat as he flicked through my file. At least she didn't say anything or demand to know how it was possible when she was mostly giving me less to eat.

"Perhaps we should have another look at your motivators," he said, unhooking the list from the rings. He put it on the table, turning it so it was the right way around for me to read. "Because clearly I think this is where the problem is lying."

I looked at the list.

"Take a look and think about whether each one is still relevant to you, because it may be they are not the right ones."

"But Yasmin made the list," Mum said.

He licked his lips, making them pinker than they already are. "Well, the things which motivate us can change," he said, "especially when we are so young."

"Right," Mum said, like she still didn't really get it.

"Let's go through," Dr. Bhatt said, smiling at Mum and tapping his finger on the paper. "So…"

"Number one," I read out, "having friends."

"Okay," Dr. Bhatt said, "well, we all like to have friends and certainly that isn't all about how we are looking. But do you still feel that making *new* friends would be easier if you were slimmer?"

I looked at him. "Yes," I said.

"Okay then!" he said, beaming as if just saying it solved everything. "But are you thinking about making new friends when you get the urge to eat outside of your regular meal-times?"

"Not really," I said.

"And that is the problem," he said.

We went through the rest of the list like that and then he asked me if there were any new motivators I'd thought of that I'd like to add to it, and like always I told him I'd forgotten to think of any and he told Mum to remind me to try.

Then he went over my diet plan, which was awkward because with Mum there I had to keep lying about not eating any sugary foods like biscuits and chocolate. He knew I was lying, too, but he didn't say anything. He just looked down at his hands. Then, without getting up, he walked his chair around the desk, wheeling it across the shiny floor, and when he got to me, he leaned forward, his elbows on his knees, and licked his lips again. "If you stick to the plan," he said, his Indian accent even stronger up close, "you *will* lose the weight." Then he put his hands together and for a second I thought he was actually going to pray for me. "Try to take each moment as it comes," he said. "Think only of your goal. It will take courage, but once the weight begins to come away, I promise you this—it will feel like the sun is coming out."

On the way home in the car it was raining. I could feel Mum wanting to ask me about exactly when and what I'd been eating without her knowing, but also that she didn't want to ask me. Maybe because she was feeling guilty about the Maltesers and about saying that it's what's on the inside that counts when it isn't really true. I closed my eyes and tried to imagine what it would feel like *physically* to be thin: to have thin arms, thin legs, a flat stomach. But even though I haven't always been fat, I couldn't do it. I couldn't remember. Instead, my body just felt even bigger than it is, then started swelling till it was taking up the whole car and pressing against the windows, which were going to explode any second if I didn't stop…

So instead I imagined what it'd be like to go into school thin. I imagined Alice coming out of the English room at the other end of the corridor, chatting to the girls around her and walking toward me. She loops her bag over her head and that's when she spots me. She stops—stops dead in her tracks, peering in disbelief at me. Then, breaking free from the others, she comes running up, smiling in amazement, her mouth open in shock and saying *Yasmin, is that really you?* and then everyone else crowds around saying that, too.

I went up to my room when we got home. I wanted to be on my own. I sat on my bed and thought about really trying to make an effort to lose weight this time. I thought about getting the chocolate and Hobnobs out of my suitcase and bedside table and throwing them all away. I thought about giving up on the idea that you were going to take Alice and me being a hero and all of that as well, because it was pretty much all I'd been thinking about and Dr. Bhatt said I should focus only on losing weight.

My file says I tend toward obsessive thoughts, which is how I got fat in the first place, so I knew I'd been obsessing about you. And I didn't really know anything about you anyway. I'd seen you only once. I thought about how you could just've been a completely normal person who was staring at Alice for some innocent reason, like because she reminded you of your granddaughter who'd died in a horrific car accident, or something like that—and not at all because you were going to do something very bad.

I thought how your taking Alice was just a stupid fantasy, the same as all the other stupid fantasies I'd had like Alice getting ill and me researching her symptoms online for weeks and weeks till suddenly I figure out what it is that's wrong with her just as she's about to die... That one never happened for real either. I thought about Miss Ward telling me last year how it was high time I realized that this life was the only one I was going to get and that I should start living it that way before it was too late. I remembered thinking what a load of horse crap—"before it's too late"—but even though I knew it was the kind of dramatic rubbish that teachers come out with that *sounds* like it means something when it doesn't really mean anything at all, and even though I walked out of her office telling myself that joke that isn't really a joke because it's true: *Those who can, do; those who can't, teach*—what she'd said got into my head. I'd remembered it, anyway.

I thought about Dr. Bhatt's hands pressed together and his worried eyes looking into mine and I thought, I'm going to do it. I'm going to forget about you and I'm going to live in the real world and not let myself imagine stuff anymore. I'm going to lose weight and become so gorgeous that no one'll even believe it's me. So gorgeous that even *I* don't believe it's me. Because more than anything, I wanted to feel like the sun was coming out.

The next day was Saturday and I decided to walk into town, even though the insides of my thighs were still sore with angry red spots on them from going up and down the wooded path looking for you. My plan was to get a Diet Coke in McDonald's, then look in some shops and walk home again. I put loads of talcum powder on my legs but they were already stinging by the time I got to Deacons Hill.

It's *a lot* farther into town than it seems on the bus and by the time I got there my feet were killing me and my stomach was like a cave. I stood in line in McDonald's feeling the coins in my pocket and staring at the menu board. I was thinking I should've brought only the exact money for a Diet Coke and that I definitely was *not* going to get a vanilla milkshake and a McChicken Sandwich with large fries, even though I had enough, when I got the feeling I was being watched.

Sophie reacted with a shriek when I looked over, then "hid" behind the collar of her denim jacket. She was with Alice, Katy and two boys who aren't from our school. She'd been telling them what a legend I am, I expect.

I took my Diet Coke into Gap across the road and went upstairs to the little kids' section. I stood by the window between the rails of doll-like dresses, chewing the end of the straw and sucking tiny amounts through it, waiting for them to come out.

I'd never seen Alice out of school. She was wearing faded skinny jeans, flat pumps and a long, pale blue cardigan. Her hair was in a loose plait over one shoulder. She looked *effortless*— that's the best word I can think of—like that, even though all the world was hers, she'd chosen to set it free.

She was laughing, her arm draped over one of the boys' shoulders. He was black—really black—and doing all the talking. He kept covering her hand with his, then taking it off again to gesture around, like it was no big deal that she was touching him. It's only because she's so nice that she didn't mind. I thought it was pretty rude, though. I thought, who does he think he is?

They headed down the High Street then, so I went back

downstairs. They were standing outside Waterstones, looking in at the display. Alice was telling them something, about a book, I suppose. I imagined it was *The Poems of Robert Browning*, even though I knew his book wouldn't be in the window because he's really old, dead, even. I hate English, but the poem of his we did in class was brilliant. It's about a man who's Porphyria's lover (they had funny names then). He knows he can't have her, even though they're in love, because she's upper class and rich, so to make sure she'll always be his, he kills her. He says:

> That moment she was mine, mine, fair,
> Perfectly pure and good: I found
> A thing to do, and all her hair
> In one long yellow string I wound
> Three times her little throat around,
> And strangled her.

I love imagining the two of them in his little cottage in the forest: him pressing her soaked crimson dress and ample tits against his shirt as the storm lashes at the windows, possessing her with his mouth as he twists her hair into that long, wet rope.

Anyway, it wasn't *The Poems of Robert Browning* in the window. When they walked on down the High Street, I stopped in the same place they'd stood and looked at the books. There was some crappy-looking vampire trilogy, a book with a shiny black cover called *The Doll* and, up on a plinth, *Alice in Wonderland*—a big hardback. Probably a new edition or something, seeing as it was in the window.

I thought Alice'd probably been telling them something about that one—like that maybe when she was little, her parents told her that *she* was the Alice in the story. She did look a bit like her. The Alice on the cover was kneeling and looking down into the rabbit hole at me, as if I was down the hole already and would be going into Wonderland with her. She had a funny expression on her face, though, like she might decide to bury me there instead.

I kept a good distance behind when I carried on down the High Street, and I made sure there were always people between us so that I'd catch only a glimpse of one of them every few seconds. Then I thought I'd lost them till I passed the cinema and saw them inside. They were waiting in line to get tickets.

I didn't go in: I wouldn't know what they'd all be going to see and anyway, I didn't have enough money. I hung around outside, finishing my drink and thinking I should go home. Then I saw them disappearing into the gloom of the foyer and went up the steps. I watched them hand their tickets to a girl and go into Screen 4.

I was so hungry the smell of popcorn nearly made me faint, so I counted the change I had and got an extra-large box— sweet, because the Odeon hasn't caught onto sweet 'n' salty yet. I asked the boy serving if he could do half 'n' half, but he looked at me like I was out of my mind, so I left it.

I went to the bathroom. I was still in one of the cubicles (thinking it would've been cleverer to go for a pee before getting the popcorn) when some girls came crashing in, laughing and screeching and going "Quick, we'll miss the beginning,"

and that kind of thing. I hate it when girls get all excited, so
to avoid them, I went back out to the foyer without washing my hands. Just as I was heading for the steps to the street
again, though, they suddenly burst out behind me, all cack-
ling idiotically, one of them saying she couldn't remember
which screen they'd come out of. Then her friend pushed her
sideways, saying, "Four, you idiot" and holding four fingers
up in her face.

And I went with them. Just like that.

I turned around and stuck close behind. The girl taking tickets looked at me like she didn't remember me from
before, but then she looked at the popcorn in my arms and
didn't say a thing.

It was dark inside. The film had started.

I headed up near the back and shuffled in past a few people
to a seat in the side block. It took me a while to find where
Alice was because it was pretty full in there. When I did
(they were in the center block in front of those VIP seats),
it was Katy I saw, only she wasn't looking at the screen, she
was twisted around and looking at me. Then the boy who
was sitting the other side of Alice—the black one—turned
and looked at me, too.

I concentrated on the shapes moving on the screen. I ate
my popcorn. I told myself it wasn't a crime to be watching a
film just because it happened to be the same one they were
watching. When I dared to glance at them again, though,
they were still looking. Not Alice; the other two.

Then the boy got up. He jigged sideways along the row,
his hands held in fists like a boxer, hood bouncing. I thought

he was probably going to the bathroom, but when he got to the aisle, he clocked me again and started up the steps.

I felt my skin burn and prickle, my heart start to thump.

"Hey, Yasmin!" he called when he got close enough for me to hear.

I put more popcorn in my mouth. I told myself I had no idea who he was, that he must want someone else because my name's not Yasmin. It's Doner. Doner, Fatso, Blubber-butt…

He kept coming, though, the whites of his eyes shining in the changing light.

The people sitting around me looked at him. Someone shushed. A woman on the row behind said, "'Scuse us, d'you mind?"

But he didn't. He didn't mind at all. He just stood there, staring at me. Then he said, "Come out," like I'd better do it quick. There was another angry shush.

He said, "I've got a message from Alice."

I thought, why would Alice have a message for me? But I stood up anyway. I squeezed past the people, spilling my popcorn, saying sorry, thinking maybe she wants me to sit with them; *would* she want me to sit with them? Then suddenly, before I was even properly out in the aisle, he grabbed my arm up near the top and pulled me so my ear was right up against his mouth. "Leave her alone, yeah?" he breathed. The words were hot. They filled my ear and spilled down my neck. Flecks of his spit hit my cheek. "You're really creepin' her out." Then he tightened his grip even more, making me cry out, and hissed, "Got it?"

I nodded quickly, just wanting him to let go, then as soon

as he did, I stumbled away up the steps toward the exit door at the back. My throat and chest felt like they were being squashed. I turned, afraid he was following me, but he was gone, jogging back down to the others.

I put the popcorn on the floor, whispering to help myself think which pocket my inhaler was in, and reached out to steady myself on the back of an empty seat. And there you were, on the far side near the wall, your face pale like milk in the darkness, your eyes staring blankly ahead at the screen.

STRAWBERRY TART

"LESBO," DAN SAID WHEN I walked into Maths on Monday.

Robert put his arms up high, his eyes wide like a ghoul, and said, "Oh no, it's the Lesbian Psycho-Stalker!"

I ignored them (obviously) as well as the death rays Katy kept firing at me from across the classroom. Aren't bullies meant to get bored and leave you alone if you ignore them? That's what adults tell you, but it's a lie. I've been ignoring them all my life. They go away only if they go to a different school.

The morning went on like that, with looks and insults. I went to the gym in first break. I knew no one would look for me there. I sat on one of the low wooden benches along the wall eating Maryland Chocolate Chip Cookies because the corner shop was out of Hobnobs, and for some reason Marcy Edwards popped into my head.

Marcy was a girl in my year who got anorexia. She got so

thin she had to go into the hospital. I know it's a stupid thing to say, and that I don't know what I'm talking about, but when she collapsed in PE and the ambulance came and she was carried into it on a stretcher, I wished, wished, *wished* it was me. It's not fair that you can get too thin to go to school but not too fat.

I wondered what she was doing now, like if she was lying in a hospice bed somewhere, looking out through a big window onto lawns with bushes and trees, with chocolates and flowers on her bedside table, or if she was in Paris twirling around one of those fancy lampposts with a million-dollar modeling contract. Or maybe she was dead. Maybe they couldn't make her eat, like Dr. Bhatt can't make me stop eating, and she died. I thought any of those things would be better than being me.

I couldn't avoid Katy at lunch, though. She was eyeballing me the whole time, then the second I got up with my tray, she got up, too—then Sophie, Beth and Alice. I glanced over at Mr. Holland, who was on duty, but he was looking the other way.

They followed me down the corridor, through the changing room and out past the music hut, not saying anything but sort of closing in on me. I started whispering, hoping they couldn't hear, then when I couldn't stand it anymore, I turned around and said, "Leave me alone."

"Ooh, don't like being stalked, then, Doner?" Katy said.

"Lesbian," Beth added.

I looked at Alice. She was watching me, but not like the others. Her eyes weren't sparkling with the same viciousness.

I don't think she even wanted to be there. "I wasn't stalking anyone," I said.

"You're a *liar*," Katy spat, leaning in. She twisted her face at me. "I saw you. In the window of Gap upstairs in the kids' department, staring down at Alice like the saddo you are. You make me sick."

"Alice was scared," Sophie said.

"Alice *is* scared," Katy cut in. "Jesus, *I'd* be scared, too. Look at you! You're a freak. You're disgusting."

Tears stung my eyes. Not because of what they were saying. I didn't care what they said. They're idiots, and I'd heard it all before anyway. It was because Alice was there.

"Leave me alone," I said and I walked back past them. I thought one of them'd shove me, but they didn't—they let me through—and for a second I thought I'd got away.

But then Katy said, "Oh, I don't think so," and I heard her shoes scuffing the concrete as she ran up behind me. I turned, but too late, crying out as her fingers stabbed into my neck, in the place where it kills, my knees giving way. I grabbed for her sweater, but she threw my arm off, going "Eurgh," so I fell onto my hands.

"I didn't do anything!" I said, standing up again. "I was trying to protect her! There's a man…"

Then she spit—right in my eye where she'd aimed it. "Just fuck off," she said. "Leave us alone. Leave *Alice* alone."

After I'd rinsed my eye in the bathroom, I left. I just walked out the school gates. I couldn't stay, especially not for PE, where Mr. Faraday wouldn't care if they carried it on. I crossed to the bus stop over the road. I wanted to go home, but Gary might be there and I couldn't face him. So I thought I'd go into town to kill the time, calm down a bit. I thought I'd get myself a Yog in the shopping center, or some churros with hot chocolate sauce that smell so good they make you want to empty your pockets on the spot. If I'm ever rich (which obviously I won't be), I'll have to live somewhere they don't make churros or I'll end up so fat I'll be like those people who can't even get up anymore and have to lie on their beds staring at the ceiling till the day they die.

I sat in the bus shelter and tried to blank Alice from my mind—how she'd looked when Katy spat. I couldn't do it, though. I kept seeing her face over and over—the shock in her eyes as her mouth opened wide, the laugh stifled behind her hand—so I saw the bus only at the last second, just as it was about to fly past. I stuck out my hand.

It lurched to a stop, squealing and bouncing on its wheels.

The driver threw his arms up when I got on, like to ask is this how I get my kicks, hanging around bus stops hailing buses at the last second, and when I got my pass out he wouldn't look at it. He jammed his foot on the accelerator so I had to grab for the pole.

I went upstairs where it was empty and looked out through the scratched plastic window at the trees and the people, at mums pushing strollers, joggers jogging and dogs chasing Frisbees on the common. It all looked so beautiful, so green and blue and full of life, but also like it wasn't real—like it was a dream or a memory of some place I'd been before, long ago. And it was. It was the world I used to live in, when Dad was alive.

I wished he could come back and everything could be like it was before he got too ill to stay at home. I wished he could come back for just one minute so I could feel his arms around me, holding me tight like he used to, because if that happened I'd be so grateful I wouldn't care if everyone else I ever met hated my guts. And then I was pressing the bell to get off because suddenly I knew where I wanted to go.

I didn't remember the gates because I hadn't been there for years—not since I was about ten. They were like those Gothic ones you see in films that have a winding path beyond them, leading up to a scary house on top of a rock. The metal letters in the top spelled out Bushgrove Cemetery.

I went through. Everything was quiet and still. It was so neat, the grass all mown, the flowers all red and pink in the beds along the driveway. I walked past the low brick building. Three pathways led off into the distance like massive wheel spokes through a hundred thousand graves. It was just as big as I remembered, and being the only person there who was actually alive made me feel a bit weird—like that if I stood still too long, I might start sinking into the ground without even realizing what was going on till it was too late, and I was under a headstone, too. Like the graveyard would swallow me.

I went down the left path. I wasn't sure, but I had a feeling it was Dad's. The only thing I could remember from the funeral was a big tree near where they put him. I remembered sitting under it away from the huddle of people around his grave. I'd picked the petals off daisies, whispering that old-fashioned thing, "He loves me, he loves me not"—only I kept saying, "He loves me, he loves me, he loves me…" Maybe that was the day I started with the whispering thing.

I looked at the gravestones as I walked. They were either incredibly old or just quite old—like either so old you couldn't see what words had been engraved on the stones anymore, or like people who'd died in the '70s or '80s, like Annie Stott, who was nineteen when she died. Her grave had fresh flowers on it—yellow-and-white ones—and little china fairies were sat all around the headstone. I wondered who'd keep coming all those years with fresh flowers. Someone who really loved her. Her stone said 1959–1978: Snatched away too soon. But it didn't say how. They seemed like funny words to put on a gravestone—"Snatched away"—as if the person who'd chosen them (probably the same one who was still bringing flowers) was pretty mad. Mad at God—or mad at someone, anyway. I wondered if Annie had literally been snatched away by some-one like you—maybe even *by* you. Maybe you'd been tak-ing girls for years and years and years…so long you couldn't even remember how many you'd snatched away. If that was true, I thought you must be really clever, not getting caught.

The tree I remembered was up ahead, off the path on the left. It was big with a great thick trunk. An oak, I think. Ac-tually I have no idea what it was. Maybe it was an ash or a cedar or something else. Tree identification isn't one of my stronger points—not one of my areas of personal expertise. Anyway, I traced an imaginary line from it to the place where I remembered everyone standing, and there it was. I saw it even though I was still quite far away—standing out from all the pale stone ones around it—black and shiny like a rich person's kitchen worktop: Dad's grave.

I turned away, my cheeks burning. I thought, what am I even doing? He won't want to see me—not like this! What if he doesn't recognize me? And I wanted to run, but then I thought, oh God, what if he's seen me and he *does* know it's me? I thought how awful it'd be if, after five years of waiting and waiting for me to come, he had to watch me running off, having no idea why. So I pressed my cuffs into my eyes till I could breathe again and told myself to turn around. "Turn around," I whispered, over and over. "Turn around, you useless cow!" So I did (after about five minutes) and I made myself walk straight over to him, gripping my hands in fists and clenching my teeth so I wouldn't chicken out.

The gold letters shone out of the smooth shiny black:

Thanos "Terry" Laksaris
1963–2006
Beloved husband to Jennifer
And dad to Yasmin
Forever in our hearts.

The ground over his coffin was filled with that gray gravelly stuff that looks like cat litter. There was grass growing up through it and a rusty metal vase on top.

I touched the stone. It was so cold. "Hi, Dad," I said. I had to look away over the graveyard so I wouldn't cry. I didn't want to cry. Not after making him wait so long to see me. Then, when I thought I could go on, I said, "It's me."

It sounded stupid saying that but he might not've known. I don't exactly look like the skinny kid he used to swing around by the ankles and give piggybacks to. I stood there in silence then, feeling him there—his eyes on me, unbelieving, taking me in bit by bit—and I felt fatter than ever. "I'm sorry," I said, and then without any warning, this giant sob sort of unfolded out of me, making me fall on my knees.

When I'd recovered a bit, I traced over the word *dad* with my fingers. Then I ran my hands over all the gravel stuff with grass growing through it, moved the vase and climbed in. I sat with my back against the stone and my legs on the gravel and after a while I started talking.

I told him everything. I told him how I hadn't come for so long because I didn't want him to see what a mess I was. How I'd tried really hard to be okay in the world without him, but how everything I did after he died felt wrong or bad, and how eating was the only thing that felt good, and then how I hadn't really noticed I was getting big until it was too late and I couldn't stop. I told him how everyone hated me, how Katy had spat at me. Sitting there, I remembered something the vicar said to me at the funeral. It was after the service, I think, when we were outside the church. He put his hands on my shoulders, bent down to look me in the eyes and told me, "Talk to him. And don't ever stop because he'll always be listening. It'll help." I thought it was odd that I'd remembered that only then, leaning against Dad's stone. But he was right. It did help. It was nice. I could feel Dad listening.

I told him Mum was fine and that she missed him, too. I didn't mention Gary because, even though Mum's always saying Dad would be pleased she'd met him, I wasn't sure that was true. I thought it was probably just easier for her to think it was true. *I'm* not pleased she found Gary, so why would Dad be? And Dad would never have gone off with someone new. He loved us. He would've gone on loving us. I didn't tell him about you either, in case he worried about me. I thought I'd already given him enough to worry about just by turning up.

It was getting dark when I got up to go. I had to pick off about a million bits of Dad's gravel that were stuck to the back of my legs first, because I didn't want to take any of his gravel away from him. It wasn't like he had much else. Then I promised him I'd come and visit again soon. I told him the next time I'd bring flowers and make his grave nice like Annie Stott's.

Mum and Gary weren't in when I got back from the grave-yard. I remembered they'd gone out to a restaurant because it was their anniversary. I went to my room and lay on the bed and looked at the galaxy on my ceiling and thought about nothing.

I must've fallen asleep because the next thing I knew Mum was standing in the doorway, silhouetted by the yellow land-ing light.

"You all right, Yaz?" she whispered.

"Yeah," I whispered back.

"D'you want some curry? I brought you some back."

"Oh, thanks," I whispered. "I'm not really hungry."

"Sure?"

"Yeah."

She didn't go, though. She waited in the doorway for a minute, her hand on the handle. Then she whispered, "Okay, love. Night."

The next day started off like normal, like any other day. I walked into the English room and Robert said, "Here's Johnny!" in this dramatic way, though I have no idea why. I don't think anyone else knew either. Even Katy ignored him, settling for her predictable death stare instead.

But then, next lesson, it was Drama. We were all sitting around randomly, Alice over the other side with Avril.

"So…" Mr. Webb said, wringing his hands together like the gay he is and running his eyes over us all as if this lesson was going to be the highlight of our lives, "physical theater." He'd already told us we were going to be doing physical theater at the meeting. Apparently, we were going to put on an *impromptu* performance after our exams the next term. In case you're wondering, "physical theater" is acting with your body rather than just with the words, and using your body to be the props as well, like being a tree or a cupboard or something (even though that makes it sound a bit shit, like what little kids in primary schools do).

Anyway, no one yelped with excitement, but we were all watching him. Mr. Webb's nice. He's a bit overenthusiastic, which is a complete understatement, but it kind of adds to how he is. Gary met him at parents' evening and said afterward, "All that man needs is a tutu and he'd be away." That made me laugh because I could see Mr. Webb twirling around

like a walrus in a tutu with his big brushy moustache and not
a care in the world. "So…" he said, looking around at us all
again with big eyes, *"Romeo and Juliet."*

Everyone groaned except Maddie King, who clapped her
hands and bobbed up and down like a spaz. It's torture for
Maddie having to wait till June to get in through those exam
doors and finally see her GCSE papers. Mr. Webb put us all
in pairs and even though we were sitting miles apart, he said,
"Alice, you go with Yasmin here…" The way it worked was
two pairs of people were given the same scene and the scene
had two characters in it. One person from each pair had to
act one part, concentrating on really using his or her body to
show the meaning, and the other person had to be the voice
from offstage. Alice and I got the same scene as Maddie and
Steph—the one where Juliet's asking the Nurse what Romeo
said. Mr. Webb said we were Juliet, and Maddie and Steph
were the Nurse.

I said to Alice she should do the acting.

She looked at me for a second, then she said, "Okay."

Then Maddie and Steph came over and Maddie said
straight off, "Well, obviously Alice has got to be Juliet, and
I'll be the Nurse." She glanced at Steph and said, "You and
Yasmin can do the voices."

Nice, I thought.

Steph opened her mouth like she was going to try to stand
up for herself, but then looked at me and changed her mind.
When we practiced it, Maddie kept stopping to have a go at
Steph, saying the lines for her, to show her how she should
do them, and the third time she did it Alice caught my eye

with a flicker of a smile on her lips. My heart started thudding. I had to look away and pin my eyes on the text so I didn't spontaneously combust. It made me want to do a really brilliant voice for Alice. Or rather for us—Juliet.

We were first up. I sat at the side Alice was on and Steph sat the other side for the Nurse part. And it was *amazing*. Really. Alice was amazing. I could see her over the top of the page— jumping up, holding her hands out as we begged the Nurse for news: "I pray thee, speak! Good, good nurse—speak!" And as it went on, I can't explain, but it was like we were so *together*, it really was like we were one person. Herandme. Meandher. The A Team. The AY Team.

"Oh, bravo!" Mr. Webb said when we finished, clapping, his eyes twinkling, and you could see he meant it. He was looking at me like he didn't know I had it in me, and I wanted to tell him, Mr. Webb, I *don't* have it in me—it's only because of Alice being with me, being part of me!

It felt like God had finally noticed what a shit life I was having and actually decided to do something about it. And after, when we were watching some of the other groups, I got this wild and free feeling right in my heart that made it okay not to look at her—like that all of a sudden it was easy not to look. Which was crazy, because ever since Year Seven I'd had to literally do battle with myself (the *How Long Can I Go Without Looking at Alice* game). But right then, I didn't even need the game. I could just watch the scenes and relax. Because I knew something special had happened—and because I knew she knew it, too. I even left the drama studio first instead of waiting behind so I could follow her, like I normally did. Then, as I was going up the corridor past the dining room, I heard her call my name.

She was sort of half running up to me. "Listen," she said, looking around, tucking her hair behind her ear. She wanted to make sure no one was watching. She didn't see Big Mary through the kitchen doors staring at us as she stirred the daily broth. She was too busy rummaging in her bag. Then she pulled out her sketchbook and opened it and, looking around again, handed me a piece of paper from inside it.

It was the drawing. The Manga girl. She'd cut the page out. I didn't take it.

"I thought you'd like it," she said. She looked a bit embarrassed.

I was trying to compute what was happening. I was thinking, if I put my hand out, she'll snatch it back and say *As if, you freak!* or something, only she didn't. Katy or Sophie or Beth or anyone else would've done that, but she was Alice. She let me take it.

Then she glanced around again. She said, "It's nothing special." She looked in my eyes. "Don't tell anyone, okay? I just thought, after what happened, you know, with Katy…" She shrugged, her cheeks going a bit pink. "I felt bad. Anyway, it's nothing, 'kay?" And then she walked off, leaving me standing there with her drawing in my hands and thinking the only explanation was that any second I was going to wake up.

I thought Alice giving me her picture must've happened because God was pleased with me for going to see Dad. Then I thought maybe it wasn't God but *Dad* who'd made Alice like me, and I loved the idea of that so much it made my heart want to burst—like Alleblimminluia burst.

I gave the Manga girl a name—Juliet—and sat on my bed that evening staring into her black eyes, rerunning in my head what'd happened from the second I'd heard Alice call my name to when she'd turned the corner at the end of the corridor. Every time I saw her face again, her pale skin turning pink, I had to bite my bottom lip and close my eyes—and every time I heard her voice in my head going "It's nothing, 'kay?" I had to laugh out loud and hold my hand over my chest to stop it from exploding. Nothing? *Nothing?* I thought. If that's nothing, then nothing's all I ever want, Alice! And I kissed Juliet all over.

When I got into bed, I propped her up on my bedside table. Then I snuggled down, kissing the tips of my fingers and touching them to her lips one last time before I turned my lamp off. In the dark, I closed my eyes. "Don't be scared to love me," I whispered, hoping I'd drift off into an Alicey dream. "Don't be scared to love me."

I couldn't get to sleep, though. I was too happy, too excited about seeing her again. I thought, there's no way you're going to get your hands on her now, Mr. Badass Pedophile. I'm going to find you and find out everything about you and get you put away, because she's mine now. She's my Alice. And I've got Dad and God helping me, too, so you don't stand a chance!

I got this picture in my head of me and Alice walking up the High Street in town, her arm linked in mine, and I knew what I should do... I should ask her out—like on a date, only

I wouldn't say it was a date. I had enough money on my debit card. I didn't know how much, but enough to get us something to eat. I thought I had to do something to show her how much I loved her Manga drawing, or she might think I didn't. She might even think I didn't like *her*, and I didn't want her to think that, not even for a second. I wanted her to know she could rely on me, that I'd never play any games with her feelings, that I'd just love her and love her and love her forever.

I thought about taking her to Yog first, but it's right in the middle of the shopping center and much too conspicuous for a secret affair (not that this was going to be just an affair). Anyway, I thought Yog might not take debit cards, so I moved us somewhere more private—first to Starbucks, in the bit around the back near the toilets where it's always dark, then to the café on the top floor of John Lewis. We'd definitely not be seen there. Not by anyone who mattered anyway—only middle-aged women. I've no idea what they serve in the John Lewis café, but for some reason strawberry tarts kept coming into my head, the strawberries all juicy and chopped and pushed into the vanilla cream on the top in a spiral pattern and sprinkled with icing sugar. I imagined me spooning one of the strawberries from my tart into her mouth, only some of the juice from it dribbles down her chin and it makes us laugh so much we're crying and clinging to each other and all the old ladies are staring in horror.

I tried to remember what my PIN was after that, because I hadn't used my card for so long I'd forgotten, and then, even though I knew Mum would've kept the bank letter that told me, I had numbers pedaling around in my head for the rest of the night. It was getting light outside when I finally dropped off.

Things didn't go exactly as I'd hoped the next day. I never ate strawberry tart, put it that way.

Basically, Alice ignored me. I told myself she'd probably had a sleepless night, too, worrying that she'd shown her feelings too quickly and frightened me off. Or maybe she'd frightened herself off with her feelings. Either way, I thought, watching her gather her hair in her fingers at the back of her neck and pull it so it all went over one shoulder, I've got to be patient. I've got to give her time to come to terms with how she feels about us. I thought, don't screw this up, Yaz. Keep Calm and Carry On. Keep Calm and Carry On Loving Alice.

I told myself she was ignoring me only because she wanted to keep us a secret, which was definitely a good idea, because if anyone at school got a whiff of us, it'd be *ceaseless*. We'd have to go into hiding… Elope. I told myself not to even get started on that fantasy because I could probably write a trilogy about eloping with Alice. The first one would be *Eloping with Alice—Europe* (because that's probably where we'd go first), then *Eloping with Alice—The Far East*, then *Eloping with Alice—The Americas*. It'd be like an amazing adventure and romance story and travel guide all in one. And somewhere along the way—probably on a beach somewhere in the Far East—we might even get married. It'd be incredible (the wedding *and* the trilogy) and by the time we got back I'd be skinny and we'd both have bronze skin and we'd be this glamorous celebrity couple—like Posh and Becks only a younger, lesbian version—and people would line up for miles at our book signings. I thought it was a shame I'm rubbish at singing, because if I wasn't, we could release an album, too, because Alice was pretty good. Her voice wasn't powerful but just like I'd imagined it before I ever heard it—understated and sweet and a little bit different. Then I thought maybe we could do the album anyway. I mean, if you look good having a rubbish voice doesn't really matter, does it? We could call it *Eloped*, or, if it had more of a rock vibe, maybe even *Lesbian Psycho Stalkers*.

Alice did such a good job of ignoring me that I couldn't get anywhere near her. She didn't even *go* to lunch because after I'd eaten I hung around the entrance right till the end of lunch break. I wrote her a note while I was there. I thought that'd be the most secret way to let her know my plan. It said *DO YOU WANT TO GO INTO TOWN? MY TREAT.* I didn't put a kiss or anything sappy like that and I wrote in capitals and left off names in case someone got hold of it.

I never even got to give it to her. She came into Science late, which wasn't like her, and sat on the other side of the room where Sophie'd kept a space. Then, at the end, she rushed out, looking at her watch, and Sophie came and asked me if I'd heard what the homework was. It was obvious they'd planned it because Sophie'd rather stick pins in her eyes than talk to me. I told myself I was being paranoid, though—that Alice might've had something really important to get to. And maybe Sophie felt bad about the spitting thing, too, like Alice. Maybe Katy'd dug her own grave spitting at me like she did, and now she was gonna pay for it and be the one *we* all hated: Alice, Sophie, Beth and Me.

I went into town anyway. I thought I'd go to the John Lewis café and see if they really did do strawberry tarts. I thought I'd go and see what else they had there, too, because I was starving and felt like eating—as in *EATING*. I got off the bus at the bottom of the High Street and started walking up toward the shopping center. I was about halfway there and thinking about when Alice'd given me her drawing, when I saw your dog. I could've missed it, because I was staring at the pavement, my head filled with Alice, but I saw it out the corner of my eye. It was sitting on the other side of the road outside Boots, tied to the bike rack with the brown leather lead that was looped around your wrist when I saw you by the school fence. I told myself there were lots of small straggly brown dogs around—the kind that'd make Gary say, *That's not a dog, that's a rat*—and lots of brown leather dog leads, too, but I knew it was yours.

My heart thudded in my ears because I didn't know what to do. I had to do *some*thing, though, for Alice. Alice needs me, I thought. I let the whispers out to do their thing, help me think. I thought, maybe I should hang around, then follow you to your house. But you could've lived miles away. You could've driven into town. Then I spotted the little silver barrel dangling from your dog's collar and saw what I could do.

I crossed the road.

Your dog saw me. I think she heard my whispers, too, because she went up on her back legs and started paddling her paws in the air. I say "she" because once I got up close it was obvious she was a girl dog.

"Hello," I said, squatting down to take her little feet. Her tiny pink tongue licked my hands, one then the other, over and over, the silver barrel on her collar jiggling about. "Aren't you sweet," I said, and she was—*so* sweet—only then I remembered about pedophiles having cute props and thought I'd better hurry up and get your address out of the barrel quick before you came back.

I stood up and peered through the shop window to check you weren't paying or on your way out already. I couldn't see you, so I bent down again. I reached under your dog's chin and got the barrel, but it wouldn't unscrew. My fingers were too sweaty. And she wasn't helping any, either. She kept making gruff little noises and bouncing on her front legs, the whites of her eyes showing as she strained to lick my face.

"Stop it!" I told her as I tried to unscrew the barrel again, but it was so tight it wouldn't budge.

I started to panic. I was thinking, You're gonna be here, like any second. Then *take her* came into my head. Just like that: TAKE HER!

I fumbled with the knot around the metal bar, my heart thumping like crazy. I knew if you came out, I couldn't pretend I was just tickling her under the chin anymore. Then her lead came free. I stood up, my legs so wobbly I thought they might not even work, put my hand through the loop, wrapped some of the lead around my wrist and tugged on it. Your dog tried to plant her feet in the pavement but when I pulled harder, she came.

You know how when teachers say they've got eyes in the back of their heads? Well, I had eyes in the back of *my* head then—eyes that could see you coming out of the shop, looking up and down the High Street and clocking me...

"Stop it," I whispered, walking as fast as I could.

I took the first turn off, down Market Street, and realized then where I could go. Without even knowing it, I'd gone the perfect way. I went left into the alley that's dingy and always smells of pee, then across the outside parking lot toward the common land where the gypsies keep their horses.

Your dog was going so fast, her little legs were a gingery blur, and I was wheezing, but I kept on because I could still see you with those eyes in the back of my head, striding after me, coming out of the alley, your hands open at your sides ready to clamp around my neck.

Then I was through the gate and into Lower Field.

I stopped by the first tree with a big enough trunk to hide behind. I pulled the lead short to keep your dog close. It was a few minutes before I dared to even peep around it, back across the parking lot. Nothing. Just a woman tipping the front wheels of a buggy up onto the curb.

I took my bag off, had about five puffs on my inhaler, then sat on one of the tree roots. Your dog looked like she could use some of my inhaler, too. She was panting like mad, looking around everywhere—out across the fields toward the gypsies' horses, behind her toward the train station, back across the parking lot.

"It's okay," I told her. I felt bad that she was worried.

I pulled her closer, stroking her soft, straggly fur.

She made little whimpering noises, licked my hand, then sort of dumped her chin on my leg and looked up at me with her big brown eyes. "Awwww!" I said, stroking the silky soft fur between her ears. "It's not for long, I promise. I'm gonna take you back."

Then I had a go at her barrel again. It came apart easily this time and a tiny scrolled-up bit of paper fell out onto the grass.

No address.

I turned it over.

No address. No number, even. Just: "I am microchipped."

Brilliant, I thought. Fan-bloody-tastic. Apparently people don't put their address or phone number on animal tags anymore. Everything's computerized instead. I got brain freeze then, thinking that, because I realized that *I'd* probably been computerized, too—on CCTV. God, I thought, why didn't I think about that? I couldn't believe how stupid I'd been. I've seen *Crimewatch* and *CSI* enough times to know that *everything's* on CCTV. Especially on a bloody High Street!

I thought you were probably at the police station right that second, watching a replay of me untying your dog and pulling her off down the street, the policeman next to you smirking as he slurps on his tea and tells you, *Well, it shouldn't be too tough to find* that *kid.* There are a lot (at least a million) of not-so-brilliant things about being ninety-nine and a half kilos. Being *highly conspicuous* is one of them.

Seeing as my idea had failed spectacularly, and the police were probably on their way to Lower Field to arrest me, I thought maybe I should just leave your dog there and go back home. I couldn't do it, though. She's too sweet and

anything could've happened to her—she could've got lost
for real or run over or something. I mean, what do dogs do
when they're lost? I don't know. "You'd probably follow me,
wouldn't you?" I said to her. She lifted her head up and put it
on one side, cute as can be. I bent my face closer and let her
sniff all around my ear, making me laugh because it tickled.
"Are you hungry?" I said, and I got the Maryland Chocolate
Chip Cookies out of my bag (the shop was still waiting for the
Hobnob delivery). There was one left. I broke it in half and
held it out. I thought some food might cheer her up. "I know
it's no Hobnob," I told her, "but beggars can't be choosers."

Dad used to say that—*Beggars can't be choosers*—quite hap-
pily, though, like he didn't mind being a beggar in the least.
He was always happy. Mum used to hate the way he'd trot out
little sayings, but he loved them. He said they were some of
the first things he learned to say in English when he moved
here. I wondered if he could see me—like, if no matter *where*
I was, he could see me from up there in heaven, even though
I don't believe heaven really exists. I used to, when he first
died, and I suppose I still think of him as being somewhere,
even though I know it's really all a load of story made up to
make the people left behind feel better.

Anyway, I wondered what he'd say, supposing he was
watching. Something like *What the hell are you doing?* probably. Then I started to think about what he'd *really* think,
like if he knew the whole story about you watching Alice
the way you were, and I thought, if he knew all that, he'd
think I was doing the right thing, and even though taking
your dog was crazy (as well as illegal) he'd say something like

Good on you, girl, and *Don't you give up*. Or, *I'm proud of you, love*. He used to say that a lot, even though I never did anything to be proud of.

This was my chance, though. I thought I'd definitely make him proud if I saved Alice's life and I started to feel better. I stopped worrying so much about the police hunting for me and you hunting for me and remembered how I was doing this for Alice—to save Alice. I thought, she still needs me, whether your address is on your dog's tag or not. So even though I was probably going to be arrested in the next couple of hours, I felt better. I wasn't ready to give up anyway.

"C'mon," I told her, throwing the cookie in the grass because she didn't want it, and we started across the fields.

A bell jingled when I opened the vet's door. Your sweet little dog planted her feet in the pavement again and looked up at me like, *Please no, not here*…so I bent down and picked her up. "It's okay," I told her, nuzzling her ear. "Nothing's gonna happen to you."

There was a woman behind a counter. "Hi," I said. "I found this dog."

She stood up and bent over the counter to get a better look at her. She was wearing a green smock for doing medical things in and a long thin badge that said Veterinary Nurse.

"Oh dear," she said, pouting her lips out and talking in a baby voice, which I thought was a bit unprofessional. "Poor doggy!"

"It says she's microchipped," I said and handed her the little scroll of paper.

She took it into a room behind the counter and came back with a metal scanner thing. "Let's have a look, then," she said, still in that stupid voice, and I put your dog on the floor. The nurse squatted down next to her, holding her by the collar. Then she ran the scanner backward and forward over the back of her neck, peering at a little screen on the top of it and making little cooing noises.

Your dog looked up at me like, *Is this nurse for real?* and I wanted her to be mine so much I can't tell you. "Yes, she is," I said, answering your dog in the same silly voice as the nurse and ignoring the nasty glance she shot me when she stood up and went back behind the counter. Then (in my normal voice) I said, "Has it got an address on it?"

She didn't answer. She sat down and pressed numbers into the phone, holding the scanner thing in front of her while she waited for someone to answer.

"Hello," she said. "Blythwoods. Yes." Then she started saying numbers.

I tried to remember them, thinking they were your phone number, but then there were too many. It was some sort of code, with loads of sevens and zeros in it.

She started writing on one of those yellow Post-it pads. I couldn't see what, because she had that way of writing with her hand all bent around above the words. People write like that a lot. Annabel Carver in my year does, and Kyle Lyons. And the man in the Post Office. Maybe it's genetic or something.

Then she covered the mouthpiece and said, "You can leave her here."

I wasn't expecting that. I thought she was going to peel the sheet off and give it to me.

Then she was dialing again.

When she saw I hadn't moved, she nodded at the plastic chairs against the wall and said, "You can wait if you want to." She was still pissed at me, I think.

At that moment, the door flew open and a man in work boots backed in, helping an old woman through the door. She was moaning and crying and carrying something heavy in a tartan blanket.

"I hit a dog," the man said over his shoulder. "It's been hit." The nurse rushed out from behind the counter, nearly falling over your dog, and opened a door that had a sign over it saying Surgery. "RTA," she called into the room and then they all bundled in. The man who'd hit the dog ran his fingers through his hair like he didn't know if he was supposed to go in as well, but then he did and the door closed.

I could hear the woman crying and someone saying, "*There's* a girl," soothingly, to the dog I think, not the woman. Then everything went quiet.

I picked your dog's lead off the floor and went over to the desk.

The yellow Post-it pad was sitting next to the phone.

I leaned over and pulled off the top sheet. I thought maybe I should just leave your dog like she said and go. I'd got your name now. I'd got your address and phone number, too. I looked down at the paper to check. It said "Mrs. E. Caldwell." *Mrs.?*

Then I had a horrible thought: it's the wrong dog!

I've taken some old lady's or something...

I started whispering. I tried to remember the dog by the school fence—your dog—and whether it was same as the dog looking up at me now. It *was* the same. Definitely. But I couldn't know for sure unless I waited. Or went to the address on the Post-it.

"Come on," I said.

I didn't stop till we got around the corner. Then I sat on someone's front wall and read what the nurse had written again, while your dog sniffed a poo on the pavement.

Mrs. E. Caldwell
81 Claybourne Road
01934762891

I got my phone out to look on Maps. Then I saw two girls from Heathfield School walking toward me in their black uniform with the bright pink trim. I'd forgotten about school. I'd been out only since three o'clock, but it felt like ages ago. Of course they stopped talking when they saw me, like everyone always does, and I saw the one with eyeliner that flicked up at the edges plant her elbow in her friend's arm as she looked from me to your dog and back at me again. They walked past like they were holding their breaths, then started sniggering. Yes, very funny, I thought: owners are meant to look like their dogs, not the complete opposite—not like an elephant and a mouse. Ha-ha, hilarious.

I typed *Claybourne Road* into my phone. I know quite a lot of roads around there because I've always lived in the area,

but I didn't know that one. It was on the estate, down the
bottom near the houses that are for families of people in the
military. From where I was, it was down the avenue, then
across the park. Not far—maybe ten minutes.

I wondered if I should call first, because whoever's number
it was might think it was a bit weird, their dog going missing, then me suddenly turning up on their doorstep with it.
Or they might not be in. They might still be in town trying to find it.

Then I thought of something that hadn't even occurred
to me before—that you might be married. That Mrs. E.
Caldwell might be your wife. And if she was, and she answered the phone, I still wouldn't know if I'd got the right
dog. It also meant that *you* might be the one who answered. I
got a funny feeling when I thought that—a chill went through
me—and it suddenly seemed a lot less scary to go to your
house than to hear your voice in my ear. I mean, the bad man
who's gonna slit your throat and hack you up isn't usually the
one answering his front door, is he?

He's the one talking to you on the other end of the phone.

Your dog seemed to know we were going to your house. It
was like she wanted me to stop using my phone so she could
show me the way herself, like she couldn't wait for you and
me to get introduced because she just knew in her bones that
we were gonna be best buddies or something. She kept looking up at me as if to say, "Yes, this is the way, well done, keep
going, I'll show you…" Once we got to the estate, though,
I got this queasy feeling in my stomach and slowed down. I

still let your dog pull me closer, step by step, but I was thinking, get out of here already. Just let her go. She knows the
way home. But she probably wouldn't have gone on, even if
I'd shooed her. She'd probably have gone up on her back legs
and licked my knees till I surrendered or something. Anyway I *had* to carry on. If I didn't, I'd never know if I had the
right dog or not, and I'd look pretty special telling the police I knew who'd abducted Alice and then leading them to
some dear old biddy.

I don't think it was the only reason I kept going, though.
It was something else, too—the idea of meeting you, I think.
I mean, I was scared of meeting you, obviously, but I also
wanted to. I wanted to know what you looked like up close—
to know what it was like to look into those eyes that'd stared
so menacingly at Alice.

We went down about six roads. The estate's a maze, not
that I needed to worry about getting lost. Your dog was still
skipping ahead, going "Left here, that's it, well done, left
again, now it's right..." I gave in and put my phone away. I
thought, who needs GPS with this crazy dog?

Some of the roads had blossom trees on them, but as we
got farther in, the trees disappeared and there were just houses
and lampposts. It was actually kind of a nice feeling, being
somewhere I didn't know and being led along by a dog, like
I didn't have to think about anything, just plod along behind.
Like *I* was the dog.

Claybourne Road looked pretty much like all the other
roads around it, but when we got to number 67 it started
curving around to the right. I stopped. I don't know why,

but that curve got me panicky. I knew there could be only more road and more houses around it, but I didn't want to see.

I got my inhaler out and had two puffs, doing it exactly like the nurse at the doctor's showed me: trying not to hunch my shoulders up too much, holding each one in and counting to five.

Your dog strained on the lead. Then she barked—a sharp, high bark meant for you, I think—or for Mrs. E. Caldwell anyway. She cocked her ear, listening ahead. I got a funny feeling then that you might suddenly appear from around the bend and catch me standing there by your neighbor's hedge, whispering and clutching your dog's lead like a nut job, so I started walking again.

You'll be fine, I told myself. Just stay where people can see you.

Everything was pretty much the same around the corner—road, pavement, semidetached houses—though there was a little parade of shops farther along on the other side.

Your house was the same as all the others: brown concrete with rough walls like sandpaper and joined to the house next to it. The other side of it had a narrow gravel driveway leading down to a garage, and at the front there was a small, messy front garden and a step going up to a red front door. Red for blood, I thought. Red for "Don't Do It!"

Your dog started making gruff little noises and pulled like crazy, hauling me up the driveway.

"All right!" I told her and dumped my bag.

I stood on the step and waited a second. I took a big breath in and blew out slowly through an imaginary straw, like Mr.

Webb told Steph to when she said she couldn't go on stage in last year's play. I'm not sure it worked because a second later she threw up everywhere. Anyway, I did the straw-breathing thing. Then I rang the bell.

Nothing. It didn't work. I couldn't hear anything anyway, so I knocked.

Your dog leaped up and started scrabbling at the door. "Good girl," I said and gave her a stroke, thinking there was still time to go before someone answered. I didn't move, though. I stood looking at the stone Scotty dog hiding in the nettles in the flowerbed, then at your front window. It had net curtains hanging in it, which seemed a bit creepy. I didn't think net curtains were the sort of thing a man like you would hang in his window, but then if you were married, or I had the wrong dog... Suddenly your dog stopped scrabbling and barked again. There were footsteps the other side of the door.

Then the silver latch turned and there you were.

Not an old lady. Not any lady.

You.

RUM AND COKES

I WAS RELIEVED YOU bent down to your dog because I went red. I don't know why. Because you didn't really look like I'd thought you would, I suppose. You were taller and younger. On the school field I'd been quite far away. I'd seen your clothes and your high forehead and limp black hair going down each side and I'd thought you were sixty or something, but you were only about forty. You put your knee on the floor next to a shoe rack that had two pairs of muddy sneakers on it and let your dog lick your face. She had her front paws on your shoulders and was going licklick-licklicklick like mad as you rubbed her sides with your big bony hands. Then you held her little feet in your fingers and looked up at me. I saw you clock the badge on my blazer that says Ashfield Senior School on it.

I stepped back, forgetting I was on a doorstep, and stumbled a bit. "Steady," you said, standing up, and you sort of smiled when I'd got my balance. I thought of the pedo-smile.

Your lips were quite thin, but because your mouth was wide, they were also long and curvy. Then you said, "How'd you get this address?"

I saw the blue coat you'd been wearing when you were watching Alice. It was hanging behind you above the shoes. I felt my face go even redder and my palms go sweaty and I wanted to swallow but my mouth was too dry. I took another step back, so I was next to my bag, and said, "The vet's."

"Where was she?" you said.

"On Market Street."

You looked down at your dog and shook your head like you were sad. "Must've been kids," you said. Then you looked up and fixed your dark eyes on me.

I wiped my palms down my skirt slowly so you wouldn't notice, even though I think you might have because you glanced down at them. Then you turned and went back inside, into your hallway, and your dog went in, too.

I thought maybe that was it—that you weren't coming back. I didn't move, though, because you'd left the door open. I looked around. Some little kids were playing over the road, taking turns on a tricycle, and a man walking farther up near the shops stopped to light a cigarette. I picked up my bag.

"Here," you said. You were in the doorway again, holding out a tenner. I knew it was a trick. I knew if I went to take it, you'd grab me and pull me into your house. You waggled it and smiled and I saw the gap between your front teeth. I still didn't move. I said, "The vet said she belongs to Mrs. E. Caldwell." I don't know why I said it because it was crazy enough going around there at all without asking nosy questions that might get you mad.

You dropped your hand with the tenner by your side and with the other one you started smoothing down your hair at the back, looking at the ground like you were deciding whether or not you were going to tell me who Mrs. E. Caldwell was. Then obviously you decided you were—because you thought I was doing a good job, I expect, making sure your dog was going back to her proper owner. You said, "Yeah, well, she did." You looked away across the road. I saw the muscles in your jaw move. Then you put your hand in your pocket and looked back at me. "She was my mother's. She passed away a couple of weeks ago."

"Oh," I said, then because the silence was awkward, I said, "Sorry."

You nodded slowly. "Well," you said, "thanks again," even though you hadn't thanked me before.

I wanted to go, obviously. I didn't want to hang around with a weirdo who stares at girls, but at the same time I sort of wanted to keep talking to you, so I said, "Can I say goodbye?"

You looked a bit confused for a second like you didn't know whom I wanted to say goodbye to, but then you turned and gave a soft whistle into the house—through the gap in your teeth, I think. "Here, Bea!" you said. I thought it was Bee as in bumblebee till later, when you told me it was short for Beatrice. But I still thought it was the perfect name. Small and fluffy and round, just like her. She appeared at your feet, water dripping from her chin.

"Say goodbye," you told her. You had a funny way of smiling that made you look sadder than when you weren't smiling. Bea looked at you like she didn't know what you were talking about, which she probably didn't. Then you looked at me, still smiling, but squinting a bit because the sun had come out and was shining on your face. "You'll have to forgive her," you said. "She's not really herself right now."

Then she did the cutest thing ever. She came running over and sat at my feet, her little tail brushing the path, her little nose pointing up at me. I bent down and stroked her head. I wanted to kiss her, but that would've been a bit weird with you watching, so I just did a kissing noise instead and said, "'Bye, Bea."

"Looks like you've made a friend," you said. Then, when I'd given her a bit more fuss, you held the tenner out again. "Change your mind?"

I stood up and shook my head.

You started smoothing down your hair at the back of your head again—probably because you didn't know what else to say, and because I couldn't think of anything to say, either, I said, "'Bye," and walked away.

I stopped when I got to the corner, though. I realized I hadn't asked you what your name was. But you weren't there anymore, and neither was Bea. The door was closed like it'd never happened.

I thought I wouldn't see you again. Maybe in court to point you out and say *It was him, that was the man I saw watching Alice,* but not at your house. There was no reason to go back there. I already had way more information than I needed, even without knowing your name. I knew your surname and your address and phone number. I even knew your dog's name and the vet it went to. All I had to do was wait.

It was like, *It's your move, Mr. Caldwell.*

I lay in bed that night and the next, planning exactly what I was going to do to prepare for when you took Alice. If she was ever more than two minutes late to class from break, I'd say I needed the bathroom so I could leave the classroom, then I'd call emergency dispatch. And if we weren't in the same class, I'd wait near the Head's office where I'd see her, no matter which door she came through, and I wouldn't go to class myself till I knew she was okay.

I kept imagining how it'd be reported in all the papers, how I'd feel, knowing I'd saved her, how I'd say it was worth risking my life to save Alice's. I imagined sitting opposite Holly Willoughby on *This Morning*'s red sofa and Mum squeezing my leg as we waited to go on air. I even imagined Gary putting his arm around me and saying something like, *I got you all wrong, kid. I had no idea.* But the best daydream I had was waiting to see Alice after she'd been rescued. I'm outside a big building—maybe a police station—with hundreds of press people pointing their cameras at the door and then suddenly all the cameras start clicking and flashing and I see Alice coming out wrapped in a police blanket, her hair caked in mud, her face all scratched and bleeding from her struggle with you, and tears running through it all as I rush over to her and she falls into my arms. I couldn't wait, couldn't *wait* for it all to be real, to actually happen. I thought, hurry up already, Mr. Caldwell, make my day!

I put Avril's password in and Googled you during a free period at school. Since I got hauled into Miss Ward's office in Year Eight for trying to Google *Most interesting ways to commit suicide* I never log in as me. It's none of their bloody business what we look at. It's abuse of our civil rights. We don't get to see what *they* Google and I'm guessing some of their searches would be pretty interesting—Mr. Faraday's, for one. Anyway, when I put your name in, nothing came up. Well, tons of Caldwell stuff came up, but nothing about you, so I tried out a few first names with Caldwell then, to narrow it down to names I thought a bad man like you might have, like Malcolm or Colin or Brian. *Brian*—I hate that name, it sounds like "brain."

None of the pictures that came up were you, of course, but it was quite funny looking at them all. There was a Malcolm Caldwell with a massive beard sitting in a giant yellow clog, which was a bit random, and a Trevor Caldwell who was probably the most good-looking guy in the world, though he knew all about it. Like Sophie does. It's something in their sparkly eyes that spells S.M.U.G. I knew I was wasting my time, but I quite like looking at pictures of people I don't know. When I'm in the mood, I can look for hours. I just type in any random name and then pick a picture and imagine their lives and what their houses look like inside and what their favorite food is.

Anyway, then I tried *Caldwell Criminal* and *Caldwell Pedophile*, as well. I knew the pictures that came up wouldn't be you. I mean, they wouldn't be, would they, because you hadn't been caught? Yet, I thought. Haven't been caught yet, and my heart started thumping again in anticipation.

It wasn't till the next day in Maths I realized that instead of looking for information on you, I should've been looking for information on the people you'd taken, so I went back to the library in lunch and looked up *Missing girls*, even though I knew I should've really been watching the path.

A site called *Missing Kids* came up. It had pages of pictures of teenagers with their ages and where they came from. The pictures were mostly of boys and any girls were either black or Asian. It wasn't till I got several pages in that I saw Amelia Bell.

She wasn't as pretty as Alice. She didn't have Alice's eyes or nose or any of the stuff that Alice has that makes her so, well, *Alicey*. But I suppose she was similarly slim with long, straight fair hair. The same type of girl. Similar enough to make me gasp, to get a funny feeling deep inside that told me you might've watched her, too, just like you were watching Alice now, only no one had seen you watching Amelia Bell…

Next to the picture of her it had a box with *Key Information* in it such as *Age: 16, Missing For: 141 days*, and under that it said *Amelia, we would love to hear from you. Call. Text. Anytime. Free. Confidential. 116000.*

When I Googled her name, the *Nottingham Post* came up. The article said *Amelia went missing on November 9. She was last seen walking to a friend's house in Mansfield at around 4:00 p.m., wearing a white top with three-quarter-length lacy sleeves and black leggings.* It had a different picture of her, smiling this time, with her arm around someone. It said, *It is possible she could have traveled to and be residing in the London Brixton area. Anyone with any information, please call the Nottingham Missing Persons' Unit.* I thought, it's also possible she's dead and rotting away somewhere and that the only person who knows where she is, is you.

Nottingham looked quite far away on the map. When I did directions from Claybourne Road, it said it'd take two hours and seventeen minutes to drive there. I've no idea if two hours and seventeen minutes is too far to go to take someone. I suppose it depends if you like driving. I thought if you had some good music to listen to, it'd be okay, but it was probably too far to go just to watch someone. Then I thought how, seeing as it was your mum's house on Claybourne Road, you probably didn't live there (which would be pretty weird, living with your mum when you're forty-something). Maybe you lived in Nottingham.

When I got home, I typed *Murderers* into Google Images, just to see what murderers look like—to see if any of them looked like you. I was still looking when Mum came in, knocking as she opened the door. She pretended she wanted to know what kind of salad I'd like for dinner.

Salad. Yeah, sure, Mum—like I'd like *any* kind of salad for dinner.

She took my "Are you all right in the mind, Mother?" face to be an invite into my room and sat on my bed. "What's that?" she said, looking at my laptop screen.

I sighed, stating the obvious. "Pictures of men."

"Oh," she said, wrinkling her nose up and leaning forward to get a better look.

I closed the lid. "What d'you want, Mum?" I said. "I'm busy."

"So I see," she said annoyingly, her eyes going all twinkly like she knew exactly what I was doing when she had absolutely no idea at all.

I sighed and turned away from her. She could think what she liked. If it made her happy to think I was lusting after men, that was fine by me. "Whatever."

"Well, it's only natural," she said. "Getting interested, you know…"

I rolled my eyes at Juliet, whom I'd tacked to the wall over my desk. She looked how I felt: *indignant*—like, Yeah, lady-in-Yaz's-room, go away already. You're trespassing.

Mum didn't go, though. She said, "It'll be a nice salad. Gary's—"

"I don't want salad!" I said, spinning around to face her. "I don't *like* salad! Salad's disgusting!"

She looked down at her lap, nodding like she was suddenly upset and picking at imaginary bits of dust on her trousers. Then she said, out of nowhere, so I knew Gary had put her up to it, "I think we need to talk."

"I don't want to talk!" I said. "I'm busy."

She looked at me, her eyes all big and pleading. "It's getting out of hand."

I threw my hands up. *"It?"* I said, then, "Oh, you mean my obsession with Googling pictures of men?" Of course I knew what *it* really was. *It* is our Voldemort. The F-word (the one with the letters *at* after it). The one that cannot be said out loud, that must be tiptoed around at all times.

She knew I was being deliberately obstructive and sighed. "Well, don't *you* think we should talk about it?" she said. "I mean, are you *okay* with being heavier every time we go to the hospital? Don't you *care*? Don't you want to be—attractive?"

I turned away again and closed my eyes. I wasn't going to rise to it. I've done all the crying and despising myself that it's possible for a person to do, followed by all the promising and list-making and willpowering, and all any of it does is make me want to eat and eat and eat and eat and eat and eat and EAT. In fact, her just bringing up the subject made me think about chocolate cake coated with thick chocolate butter icing, and before she'd mentioned it I hadn't even been thinking about food. So I shrugged. "Not really," I said, "no."

That stumped her. I could feel her staring at me, lost for words—wondering, probably, why she'd got stuck with such a nightmare of a daughter when all she wanted was to enjoy being *in love* in her happy new life. Then she got up.

"Well, that's fine," she said, "but salad is what Gary and I are having, because even if you don't care, *I* do. *I care*. And we're going to be eating better things from now on. No more Pizza Hut. No more junk."

When she went out I shouted after her, "I thought you said it's what's on the inside that counts." Of course she didn't have an answer for that.

Bloody Gary, I thought, because I knew it'd come from him. I hate bloody Gary! At least Mum wasn't deluded enough to have said "*We* care," as in "your loving stepdad and I," because she knows that's not true. She knows he wishes I didn't exist. I'm just baggage to him—the extra-weighty kind that comes with Mum—like it or lump it.

That night, I don't know if I was dreaming about her, but when I woke up, she was there in my head—Little Bea. All alone and sitting by the front door underneath where your blue coat hangs, wondering if Mrs. E. Caldwell was ever going to come back.

"She won't, little Bea," I whispered and I sat up clutching myself because I couldn't stand thinking of her, all alone and sad like that. I didn't know why I hadn't thought about her before—why I hadn't thought about what you'd meant when you said, "She's not really herself right now." You'd meant she was grieving, didn't you? That she was miserable without your mother.

I stared into the dark of my room and wished I could cuddle her up in my arms like I had in the vet's. I thought about how she wouldn't even know where Mrs. Caldwell had gone—not unless she was there when it happened like if Mrs. E. Caldwell had a heart attack or something and died right in front of her. But what if Mrs. Caldwell had been taken to the hospital? Bea would've been left at home, feeling like she never got to say goodbye.

Like me when Dad died. I never got to say goodbye, either. Mum didn't tell me till after school when we got in the car. I remembered the trees outside lurching across the windshield, the car tilting so it felt like we were falling through the branches and me whispering, "When?" because I could tell from the way Mum was being that it hadn't just happened and I couldn't bear to think he'd been dead for a second without me knowing. She told me his heart had stopped at about 10:30 a.m. I wanted to beat her with my fists and shout, *What do you mean, about 10:30 a.m.?* But I was falling, and all I could do was cling to the car seat and think that was this morning, and how since 10:30 a.m. I'd stuck shells on my Mother's Day box and scored a goal in netball and laughed so much with Ella at lunch I'd nearly wet myself...

I couldn't forgive Mum for that—for those hours when Dad was dead and I didn't know and was happy. Those hours haunt me. I still have the nightmare where I'm standing over him in his hospice bed, laughing and laughing, while he's gasping at the air like a fish in a boat, trying to tell me goodbye.

Bea must feel like that, I thought, only it's even worse for her because she probably doesn't know where Mrs. Caldwell is. She probably thinks she just walked out the door and *chose* to never come back. I closed my eyes, whispering, "Poor little Bea," over and over and praying that she was curled up next to you on the bed and not in some cold, dark corner of your house all alone.

Then I told myself to calm down. I told myself I was obsessing and letting things get out of perspective. I put my bedside lamp on and remembered how you'd held her feet in your fingers and let her lick your face, and thought how actually you'd looked kind and how you were probably really nice to her and I was worrying about nothing. But then I thought about who you *really* were—how you'd looked when you'd been staring at Alice—and I got worried again. I thought, people say it's the nice ones you've got to watch, don't they?

Or is it the quiet ones? I thought, you were nice *and* quiet. Then I thought how, seeing as she wasn't even your dog, maybe you didn't really want her, that you were planning to give her away...get rid of her... I remembered you saying, "Looks like you've made a friend," and I thought, maybe if I go back, you'll give her to me.

Gary's never let me have a dog because he's allergic (supposedly). I begged and begged when I first moved into his house till he lost his temper and forbade me to mention the word *dog* again—even *hypoallergenic dog*, which proves the allergy thing's just an excuse. But if I was *given* a dog—one that would have to be put down or something if I couldn't take it—I thought maybe Mum could convince him. 'Specially as he's so keen for me to lose weight (more for his sake than mine, in case you're wondering, so I won't be such an embarrassment to him). He hates being anywhere in public with me. He literally squirms when people look at us, because he thinks they'll assume he's my real dad. He'd get a T-shirt that says I'm Just the Stepdad if he could. Anyway, I thought if Mum told him I'd be walking Bea every day and out of the house more, he might say yes.

Then I caught sight of Juliet. She was glaring at me from the wall and she didn't look like she was very happy at all about the way I was thinking about your dog. I told her sorry and that she was right—the last thing I needed to do was start obsessing about the dog of the man who was going to take Alice. I told myself, get a bloody grip!

School went so slowly those days, I thought my heart might literally stop beating out of boredom. The only remotely interesting thing that happened was that I found one of Alice's hairbands when everyone had changed and gone after PE. I was doing the buttons up on my shirt and saw it under the bench where she'd been changing, so I went over and moved it out with my toe. I knew it was hers. It's that thick elastic threaded with gold that she always has, and loads of her hair was tangled in it.

But even that wasn't *that* interesting—not as interesting as it should've been. And that was weird. I stood there looking down at it, thinking, why doesn't it feel like it normally does? I didn't get any of the usual tingly feelings in my legs and arms, my mouth going dry, my breath going fast and shallow. But why? Nothing's changed, I thought. She's ignored me forever, so just because she's going out of her way to ignore me now—like I'm the one who chased her up the corridor with a present—what's the difference?

I thought I might not even bother to pick it up. Then, when I did, I thought I might just drop it again. I thought, I'll be late for History if I don't hurry. I thought, I'm late already— but I didn't move. I stood there, turning the hairband in my fingers, gently pulling on the strands of Alice's hair and wondering why it didn't feel like it should.

I kept it, though. More out of habit than anything else. I put it in my coat pocket.

Gary was outside school when I left. I suppose he was finished for the day and driving past when he saw all the kids coming out.

"Hey, Yaz!" he called when I was heading for the bus stop.

I generally walk around keeping my head down, so I hadn't seen him. He was parked by the side of the road, leaning out the window of his van and drumming a rhythm on the door with his thumb. "Want a lift?"

I never want a lift—not with Gary. I'd rather sit on the bus with everyone from school hurling abuse at me than be trapped in Gary's van, knowing that even though he's being all jolly-jolly-stepdad, what he's really thinking about is how, if I was his child, he'd take me in hand and whip me into some kind of a shape he didn't have to feel so ashamed of.

After he'd pulled out into the traffic, he turned the radio down and said, "Good day?" and I got the idea this might not be just a lift because he happened to be driving past school. This might be a lift because he wanted a *little chat* about eating salads and being more respectful to my mother.

"Yeah," I said, feeling even more uncomfortable than I usually do around him, and adding, "Not bad," when he glanced across at me. I pulled my skirt down so it was covering as much of my legs as possible and looked out the window.

"Bit nippy out, isn't it?" he said.

"Yeah," I said, remembering Alice's hairband in my pocket and taking it out for something to fiddle with.

When we pulled away from the lights, he said, "Everything okay? Only your mum said she thought you seemed a bit down."

I rolled my eyes at my reflection and said I was fine, praying he'd leave it at that, and he did for a bit. Then he said, "Well, you're in luck tonight. It's going to be veggie curry—made by my own fair hands."

One thing I absolutely hate is when people start talking
about food when they think I'm unhappy or being too quiet.
As if talking about food will cheer me up, like I'm a simple
idiot or something.

I stared out the window and let him blab on about what
kind of curry he was going to make and what things he was
going to put in it, when I realized I'd done the same thing to
Bea in Lower Field when I'd shoved the Maryland Cookie at
her. She'd looked pretty upset. Thinking about it, and even
though she's the sweetest dog ever, she'd probably been pretty
insulted, too, like, *Oh that's right—just abduct me, why don't you,
then make it all A-OK with a cookie?* She'd have probably rolled
her eyes if she could, which was a funny thing to imagine—
Bea rolling her eyes.

Then Gary pulled over. We were at the top of his road.
I looked at him. For a moment I thought he'd stopped be-
cause he was going to give me a lecture, but then he said,
"Come on, then."

"What?"

He lifted his hand off the steering wheel and thumped it
back down again. "Chrissakes," he snapped, letting his jolly
mask slip. I realized he'd been saying something about going
to the co-op. He was dropping me off. "It wouldn't kill you,
would it?" he said.

"Sorry," I mumbled, getting my bag and getting out.

"I mean, I'm trying here," he called, leaning across my seat.

I swung the door shut and walked off and didn't look back.

When I got in, Mum wasn't in the kitchen or the living
room. "I'm up here," she called.

She was in my room, standing with her arms folded like she was waiting for me. My drawers and wardrobe were all open and the Cadbury's Dairy Milk Turkish Delight bars from my suitcase and bedside table were on the bed with half a packet of Maryland Cookies lined up like exhibits.

"What're you doing?" I shouted. "Get out!"

She didn't move, though. She said, "Yasmin, someone has to…"

Then I saw Alice's Box on the bed behind her, lying on its side, Alice's things tipped out over the duvet.

I lunged for it, pushing her out of the way, picking up the green foil and holding it up. "You *ripped* it!"

I felt dizzy suddenly, my stomach like liquid, and I thought I was going to heave. Just the thought of Mum touching them, touching Alice's things…

I could see the shock on her face—the incomprehension at why I was completely freaking over a biscuit wrapper. I spun away and started putting the things back in the box—the sock, the hair clip, the pencil, the foil—then realized the heart wasn't there. "Where's the heart?" I said. *"Where's the heart?"*

"I don't know… I didn't move anything…" Mum spluttered, coming to help, but I pushed her away again. I pushed her so hard she hit the wardrobe door.

"Get off," I shouted. "I hate you!"

She was looking at me like she was scared of me. "I *hate* you!" I screamed. "I wish *Dad* was here!"

Then she stepped forward—suddenly, like she was programmed to do it, like that whatever else was happening was instantly wiped the second I mentioned Dad. Her face was full of sympathy, her arms going out to wrap around me.

I batted them away. "Don't you get it?" I said. "I mean I wish Dad was here *instead* of you!"

She looked like I'd punched her. *I* felt it, too—the force of what I'd said and how horrible it was, but worse than that, how *true* it was, because I *do* wish it'd been her who died instead of Dad.

She put a hand over her mouth and stared at me with hurt eyes, then left.

I sat on the bed and tipped Alice's things out of the box again. The heart was there, caught in the bottom. I put everything back in and laid the torn foil carefully on the top. Then I put the box under my bed, took it out and put it in the bottom corner of my wardrobe under a pile of sweaters. Then I grabbed the chocolate bars and went downstairs and out the front door.

As soon as I'd shut it, of course, I realized I didn't have my phone or any money, so I couldn't go to the chip shop and get chips with curry sauce, which was what I really wanted. I thought about going and asking if they'd just give me some, or let me pay later, but they wouldn't, and anyway I was shaking so much I wouldn't be able to speak.

So I went to the park.

I shoved the chocolate in my mouth row by row as I walked, chewing and swallowing. When I got there, I didn't stop, though. I carried on right through it till I was on the edge of your estate. Then I was walking down all the roads to you, not knowing if I was going the right way but just going anyway.

It must've been right, because I got to your road and your neighbor's hedge where I'd stopped when I was with Bea. All four Turkish Delight bars were gone and my jaw was aching like crazy, but I still felt shaky and like I was going to cry. Only now I felt sick, too.

I tried to take deep breaths, whispering to steady myself, but my chest was juddering. I knew it was stupid to be going to you—stupid, stupid, stupid—but I wanted to see Bea. I wanted to cuddle her, bury my face in her fur, tell her I knew how she must feel, losing Mrs. E. Caldwell. Then I was knocking on your door and Bea was barking and you were there and I think I was so *afraid* of you being there and then so relieved that you *were*, I burst into tears.

"Whoa," you said and you ran your fingers through your hair. You looked like you couldn't believe I was really standing there on your doorstep. Then Bea came running out of the hallway barking at me, and instead of thinking how you were this very dangerous man and that this could be the last time I was ever going to see daylight, I thought how she was probably warning you that you shouldn't let me in because I was the bad person who'd taken her and I said, "I'm sorry," only I was crying so much it just came out like massive sobs.

You put your hands out then to tell me to stop crying or calm down a bit, but I couldn't. "Shush, Bea," you said. "Look who it is! It's that nice girl who rescued you." You weren't looking at her, though. You were looking over my shoulder, out at the street, one way then the other, like you were checking no one had seen me.

Then, when I kept on crying and Bea kept on barking, you stepped back, pulling the door open. .

Normally, I never would've gone in. I'd have said, *Nooo, Mr. Caldwell, I am not coming into your evil lair*, but right then I really didn't care if you killed me or not. I thought how it'd actually be a bonus, a double bonus even, because if you did and then got caught because of it, I'd have saved Alice by sacrificing myself in her place, which would be even more heroic than just telling the police about you (except that no one, including Alice, would ever know that that's what I'd done because they'd never know how all along you were really planning to kill her).

You ran your fingers through your hair again like you weren't at all sure about me coming into your house, but then you closed the door and followed me down your hallway, touching my shoulder lightly to tell me to go into the room on the left.

It was small and dark because of the net curtain, and smoke was hanging in the air.

"Take a seat," you said. I sat on the sofa—sank into it, it was so spongy—and Bea came and stood at my feet, panting up at me, her sharp white teeth showing. I could feel your eyes on me and even though I was still blubbering like a little kid, I wished I wasn't wearing my school uniform and had changed into something a bit nicer. I wished I'd put my jeans on with my black mohair Evans sweater that's got a peach on the front of it.

You went out and Bea went up on her back legs in front of

me and started paddling her paws in the air like she had outside Boots. Then you came back with a handful of toilet paper.

I pressed it to my eyes, my chest jumping in spasms. Then,
because it was making me feel pretty self-conscious with you
standing there at the end of the sofa watching me, I leaned
forward and stroked Bea.

You said, "Do you want a drink? Tea?" I nodded and you
went out.

Then you were there again. "Or a rum and Coke?"

I said, "Can I just have Coke?"

Bea lay down at my feet while you were in the kitchen,
her chin on her paws. I could hear you opening the fridge
and cupboard doors.

"Hello, little Bea," I whispered. I could smell the cigarette
butts from the ashtray on the floor next to the chair. There
were five in there, all roll-ups, skinny and folded where you'd
pressed them out. The chair was blue velvet with a bit of
lace hanging over the back and the only thing in the room
that wasn't brown. The carpet was brown with swirls on it,
the curtains were brown, the table and sofa were brown and
the fireplace had beige tiles around it with pictures of plants
growing up them. Above that, lots of little china dogs were
lined up along the mantelpiece. I started to feel better. Calmer
anyway, even though I was still having to catch at breaths.

You came in with a tray. Bea's tail wagged, but she didn't
move. "It's Diet Coke," you said, stepping over her. "That
okay?" And because it seemed funny asking someone as fat
as me if Diet Coke was okay, I laughed. I said Diet was prob-

ably a good idea and you smiled, even though you didn't look at me.

You pushed the tray onto a round side table next to the velvet chair, making some letters fall off. You picked them up and put them on the tray next to two wineglasses with ice in them, two cans of Diet Coke and a bottle of Captain Morgan rum that had a picture of a pirate on the label. Then you pulled a dark blue packet out of the back pocket of your jeans and sat down, putting it on the arm of the chair. It was tobacco. The packet said Drum on it in big white letters.

Neither of us said anything while you poured Coke into the first glass. It fizzed on the ice. I looked at your skin, pale and yellowy against your dark hair, at your big muscly nose and the dimple in the middle of your chin. You handed me the glass, then poured some rum into the other one and topped it up with Coke from the open can.

I could feel a faint breeze on my face from the bubbles popping in my glass, and because I thought you might notice I was staring at you, I looked around at everything in the room again.

There was a cuckoo clock on the wall next to the chimney breast. I hadn't even heard it ticking till I saw it, which was crazy because it was really loud, like *tock-took, tock-took*. It was in the shape of a house covered in blue and red flowers, with green leaves and little birds, and every time it *tock-took*ed, a girl on a swing with blond hair in a blue dress and puffy white sleeves went left, right (instead of backward and forward) underneath it.

"Do you live here?" I said.

"Me?" you said. You picked up the Drum and opened the flap. There was a packet of green Rizlas inside and you pulled one of the papers out. "No. Well, sort of. I do now."

I nodded even though you weren't looking at me, and watched you pull some tobacco along the Rizla with your fingertips. I'd seen roll-up butts lots of times, but I'd never seen anyone make one. You were so quick it was almost like it was making itself. It made me think of a video I saw on YouTube where someone scrunched a piece of paper up, only the film was played backward so the paper started off in a ball and then went flat.

You put the roll-up in your lips and started rooting around in the front pocket of your jeans—the same pocket you'd had your hand in when you were watching Alice. You pulled a silver lighter out, flipped the lid back and lit the roll-up, screwing your eyes shut as you dragged on it. A thin line of smoke went up into the air, then curled out like the branches of a tree.

When you'd had a couple of more drags, I said, "Where were you before?"

"Oh," you said, "farther north." You pulled a bit of tobacco off the end of your tongue and wiped it on the chair cushion.

I thought of Amelia Bell, the girl who went missing in Nottingham, and said, "Whereabouts?"

You glanced at me again, but only for a second. "Here and there," you said.

I nodded. Then I said, "I had a friend who went to live in Nottingham." That wasn't true, but I wanted to see what your reaction was.

You picked the ashtray off the floor, put it on your leg and tapped the ash from your roll-up into it. Then you looked at the wall behind me. "I'm going to redecorate," you said. "Do it up, you know."

I nodded, thinking, nice "changing of the subject" there. I also thought how I probably looked like the Churchill dog from the television commercials, nodding all the time, with my face all swollen from crying so much. I looked at the china dogs on the mantelpiece again.

You saw me looking, but you didn't say anything, so I said, "Can I have a look?"

"Oh, sure," you said, "have a look."

I put my drink on the floor and had to pretend it wasn't a major nightmare trying to get off the sofa, even though you could probably tell. Then I went over to the fireplace.

You leaned forward like you might be going to get up as well, and the thought crossed my mind that these could be the last moments of my life—that in a second or two you were going to whip a rope or a shoelace or something around my neck. I still didn't really mind, though, which was weird. I mean I even felt okay about it, like, Well, I guess that's up to you, Mr. Caldwell. You didn't get up. You had another drag of your roll-up, tapped more ash into the ashtray, then took your glass off the tray and had a sip.

There were loads of china dogs, probably thirty or something, and all of them were like Bea. They'd been positioned so they were acting out little scenes, with one crouching forward, its bum in the air like it was about to pounce on the one next to it that was rolling on its back. It was nice thinking of Mrs. E. Caldwell putting them like that so carefully. I wondered if she used to change them around so they all got to play with each other.

Some had really long silky hair and others had shorter hair more like Bea's, and they were different colors—white, black, gray, brown—but they were all the same kind.

"How'd your mum die?" I said, without really meaning to.

You swished your drink around slowly, making the ice chink, then had another sip. "Stroke," you said.

"Oh," I said, then because you didn't say anything else and because I thought you might've thought it was a nosy question, I said, "The dogs are really sweet. What are they? I mean, what's Bea?"

"Havanese," you said, still swishing your drink around and then, as if you were quoting from a trailer for a film or something, you added, "The little dog with a big heart."

"They're so cute."

You nodded. "Queen Victoria had two of them," you said. Then you shrugged and did that smile that makes you look sad, the skin around your eyes going crinkly like the pictures of dried-up riverbeds in my old geography textbook. You said, "Mum used to tell everyone that."

I looked at the dogs again. Then I spotted a brown one that was just like Bea. It was even up on its hind legs, with one front paw higher than the other, like it was paddling in the air. "That one's her!" I said, a bit too enthusiastically, but it was *so* like her. I pointed.

You stood up, putting the ashtray back on the floor and

your drink on the tray, and stepped forward so you could see which one I meant. "Oh, yeah," you said. "I got her that one."

"Where from?"

"From Harrods," you said.

"*Harrods?*" I had to stop myself saying it must've cost a hundred quid, or maybe even a thousand.

Then you reached past me and, careful not to knock over any of the other dogs, you picked it up, holding it out to put on my hand.

The base felt cold on my palm and as I stood there looking at it—at the darker streak down its back, its ginger plumy tail and tiny pink tongue hanging out on one side—I could feel you standing there. I don't know how I mean that really. I mean, we weren't touching or anything, but it was like my body knew your body was there, even though I was looking at China Bea and could hardly even see you out the corner of my eye. And then suddenly it was like my mind froze— like I couldn't move, couldn't look away from China Bea or think of anything to say, and because you didn't move or say anything either, it was like we were stuck there together in suspended animation.

Then you had another drag of your roll-up and I *did* look up and even though your eyes were only on me for probably a second before they flicked away, I'll never forget how they looked. They were so dark I couldn't see where the pupils stopped and the color bit began. They looked endless in the gray light of your mum's front room—like black holes in space—and I know that sounds creepy, but they weren't. They were nice.

You were embarrassed, I think, because you went and sat down again, pushing your roll-up into the ashtray.

I put China Bea back in her place on the mantelpiece and went and sat down, too. I watched you seal up the Drum and put it on the tray with the Rizlas and the lighter. "Sorry for coming around like this," I said. "All upset."

You didn't say anything. You looked at my drink. Then you were looking at my legs. I could feel the black hairs on them prickling and wished I could cover them up or that I'd shaved them like girls my age are supposed to. I had a feeling you might be thinking about what you were going to do with me—like if you were going to let me go or keep me in your cellar or just kill me. I thought you'd kill me because what'd be the point in keeping me? You'd keep a girl like Alice, but not me. I thought you were probably wondering how you were going to get rid of my body, about how you'd have to cut it up because it'd be too heavy to carry. I wondered if I should ask you—just come out with it so there wasn't such an awkward atmosphere—say something like, *So have you decided if you're going to kill me yet, Mr. Caldwell?* Obviously I didn't, because you can't ask that kind of thing—especially if the person you're asking's being kind and has just given you a Diet Coke with ice in it.

You took your drink off the tray and downed it in one gulp, even though there was more than half of it left. Then you looked at my drink again and gripped the arm of your chair, like to get up, and said, "Well, I'd better get on."

I wasn't expecting that. I'd hardly had any of my Coke, just a few sips. And I didn't want to go. It was nice sitting there in your mum's house with Bea lying quietly on the floor and your mum's clock going *tock-took*. I said, "Don't you want to know why I was crying?"

You looked a bit alarmed, probably because you're a man and men don't like talking about feelings, do they? So before you could say anything to stop me, I said, "My dad died."

It was weird saying it out loud like that, because I never tell anyone. I don't think anyone at school even knows my dad died. No one's ever asked.

"Oh," you said and sank back into your chair a bit. "That's…that's a shame."

I knew from the way it sounded and the way you reacted that you thought Dad had only *just* died and not six years ago, but I liked the way you were looking at me, your dark eyebrows pinched together, your eyes shining like you understood how terrible that must be. "On Tuesday," I said and even though it wasn't *that* Tuesday, telling you made it feel like it was—like it'd all only just happened. You looked down at your empty glass.

"I never got to say goodbye," I said. "That was the worst bit. I was at school and didn't find out till the end of the day." I glanced at you to check I wasn't saying too much and boring you, but you didn't seem to mind. You were tracing around the rim of your glass with your finger.

Then Bea jerked her head up and this sound—this *incredible* sound—filled the room. It was mad. I didn't know what was going on. It was like something from a spaceship—like singing—filling the room from inside and out at the same time.

You looked up, your finger still moving around the top of the glass and your black-hole eyes telling me...what...*what*...?

Then I realized. "It's you," I said. "Is it you?"

You didn't say anything. You just let your finger sort of slide off the glass like it was ski-jumping off or something, and the sound vanished.

"That's amazing!" I said. "Can you do it again?"

You shrugged, smiling like it wasn't that big of a deal, but then you reached a finger down into the melted ice at the bottom and started moving it around the rim again, looking up at me like looking at me was part of the magic, and the singing sound was back.

Bea stood up and shook her head, walking around in circles. I leaned forward to pat her and when you stopped, I said, "She doesn't know what's going on."

You smiled and did a small, silent laugh, looking down into your glass, and you said, "Does anyone?"

Then I said, "Are you going to keep her?" hating myself the second I had because you'd just said something really deep and amazing and I'd ruined it, and also because I knew it sounded like I wanted you to give Bea to me—as if that was the only reason I'd come around.

You didn't answer straight away. You put your hand out for her, clicking your fingers softly. When she came to you, you put your hand on her head, then moved it around her ear. You said, "She's all I've got now."

I told you I wasn't allowed a dog because Gary's allergic. Then I had to explain who Gary was, of course, and how I had to live with him because of Mum. I couldn't say she'd married Gary after Dad died obviously, because you thought that'd only just happened, so I suppose you thought Mum and Dad had split up.

You didn't ask about that, though. You just said it was a shame I couldn't have a dog of my own, and then I got an incredible idea that made my heart go fast all of a sudden. I said, "I could take Bea for walks."

You turned away and put your glass on the tray.

I said, "It'd help you out, wouldn't it? You could get on with doing the house up and I could take Bea for walks." I thought about it being the weekend and said, "I could come tomorrow."

You stood up. "I don't know," you said.

"Or Sunday?"

"I'm a bit busy," you said and you picked up the tray and went out.

I had one last gulp of Coke, getting up to follow you, but by the time I got to the hallway you were there without the tray, standing in the kitchen doorway, so I went down the hall. When I got to the front door, though, I got that feeling again, like I didn't want to leave. I turned around. I couldn't really see your face because the light in your hallway was so dim, but I said, "What's your name?"

You didn't answer for a second. Then you said, "Samuel." You didn't ask my name, though, so I told you. Adults usually say what a lovely name it is, but you didn't say anything. You started smoothing your hair down at the back. I knew that's what you were doing, even though you were only really a silhouette. Then, because I couldn't think of anything else to say, and it felt a bit weird just standing there looking at you, I opened the door.

"Actually, Yasmin," you said.

When I turned back, you were still smoothing your hair down.

"Sunday'd be all right. I mean, if you want."

"Okay," I said.

You folded your arms and leaned against the stair banister. "It's just I've got something planned and didn't think before, but it'd be easier without Bea."

"Okay," I said again.

"She doesn't like being left here on her own. Barks the place down."

I told you I'd really like that. "Five be all right?" you said.

I said five o'clock was great. I said thanks for the Diet Coke, too, and went out and started to pull the door behind me, but you caught it—grabbed it so fast and tight, it made me jump. I didn't know how you'd got to it so quick. I stepped back onto the path. I still couldn't see you properly because my eyes hadn't got used to the light, but you weren't smiling. You were serious and so was your voice.

"Don't be late," you said.

Mum was obviously still upset because when she opened the door for me she just said, "Dinner's on the stove," her voice all flat, then went back into the living room. Gary's curry looked like a kind of alien autopsy—brown goo with strings of onion and pepper in it. I spooned some into a bowl and stuck it in the microwave, then took it upstairs.

She hadn't told Gary what I'd said, though. If she had, he'd have dragged me in to make a public apology. I knew she was waiting for me to say I was sorry on my own, but I couldn't. Not yet anyway. And I wasn't even sure I *was* sorry. I thought how she'd never cared about what I wanted because if she had, she wouldn't have moved in with Gary like she did—like Dad never existed. I thought it was probably about time I started saying what I really thought.

Anyway, it was good I didn't have to talk to Mum because I wanted to be on my own. I wanted to think about everything that'd happened—everything you'd said to me. I thought how you'd definitely acted suspiciously when I'd told you I had a friend who went to live in Nottingham. I thought maybe I should go to the police right then and tell them that—how I'd seen you staring at Alice and how, after investigating you, I also thought you'd taken Amelia Bell. Because if you *had* taken Amelia Bell, I bet they could prove it once they had your name, and then I wouldn't have just prevented a murder, I'd have solved one, too. And I'd still be Alice's hero.

I thought about how you'd stared at my legs and how the only thing that'd probably saved my life was telling you that Dad died, because once I'd told you that, you couldn't do it. Not when you'd just lost your mum and knew how awful losing a parent is. I know it sounds stupid because it's obvious, but I think I realized only then that losing a parent was something else we had in common—something much more important than being freaks or fantasizing about Alice—except you were really the only one fantasizing about Alice now, because she'd pretty much spelled out that she liked me when she'd given me her drawing.

I remembered how her cheeks had gone the palest pink, how she'd said, "It's nothing, 'kay?" and I knew she'd never have given me a drawing if she didn't like me, that the only reason she wasn't being nice to me anymore was because she couldn't deal with her feelings. I knew it'd be scary for her, realizing how she felt about me when everyone else hates me. I expect she was scared of being a lesbian, too, because people don't like lesbians, even though being gay is supposed to be all equal rights these days. I thought she wouldn't feel so scared of showing her feelings if the police told her I'd saved her life, though. I bet she wouldn't care what anyone thought then. And, in any case, if I saved Alice's life, *everyone* would like me.

I didn't go to the police because, when I went into the kitchen the next morning, Mum said Gary'd moved a job especially so we could all do something together. "Like what?" I said.

"Oh, I don't know..." she said. She still hadn't completely forgiven me. She was wiping the countertop and hadn't turned around once. "He thought the forest would be a nice idea."

"The *forest*?" I said.

She turned around then. "Yes, Yasmin," she said, "the forest," as if going to the forest was something totally normal, something we did all the time.

"Okay," I said. "I was only asking. I was going to go into town."

"Well, you can do that another day, can't you?" she said and then Gary walked in through the patio doors, his hands covered in soil, going "Ah, she's up then!" all super-jolly, and I knew I wouldn't be able to get out of it.

Actually the forest was okay, even though it was so obviously a plan to get me out of the house and doing some exercise, and even though it was the kind of place you go only if you've got a dog because everyone we saw there had one—at least one. I thought about pointing that out, but I couldn't be bothered. It wasn't like Gary'd care anyway, and he'd ignore the hint. He'd never say yes to us having one. He's the kind of person who always gets what he wants and that's what everyone else has to put up with (like going to the forest, for example). And Mum's so soft she just goes along with whatever he says, even when it means she can't have a television in the bedroom anymore. Can you believe that? Mum and Dad always had a TV in their room. I had a TV in mine. Not with Gary, though. Apparently, I should *read* when I'm in my room. Apparently, I don't know how lucky I am having a laptop, even though everyone I know has got one. So, no televisions in bedrooms. No dog. End of.

He picked up a long stick and marched ahead of me and Mum in his rain boots, nodding at every single person we passed, going "Afternoon," but apart from that he wasn't too bad. He didn't say, *I told you to put some proper footwear on, didn't I?* when I couldn't get across a massive muddy puddle. He walked back into the middle of it and said, "Here, lean on me," as I wobbled around the edge. And he laughed at Mum's story about how she'd caught one of the young lads who was supposed to be handing out shampoo samples in Asda canoodling with one of the shelf stackers.

"Did he know her?" I said.

"I don't know!" Mum said. "I've no idea!"

And when she said she hadn't the heart to report him, Gary just shook his head, smiling and tutting, and said, "Well, you can't stand in the way of young love, eh?" and Mum put her arm through his and leaned her head on his shoulder.

I thought about you on the way back in the car—how you'd said that Bea was all you'd got now and how you'd looked really sad when you said it.

Do you want to know what my favorite thing was that you said to me? It wasn't any of the things I bet you'd think of. It wasn't when you said Bea was all you'd got or when she was barking and you told her I was the nice girl who'd rescued you. It wasn't "Whoa" either, even though the way you said that was really nice, like when you said "Steady" when I fell off your step the first time we met. Okay, since you'll never guess, my favorite thing you said was the last thing... "Don't be late."

I loved that *so* much. 'Specially because you were so *serious*, like the whole time I was there you were all awkward and shy, but then when I was leaving you suddenly realized that my coming back really mattered or something, like if I was even one minute late you'd hate it.

I thought how seeing as you'd been in the area only since your mum died, you probably didn't have any friends and were feeling lonely and that that was why you wanted me to be on time. But it didn't really matter *why* you wanted me to be on time. You wanted me. And even though there was no way I was ever going to be friends with someone like you—that felt nice.

I decided there was no point in rushing to the police, because if you had taken Amelia Bell it was too late to help her now, and if I went to the police I might not get to see Bea for ages. Or maybe ever again, because I don't know what happens to the dogs of people they arrest. They might even put them down, and I wouldn't be able to live with myself if little Bea got put down. It'd be all my fault. So I decided to wait.

I also decided I was going to be the best dog-sitter ever. The next morning I went and got some dog treats. I'd Googled *pet shops* and saw there was a Pet Planet in the industrial park that I didn't even know was there. When I saw it, I don't know how I'd missed it because it's literally a planet. It's *massive*. It's got everything you never even knew you wanted, like cool T-shirts for owners with The Dogfather written on them and dog toilet seats and plastic dogs in all different breeds that come with refillable brown dog-poo sweets that drop out of the bum when you press down the head.

There were loads of treats to choose from, too. After a good look at them all, I got Betty Miller's Tasty Treats for Good Dogs. They had the same make for "Whiffy Dogs" or "Chubby Dogs," but Bea's definitely a good dog. I got an amazing idea looking at them all. I thought I could teach her some tricks and work on them with her every time I took her for walks, like in secret, and then when they were really super-perfected, we could amaze you out of nowhere. Like you'd amazed me with the singing glass.

I thought about it all the way home—my getting Bea to do all these brilliant things like dancing on her back legs and rolling over and stuff, and then me in your mum's front room drinking Diet Coke and suddenly just snapping my fingers and Bea dancing around the room and shaking your hand with her paw and you laughing because you can't believe your eyes. I thought we might even get on *Britain's Got Talent*. I thought, that'd shut everyone up at school—me and Bea on TV! It even rhymes—me and Bea! Me & Bea. Bea & Me.

I looked up *Havanese dogs doing tricks* on YouTube when I got in. There were loads of them, of course, even tiny puppies playing dead and then jumping up, their little voices like squeaky toys. It was good that I'd got bite-size treats because that's what the people on YouTube had—one treat for everything their dog did.

I'd have given anything to have my own Havanese puppy, but the only way that was going to happen was if I got a place of my own, and the chances of that were like nil—even though in theory I could because I was going to be sixteen in a few weeks—unless I won the lottery, which was unlikely because I don't play it. Or unless I got pregnant so the council had to give me somewhere, but the chances of that were even smaller than the chances of me winning the lottery without a ticket. It didn't stop me dreaming, though, about how nice I'd make a place of my own, all white and black and clean. It'd be small, of course, because I wouldn't be able to afford anything that wasn't small, but it'd be really smart, with white blinds and shiny white kitchen cupboards and a black marble worktop, and I'd get the black dog bed I saw in Pet Planet to go under the counter because when I imagined my own place, there was always a dog in it. And now I'd met you, I knew I'd have a dog just like Bea. I imagined my dog and Bea meeting up every day out on their walks and Bea being like my dog's mum or something—looking out for her and teaching her stuff that Havanese dogs need to know, like how to paddle their paws in the air and be mega-cute.

I had a shower and dried my hair upside down to give it some volume and put my peach sweater and jeans on to go to your place. I put some makeup on, too. Not much, just some mascara and lip gloss. I kept saying, "What're you *doing?*" to myself in the mirror, because I knew I hadn't put makeup on for Bea and if I'd put it on for you that meant I was putting makeup on to look nice for someone who was a pedophile or a murderer or both, which was a bit weird. But asking myself what I was doing didn't seem to spoil my happy-bunny mood in the slightest, and seeing as I hardly ever got to feel happy like that, you being a murdering pedophile really didn't seem like that big of a deal.

Bea started barking in the hallway when I knocked, but you didn't come to the door. Then I heard a noise and went to the corner of the house. The garage door down the drive was open and you came out of it carrying a canvas bag for tools toward the side door of the house.

When I called "Hello," you looked up like you were surprised, then threw your arm in the air to shoo me away.

"Around the front," you said.

Bea ran out when you opened the front door and skipped

around my ankles. "Hi," I said, bending to give her a fuss, smiling up at you, but you didn't even look at me. You just said, "You're early," and started rummaging through the coats above the shoe rack like you were in a hurry, even though you couldn't have been because you'd said I was early. Then you went down the hall, came back with Bea's lead and held it out—but you still didn't look at me. Not properly. "Probably best not to let her off it," you said.

I took it. "What time shall I bring her back?" I said. I was trying to sound upbeat, like I hadn't noticed how off you were being, how you hadn't even noticed I'd made myself look nice.

You ran your fingers through your hair and looked at the path. "'Bout nine," you said.

"Okay," I said, nodding and chewing my cheek and trying not to show how I felt, which was *stung*. Stung and stupid and unable to say what anyone normal would've said, which would've been *Nine? Are you mad, Mr. Caldwell? It's dark at nine!* Not that I'd even have had time to say that because you closed the door—*boof*—just like that. No *'Bye then* or *See you later*.

I told myself I shouldn't take it personally as I clipped Bea's lead on and led her off down the street—that I hadn't done anything, that *I* was the one helping *you* out. It didn't make me feel any better, though. I still felt hurt.

I thought then how it could be grief making you act that way and not because you wished you'd never said I could come back—because grief can make people act weird, like they're not themselves anymore. I acted weird after Dad died.

It's difficult *not* to when the whole world around you feels weird. I remember forcing myself to join in the games in the playground and to laugh at things people said, but they could tell I was pretending. I used to catch Ella watching me whenever I said something or laughed at something, a funny expression on her face, and instantly my whole body would turn to cement and I'd stop whatever I was doing and stare at the ground. Then, one day she didn't come and sit with me at lunch and that was it. That was the end of Ella being my friend. I didn't know it then, of course, but that was the end of *any*one being my friend.

"Hey, Bea," I said, realizing that trying to figure out why you'd practically ignored me meant I'd been ignoring Bea, which wasn't fair because Bea was suffering enough already, grieving for Mrs. E. Caldwell. She didn't look up. It seemed like your mood had rubbed off on her. Or mine had. Or yours, then mine. I told her I wouldn't think about you anymore.

At the park I sat on a bench, which was damp because it'd rained that morning, but because I had my long puffer coat on it didn't matter. I patted the seat and told her to get up next to me, but she didn't want to, and when I picked her up and put her there, she jumped straight down again. I roughed her head and told her her problem was she was too well brought up.

Then I pulled the packet of doggy treats out of my pocket. When I was trying to open it, Bea made a noise in the back of her throat that didn't sound very nice. I'm sure all it meant was "Really?" or "For me?" or something, but it sounded unfriendly.

"Betty Miller's Tasty Treats for Good Dogs," I read to her. "Are you a good dog?"

She licked her lips.

I leaned forward and patted her. "Are you?"

Then she barked like, "Hurry up already," so I opened the bag and gave her one. She ate it so fast she was jumping up at the packet before I could stop her, knocking it out of my hands and onto the grass, spilling the biscuits.

"Bad Bea!" I scolded, pushing her out of the way because she was scarfing them all. I smacked her nose. "Naughty!"

Then I picked the bag up and stuffed it back in my pocket and told her that if that was the way she was going to behave we'd forget the whole thing.

"Bad dog," I said again. No matter how hard I tried to make myself believe that your weird mood had been because of grief, I knew it wasn't. I knew it was because you'd decided you didn't like me anymore. I thought how it was exactly like it was with Alice, only for some reason with you it felt even worse. I mean, I never expect people like Alice to like me, but with you…it was different—because you're a freak, I suppose, because you didn't have any friends and dreamed of having Alice, and because you'd lost a parent, too. I just thought you'd like me. Wrong. Wrong again.

I thought about leaving Bea there in the park, tied to the bench, and going home and forgetting about the whole thing—going home and leaving you to your stupid murdering stuff and Alice to her stupid *being* murdered stuff and doing something far more productive like watching *Star Trek* or counting calories.

It had spoiled things, that's what it'd done. And now I didn't feel like teaching Bea any tricks. There wasn't any point anyway if you'd already made up your mind that you didn't like me.

I didn't leave Bea there. I took her to the chip shop. I thought I'd feel better if I ate some chips. I went to the Belmont Road one I usually go to near Gary's house. It's twice as far as the one on Falconer Road, but they do the nicest chips and it wasn't like I didn't have *four hours* to kill before 9:00 p.m.

The second we turned onto Belmont Road, though, I stopped.

That boy was there—the black one from the cinema who Alice was with. He was standing with his legs either side of his bike, holding a can of Fanta and talking to three other boys who were standing around him. He was waving his arm about again, like he had when he was with Alice, making them laugh.

I turned to leave before he could see me, but a woman with a Jack Russell came out of her house on the other side of the road and it started snarling and barking at Bea, straining toward us on its lead, showing its sharp teeth. The boys all turned and looked then—and he saw me, the black one. He stared right at me.

I walked away quick, yanking Bea from under the back of a parked car to make her come. She ran at my heels because she didn't like being snarled at any more than I like being stared at. My heart was thumping and shivers kept racing up my neck. I kept thinking he was going to come up behind on his bike and grab me like before and breathe his nasty, hot words over me.

By the time we'd got to the mini roundabout on Cedar Lane, though, it was obvious he wasn't coming. The streets were empty. It was getting dark. I puffed on my inhaler. I was glad he hadn't followed me, obviously, but it made me feel bad, too, because I thought why would he, anyway? Why would anyone bother following me? I'm just a fat blob no one cares about.

I squatted down and gave Bea a stroke. "That wasn't very nice, was it?" I said. I got the treats out and gave her a handful and stroked her and said I was sorry for being mean to her. She gobbled them up, then licked my nose—more to see if it was another treat, I think, than to tell me she forgave me, but it was still sweet. Then she let me pick her up and carry her for a bit.

I was going to go to the other chippy on Falconer Road, but because my feet and back were aching and my thighs were starting to sting, I stopped when I got as far as the park and sat on a bench. I thought Bea might get all fidgety, sitting and doing nothing, but she was good as gold and just lay down on the grass and looked out at the black trees reaching up into the blue night sky.

By nine o'clock I felt better. Sitting in the dark had helped put things back in perspective. Basically, I realized that it didn't matter if you'd decided you didn't like me. You were a bad man and I didn't want to be friends with someone like you anyway, so your not liking me was fine. In fact it was *better* if you didn't like me, because then I wouldn't have to feel so bad about it when I went to the police.

When we got around the bend in your road, I could see the light in your front room was on. I could hear music as well, but I wasn't sure it was coming from your house till I got a bit closer.

Bea lay across my feet on the doorstep.

I thought you probably hadn't heard me knock because of the music being so loud, so I knocked again when the track was ending. Then I heard you coming and the latch on the front door turned and there you were. Your hair was wet and combed back and you were wearing a dark blue shirt with the sleeves rolled up that made your eyes look even darker than they are.

"Hey," you said, smiling and having a drag on the roll-up in your hand. "The girls are back."

I thought maybe you were a bit drunk, smiling like that and saying, "The girls are back," but at least you were being friendly again. You didn't move, though. You just kept standing there.

"Shall I come in?" I said.

"Oh," you said, "sure, come in," and you went down the hall. I followed Bea inside and closed the door. I thought it'd be okay to stay for a bit, so long as I got home by half past ten. I'd just tell Mum I met some people from school at the chippy if she asked.

The next track was playing. It was really weird with lots of guitar and a man singing about how his mum was going to keep him safe.

You were in the kitchen, trying to push ice out of a rubber ice tray, your roll-up in your lips. The kitchen was like I'd imagined it, more or less, with old wooden cupboards and a nasty beige lino floor with dog biscuits around Bea's dirty bowl and wet mud around the door—the door I'd seen you going to from the garage down the side of the house.

A bunch of ice cubes suddenly fell out onto the countertop. You took your roll-up out of your mouth and scooped them off, plopping them into two glasses of Coke, then you turned and held one out. "For you, Madame," you said, bending forward all posh, like a butler or something.

I watched you while you mashed your roll-up out on a dirty plate, got a small tin of dog food out of one of the cupboards, peeled the lid back and tipped it into Bea's bowl.

My drink smelled of alcohol. I thought maybe you'd put something else in it, too—spiked it with Rohypnol or something, like someone did to Lucinda Wells in Year Twelve. Apparently she woke up in a strange flat on the other side of town with no pants on. She managed to escape through a window and was found wandering about, but she was still so out of it she couldn't remember where she'd come from, so the police never got the person who did it.

When you clinked your glass against mine, though, your eyes shining, I didn't want to seem ungrateful, so I took a sip. I decided to forget about the spiking thing and took another bigger sip. "What's the music?" I said.

"What's the music?" you said.

I wasn't sure what you meant—like if you were checking if what I'd said was what you thought I'd said, or if you couldn't believe I didn't know—so I nodded. You put your arm around me then, very lightly, so it was hardly touching me, and walked me through into the front room. I could smell a nice soapy smell on you under the smoke. Then you went over to a record player on some low shelves behind the sofa that I hadn't noticed before and handed me an album cover. There were four faces on it, except they were cut out like masks with holes where the eyes should've been. It said Pink Floyd in white capital letters above the masks and underneath, in red, it said, Is There Anybody Out There? You stood next to me and I thought you were looking at the cover, too, but when I looked up at you, you had your eyes closed and your glass to your lips, listening to the man on the record singing about how his mama was going to wait up till he got in and how she'd find out where he'd been… I had a few more sips of my drink while I waited for you to open your eyes again, then gave you back the album cover. I didn't say anything about it because I didn't like it very much. I thought it was pretty creepy singing about your mother like that. And the next track was creepy, too, like horror film music with bombs exploding everywhere like it was a war.

You went back to the record player and started looking through more records that were lined up next to it like books. There were probably about thirty or something. I followed you over, but I couldn't see what any of the records were because you were going through them too fast, and I didn't want to lean in. I stayed where I was and watched you in-stead, sipping more of my drink.

Before that night I thought I didn't like alcohol, especially when it was as strong as that was, but it was nice and relaxing—and it was making me warm even though it had ice in it. I thought it probably had the rum in it that you were drinking the last time I was there. It was nice watching you, too—watching your big knuckly hands flicking the records past and the ends of your dark, wet hair disappearing inside your collar.

You pulled a record out and laid it on top of the others. It said Queen on it and I recognized the picture of the man in the middle of the cover. Then you stopped the record that was playing, lifting the needle so that suddenly all we could hear was the turntable and the cuckoo clock and Bea chomping away in the kitchen.

"Close the curtains," you said.

I went behind the blue velvet chair and pulled the curtains with one hand because I still had my drink. It felt a bit weird closing them because they moved really smoothly on their runners, making me think of the ones that'd closed on their own around Nana's coffin before she got cremated. But it also felt nice closing them, like we were a family—you, me and Bea—shutting out the rest of the world at the end of another day.

Then the sound of a piano filled the room and the singer was singing how tonight he was going to have himself a real good time and I turned to see you nodding your head slowly to the beat and looking at me. I didn't recognize it to start with but then when it went faster with the lyrics going "Don't stop me now," I did and I got this funny rush, like excitement and happiness and I half danced back into the middle of the room, turning around when I got there. I thought whatever was in the drink was definitely working because normally I'd never half dance across a room or turn around in the middle of it, but it felt nice doing it and nice with you watching me, too.

When the song was ending, you took my empty glass and went out, waggling it to tell me you were going to get me another one.

I listened to the next couple of tracks, swaying along a bit, but when you still hadn't come back, I went to see where you were. I could feel cold air as soon as I got to the hallway.

I went into the kitchen. Bea was curled up in her basket, the side door was open and I could see you outside through the window.

You were smoking, a new drink in your hand. "Oh," you said, turning when you heard me, "your drink's on the side." I went back in and got it.

"It's a nice night," I said when I went out again, just to make conversation really because you weren't saying anything—just staring at the sky.

You had some of your drink and tapped the ash off the end of your roll-up onto the cracked concrete patio. "No stars down here," you said.

I wasn't sure what you meant by "down here" but I didn't ask. I just sipped my drink and stood next to you and neither of us said a word. It wasn't awkward, though it was nice standing quietly in your garden with the music playing in the house.

Then, out of nowhere, you said, "Do you believe in fate?"

Just like that. You didn't turn to me or anything, just carried on smoking and looking out at the night.

I thought of that film *Final Destination*, where the people who survive a plane crash die anyway, one by one, because it's their fate and I was going to say something about it, but then you flicked your roll-up off into the black grass and turned to go in. "You don't have to answer that," you said.

You went into the downstairs bathroom that's off the hallway and I went back into the front room. A new track was playing and it was *beautiful*. It was a piano with the voice all soft, singing about how things had started off so well and how they'd made the perfect pair. I closed my eyes and was just swaying a bit and listening because I didn't know it and it was so lovely and then at the exact same moment that he sang, "I'll love you till I die," you were there behind me and I turned and your black-hole eyes were looking right into mine and then the chorus kicked in with crashing drums and guitars going "Save me, Save me, I can't face this life alone," and I just threw my arms around you.

You flinched, stepping back a bit and saying, "Whoa," because you were surprised, I think, and because you were worried your drink was going to spill. Then there was a knock on the door—a really loud one.

You put your drink on the arm of the sofa, went over to the record player fast, turning the volume down, then over to the window. You looked out through the gap in the curtains. Then you came back past me, running your fingers through your hair and going "Shit" under your breath.

I stayed in the front room and had some more of my drink.

The woman at the door was really angry. She was saying, "It's a disgrace playing music so loudly," and, "What would Evelyn say if she was still here…" And even though she was almost shouting at you very rudely, you didn't raise your voice at all. You just kept saying you were sorry and that you'd turned the music down, but she didn't even really care about the music. She just wanted to be nasty to you, because then she started saying what an awful son you were and how it was blatantly clear you'd never cared about your mum because you'd never visited her.

In the end I couldn't stand it anymore, not with you being so polite and saying you were sorry all the time, so I went into the hall.

"And who's *that*?" she said when she saw me, looking me up and down like I was dog poo. She was a typical horrible old lady with gray, sprayed curls and tiny, peery little eyes.

"It's none of your business, that's who," I said, going up the hall and standing next to you. "So piss off."

She opened her mouth but was too shocked to think of any words to put in it.

"Mrs. Robertson, please…" you started saying, but before you could go on, I said, "Just because Sam didn't visit doesn't mean he didn't love his mum, because he did. He *really* loved her! He bought her presents from Harrods!" Then I went to slam the door, but you caught my wrist and pushed me behind you.

"Well, I should call the police," I heard her say.

"Please," you said again. "You're right, the music was much too loud. I've turned it down."

She said something back, but because she was walking off, I didn't catch what. Then you closed the door and went past me and back into the front room.

When I got there, you were standing in front of the fireplace looking at me. "I think you'd better go," you said. Your voice was quiet and tense. You were upset.

"She was being so mean to you," I said. "She wasn't listening, even though you kept saying you were sorry."

"Just go," you said, and then suddenly you turned and got one of the china dogs off the mantelpiece. "Here," you said, holding it out. It was the one from Harrods. "As a thank-you."

"What for?" I said.

"For having Bea. I appreciate it."

"But it's the one you got her," I said, taking it only because I could see you really wanted me to. "It's part of your mum's collection."

You closed your eyes and nodded like you were trying to stay calm—trying not to think about what that horrid neighbor said. Then you looked at me again, the muscles in your jaw moving, and you said, "I want you to have it."

I could see you were serious, so I said, "Okay," and I squeezed China Bea safe in my hand. Then I saw your rum and Coke on the arm of the sofa and went to get it for you, going "D'you want your drink?"

But you said, "No," your voice sharp and loud. When I looked at you, you put your hand on your forehead, then in your back pocket. "No," you said again, "I just want you to go."

I put my coat on by the front door. You didn't come into

the hall to say goodbye. I thought, that stupid woman's really upset you. Silly cow. I thought how upset I'd be if someone ever said that to me—that just because I didn't go to the cemetery, I didn't love Dad.

All the way back to Gary's, I held China Bea tight, kissing her and whispering through my fingers to her and thinking about everything that'd happened because so *much* had happened. I'd hugged you! And you'd given me China Bea! It was crazy. You'd gone from practically ignoring me when I first got there to giving me something incredibly precious that you'd bought for your mum and saying, "I want you to have it."

I wanted to do something to show you I was sorry for getting you in even more trouble with your neighbor, to show you I'd said all that only because I couldn't stand listening to her bullying you. But more than that, I wanted to show you that I liked you and that Bea wasn't all you'd got like you'd said she was—that you had me, as well. That I was your friend.

I wanted to do something to show myself how much I liked you, too. So when I got in, I took all of Alice's things out of her box, deliberately scrunching the foil in my hand before I had time to even think about what I was doing, took them downstairs and stuck them in the kitchen bin. Even the heart. Then I made sure there was rubbish covering them so Mum wouldn't see.

I went back upstairs and tore Alice's Box down at the corners so it folded flat, and took that downstairs, too, and pushed it between Gary's Stella Artois packaging in the recycling bin.

I washed for ages in the bathroom, watching myself in the

mirror. I was shaking because of what I'd just done—scared that I wouldn't be all right without Alice's things to look at and hold—but at the same time I knew it was the right thing to do. I mean, I couldn't go on fantasizing about me and Alice forever when she was never going to like me. It was a childish schoolgirl fantasy. I had to grow up some time. And I told myself that now was my chance to do it, because now I had something better than a fantasy. I had you, and I didn't have to just imagine conversations with you in my head, because you talked to me for real.

You were my real friend.

ROTTING FRUITS

THE SECOND I SAW HER, holding a police radio against the lapel of her dark gray suit, the man in uniform behind her, I knew what'd happened.

I couldn't believe it'd happened, not after imagining it so many times. Not after waiting for it. But it had.

Alice was gone.

It was right after assembly, when everyone was pouring out of the gym and past the Head's office to get to class. I must've stopped because people were pushing and elbowing me, saying, "Move it, Doner," only I couldn't move. I could only stare at her—the policewoman—waiting for her gaze to fall on me, fix on me. And when it did—when her eyes locked with mine—it wasn't anything like I'd thought it'd be, with me rushing over to say I knew who had Alice. A voice in my head was telling me to do it. *Do it!* it said, but I couldn't. And then I was looking away, down at the floor and walking off toward the Maths wing.

I sat at the back of the classroom, paralyzed and clutching China Bea in my cardigan pocket while everyone else crowded around Katy. I told myself I was just being paranoid, that there could be a million reasons why the police would be in school—but the way everyone was talking—so *intently*. They already knew about Alice, of course. Her parents would've rung around, wouldn't they? The second Alice hadn't come home, they'd have gone through their mobiles, calling every friend of Alice's they knew: "Have *you* seen Alice? Is Alice with *you*?"

If I'd got to school on time, I'd have known about it before assembly, but I'd slept through my alarm. I'd probably still be on the bus if Gary hadn't given me a lift. I wished I was.

I whispered quietly so no one would notice, telling myself that if the police were here because Alice was missing, it was nothing to do with me. And really it wasn't. But it didn't *feel* like that. I'd imagined this moment with Alice gone too many times, spent too many hours going over and over how everyone would react. Feeling like I had nothing to do with it was impossible. I'd even thrown her things away. It felt like it was my fault, like somehow I'd created it, conjured it out of my head.

Then Mr. Carter was at the door with the Head's secretary. Usually no one reacts at all when he comes in. Everyone carries on talking, sitting on each other's desks. Not that morning. Conversations *vaporized* as everyone turned.

The secretary cleared her throat. "Katy Ellis," she said, smiling despite the atmosphere in the room, "could I borrow you for a few minutes?"

Katy slid off the desk, glancing meaningfully at Sophie, and went to the door. I could hear the secretary's heels clacking as she led Katy away up the corridor.

Then Robert said, "Is it true, sir? Is Alice really missing?"

Mr. Carter put his small pile of books carefully on the desk and hung his bag over his chair before he answered. Then he looked around the class. "For the moment, it would seem so," he said. "Although I'm sure there's a good explanation."

A murmur started up again. Even Sangeet, the Maths geek, was wide-eyed and twisting around in his chair, trying to get information out of anyone.

"But while the police find the explanation," Mr. Carter went on, his voice raised, "we continue as normal. So…" He opened his textbook, told us the page number and started talking about math.

I watched the clock.

I tried to think about what could've happened and when. *When* had it happened? I thought about you standing in the hallway saying, "Sunday'd be all right…" I thought about you coming out of your garage carrying that heavy tool bag and handing me Bea's lead, your eyes avoiding mine as you said, "'Bout nine." And how you'd looked when I brought Bea back—your hair wet like you'd had a shower and wearing that nice shirt.

Then the classroom started to tilt away from me—slowly one way, then the other, like the ground under the floor wasn't solid anymore—because I knew when. I knew exactly when…

When I'd had Bea.

I put my hands over my mouth to catch the whispers that were escaping. I saw Sangeet looking, frowning at me, but then he was moving, spinning around me, along with the rest of the room—like the night before, after I'd got home from your house and thrown away Alice's Box, only *nothing* like the night before. The galaxy on my ceiling had turned in circles then, but slow circles that spiraled upward, pulling me in. This was fast. This was frightening. I closed my eyes.

When I opened them, everything was blurred. Everyone was looking at me. The secretary in the doorway was looking at me.

"What?" I said.

She glanced at Mr. Carter, then back at me. "Hurry up, please, Yasmin."

I stood up, scraping my chair, unprepared to have to do anything or talk to anyone—especially the police. Why did they want to talk to me? What did they know? *Did* they know?

Katy was back in her seat and watching me as I got up, her face set hard like she was onto me. Then the secretary was marching me up the corridor too fast, saying, "The police have a lot of people to get through this morning." When we reached the Head's meeting room, she said, "Are you feeling all right, Yasmin?"

I shook my head because I wasn't feeling all right at all, but I don't think she even saw. She was already opening the door. I'd never been in there before. It was like the other classrooms, only with framed pictures by students all around the walls and a bunch of desks pushed together to make one big table in the middle. Miss Ward was sitting at one end with the officers I'd seen in the corridor. The man glanced up from the notepad on his knee and did the Blimey-she's-big double take.

The policewoman gestured for me to come and take a seat. Then Miss Ward leaned forward. She gave me a tight smile. "Hello, Yasmin," she said. "The police are here today about a very serious matter. This is DI Burke"—she indicated the woman, then the man—"and DC Hill." The man kept his eyes on his notebook this time and hidden behind his long wavy bangs, but DI Burke was watching me.

I tried to look back at her, but it was difficult because Alice's rotting fruit picture was right behind her in a white frame, the vivid oranges and browns bulging out like they were shouting at me to hurry up and tell them about you. I wondered if DI Burke knew that it was Alice's picture behind her, if she'd sat in front of it on purpose, like it was some sort of police tactic.

She cleared her throat. "Alice Taylor's parents have reported her missing," she said. She spoke quietly and clearly even though she had an accent from up north somewhere.

"I know," I said, my voice shaking. I put my hand in my pocket to hold China Bea and stared at DI Burke's smooth brown skin and black scraped-back hair. Her brow was furrowed, her brown eyes serious. She looked like someone who never gives up till she finds the truth. No makeup. No nonsense. She said, "Your friend Katy—"

"She's not my friend," I said.

"Your classmate, then. She seems to think you're fond of Alice."

I pulled a face. What did that even mean—*fond of*? "No."

"She said you were in town on Saturday and that you followed her and Alice and a few others to the cinema."

"No," I said again. "I was in town. I just saw them."

She rested her forearms on the table then, interlocking her fingers like she was prepared to be as patient as she had to be. "No one's accusing you of anything, Yasmin," she said. She looked at me squarely, as she had when I'd seen her in the corridor. Her eyes were huge. It was like they could see more than other people's, or that what they saw went straight to her no-nonsense brain that translated it all in a flash. "It's important you know that," she said. "We're just trying to gain as much information as we can. This is a very serious matter, and it may be that you can help." She licked her lips. "If there's anything you remember, anything you saw there that day, no matter how small or trivial it seems, it could prove crucial in helping us to find her."

"What, in town?" I said.

"Yes, in town," DI Burke said. "*Any* time."

I remembered your milky-white face in the darkness of the cinema, staring ahead at the screen. I thought about how you'd bowed when you'd given me the rum and Coke in your kitchen, and the cuckoo clock going *tock-took, tock-took...* and I knew I should tell them. I *knew*. I said, *Tell them!* in my head, but I couldn't, even though their faces were all looking at me, willing me to, and even though Alice's rotting fruit was glaring at me—maybe even because of that. I was too confused. I needed to be on my own, in my room at home, away from their questions and their staring eyes. Somewhere I could think.

"There was a boy there," I said, turning China Bea in my hand. She was warm now. "At the cinema." The man wrote that down, so I went on. "He came up the steps to where I was sitting. He told me he had a message from Alice."

I glanced at Miss Ward, who was sitting back in her chair, watching me. I suppose she thought I was making it up.

"Was he with them, this boy? With Alice?" DI Burke said. I nodded.

"And what was the message?"

"There wasn't one. It was a trick. He grabbed my arm and threatened me." I let go of China Bea and held my arm to show her where. If she'd been interested, I could've shown her the yellowy bruise that was still there, but she wasn't. She just pulled a folder that was on the table onto her lap and flipped through some sheets inside it, tilting her head to read something.

"Was that Darren?" she said. "Darren Travis?"

I shrugged. "I don't know," I said. "I don't know him. I saw him again last night, though."

The second her eyes flicked up to mine, I knew I'd said something stupid—unbelievably stupid because I'd had Bea with me when I saw Darren. I'd had Bea and he'd tell them, wouldn't he? He'd say I was walking a dog. My face burned. They all saw it burn. Even the man looked up from his notepad and saw it.

I looked away, down at my lap. I bit my cheek to stop from whispering.

I could feel DI Burke staring at me—into me. "You saw Darren last night?"

I nodded. I knew if they found out about Bea, I'd have to tell them about you. It wasn't like I could say it was anyone else's dog, and in any case, they'd find out and then they'd start asking all sorts of stuff about how I knew you till they knew it all.

DI Burke put the folder back on the table and leaned forward, interlocking her fingers again. "Where was that?" she said.

I made myself look up. I said, "By the chippy on Belmont Road," but the words caught in my throat and just made DI Burke stare at me even closer, her eyes moving between mine. I knew I should've told her about you right away when I'd first locked eyes with her in the corridor. Or the second I'd come into the room. But I hadn't—and now because I *still* hadn't, I knew I wasn't going to. I'd missed my chance. It was too late. I said, "He was on his bike talking to some other boys."

"What time was that?"

I shrugged. "I don't know," I said. When DI Burke kept staring, I bit my lip and thought about what time it'd been. "Six?" I said. "Maybe. Maybe six thirty. I don't really know."

The man was writing fast, like he was trying to keep up. I watched my words scrawling out the end of his pen and thought how Bea had been behind a car and how Darren might not've seen her from where he was, and even though I still couldn't look at DI Burke, I felt a bit calmer.

"And what were you doing there?"

"Getting chips."

"And did you?"

"What?"

"Get chips," she said. I shook my head.

"Why not?" She was still watching me closely, but when I didn't say anything she started to nod slowly, her eyebrows creasing together like she understood. "Because Darren was there," she said. "You were afraid."

I nodded.

"So what did you do then?"

"Went home."

"You went straight home without any chips?"

"Yeah."

There was a silence while the man finished what he was writing.

DI Burke was still staring intently at me, but I thought even though I'd gone red, maybe it was okay—maybe she thought that was because of remembering Darren.

"Is there anything else you can think of that might help us here?" she said. "Help Alice?"

I shook my head slowly like I was thinking really hard about it.

Then she said I could go. She said if I remembered *anything at all*, I should tell Miss Ward or a member of the staff. When I got to the door, I turned back. DI Burke's eyes were still on me. "When did she go missing?" I said.

"Yesterday," she said. "Her parents reported her missing shortly after seven. She didn't come home from her singing lesson."

I felt dizzy as I walked back to class. The air around me seemed to be thick with a sickly smell like rotting fruit, but I kept going. I trailed my hand along the wall and listened to your voice in my head going "Steady… Steady…"

Between classes I avoided everyone, ignoring Katy's and Sophie's looks and saying, "Nothing," when people asked me what the police had said. I Googled Alice on my phone—just to see her, really—to look at her face because it didn't seem real that she'd gone. The first thing that came up was *Help Find Alice Taylor*, a Facebook link, and there she was in a picture I hadn't seen before, looking at me with those same steady green eyes that'd watched me in English just a few days before. She was wearing the pale blue cardigan she'd had on in town, a strand of loose hair caught in the corner of her smile.

This is Alice Taylor, it said underneath. *She's fifteen years old and missing. She was last seen walking westbound along Rectory Road in the Watford area at 6:30 p.m. Sunday, April 2. She was wearing medium-blue skinny jeans, a white T-shirt, khaki Converse sneakers and the pastel blue cardigan shown in the above photo. If you've seen her or know anything about her whereabouts, please contact us urgently.* Then, in a new post: *Please share this page with everyone you know. The more people who know about her, the more likely we are to find her. The police have been informed.*

I scrolled down. Katy'd posted a picture at 7:04 a.m. that day—her and Alice together, pouting at the camera. Under it, she'd written *Please, please call me, A. I'm so worried. Call me.*

I scrolled back up to the photo of Alice at the top, expanded it till her face filled the screen, touching her cheek with my thumb. I couldn't help smiling at her, reaching out in my imagination to unhook the hair caught on her lip. "What can I do?" I whispered. I knew I had to do something, and that I had to do it quick, but I couldn't get anything to sit still in my head. As soon as I got a thought, like, should I look for her or should I go back and tell DI Burke? it would skitter about while a new one arrived and did the same thing. By the end of morning lessons, I couldn't take it anymore, so I put my bag in my locker and left.

I had to stop myself from running to your house, because then I'd get an asthma attack and sore thighs again. I thought I'd catch a bus, but didn't know which one and I couldn't stop to think about buses or bus stops, so I kept going, sort of half running and puffing on my inhaler every minute or so. I didn't like the thought of going to your house, not now that I knew you really *had* taken Alice—but I had to. She might be there, I kept thinking. She might be there. Up till then, I'd only really thought about Alice and how she'd be when she was rescued. I'd never thought about the bit before when I wasn't there—when you had her on your own. I mean, I'd thought about how you were a bad man who wanted to do bad things to her, but I hadn't thought about what you'd actually *do*. I'd only ever imagined you looking at her, maybe giving her something to make her dozy so she'd let you. I'd thought about you stroking her pale skin till it goose-pimpled up, pushing your fingers through her hair and laying your head on her stomach to feel her warmth against your face. But now that she was actually gone and I was stumbling toward your house across the park, I knew you wouldn't just do those things. You'd do something much, much worse, and it was all my fault because I'd let you.

I didn't slow down till I turned onto your road. I puffed on my inhaler some more, trying to hold it in and count each time, but I was too out of breath. And every time I thought about what I was going to do when I got to you, my heart started banging, so I tried not to think, just to keep going.

Your house looked the same. I know that sounds stupid, because why wouldn't it, but for some reason it seemed weird. It was like it was a stage set or something. Bea started barking at the upstairs window before I even walked up the path.

I made myself knock straight off so I didn't have time to chicken out. Then I stood there, still trying to get my breath, with no idea at all what I was going to say when you opened the door. Bea went quiet for a few seconds, then started barking again, downstairs in the hallway this time. When you still didn't come, I thought maybe you were out. I moved off the step and leaned against the wall of the house. I waited till she was quiet, then waited a bit more to make sure you weren't coming.

Then I went down the driveway at the side, treading on the grassy bits so Bea wouldn't hear. The garage was closed now, but in my head I saw you with that heavy tool bag again.

When I got to the side door, I stopped and looked at the frosted glass, waiting for Bea to appear in the kitchen on the other side. She didn't, though. Nothing moved, and it was only a few more steps to the garage.

I put my hand on the cold white metal, hardly breathing and listening for any sound—any muffled cries or struggling. "Hello?" I said quietly, in a half whisper, then, "Alice?" I looked at the side door again, then went around the back of the house. It'd been so dark the night before I hadn't been able to see the garden very well. It was long, the grass overgrown with a pathway trodden through it that led to a rusty barbecue and a pile of burnt wood at the bottom. Thick bushes and trees overhung there, making it gloomy, even though it was a sunny day. I stepped onto the patio, avoiding some dried dog poo, and peered through the kitchen window. The tap was dripping into an overflowing pan in the sink, and through the kitchen door I could see the empty hallway.

I stepped back and looked up at the window above. The curtains were closed—dark pink ones, pulled firmly together, so no chinks of light could get in—and a ringing sound started in my ears and I had to do the breathing-out-slowly-through-a-straw thing because I was thinking, Alice, are you up there?

Then I thought about throwing some stones up at the window like people do in films and I went back to the driveway to get some.

"What you doing?" you said.

I stood up, stumbling I was so shocked, dropping the gravel and rubbing my palms down my skirt.

You were in the side doorway. You looked at my hands. "What you playing at?"

"Nothing," I said. "I was…" I'm usually good at coming

up with an explanation for whatever it is I'm doing that I'm not supposed to be, but I couldn't think of a single reason why I'd have a handful of your gravel, other than for throwing at a window.

Luckily Bea shot out the door barking and jumping up at me.

"I came to see if you were all right," I said, rubbing Bea's sides. Your shirt was buttoned up wrong so it showed your chest and your hair was all messy. "If that neighbor came back. That's all. Then I heard a cat." I pointed at the garage. "I think it's in there."

You didn't move. You kept looking at me.

I bit my lip so I wouldn't start whispering, because I could see you didn't believe me.

Then you turned and went back inside, leaving the door open like you did when you went to get money for me. My heart was thudding. I was thinking, you're gonna come back with a kitchen knife or a hammer or something and you're going to kill me...

You came back with some keys in your hand and whistled for Bea. Then you shut her in the kitchen and walked past me to the garage door. "A cat," you said, looking through the keys for the right one, then twisting it into the handle.

I took a few steps back when you pulled the door up. I was afraid I was going to see Alice in there, and didn't know what I was going to do if I did. I thought I'd have to play along, like I knew you had her and I'd come to warn you about the police being at school asking questions. I'd have to say, *What shall we do with her?* and *I'll help you* and stuff like that till I got the chance to knock you out.

She wasn't in there. There was just a rusty blue Nissan Micra and garagey stuff around the walls: rakes and a spade and a rolled-up rug. No cat, of course.

"I definitely heard a meow," I said, stepping closer and peering inside. I didn't go too close. Not close enough for you to grab me and pull the door down, but close enough to smell your sweat.

You grabbed a flashlight and went down on your knees, shining it under the car.

"Here, puss," I called a few times while you checked around the back of the garage and tipped a sunbed forward. I couldn't see the canvas tool bag either.

Then you hung the flashlight up again and came out, fixing me with your dark eyes. You raised an eyebrow. "No cat," you said.

I pulled a face, shrugging, and said, "That's weird," except my throat was so dry the words didn't come out properly, and then I was going to try to say something like *It must've been next door* when there was a sudden scrabbling sound the other side of the fence and a cat appeared over the top. It froze for a second, staring at us with big yellow eyes, then jumped onto your garage roof, sat down and started licking its leg. You pulled the garage door down again and went back past me and into your kitchen.

I thought I shouldn't go in your house, but then I thought of Alice and followed you. I closed the door because of Bea, even though she'd got in her basket, but I stayed close to it. "Can I have some water?" I said.

You rinsed a mug, filled it up and handed it to me. I drank it down in one gulp I was so thirsty.

Then you filled the kettle at the sink.

"So was it okay last night?" I said. "That woman didn't call the police?"

"No," you said, turning the tap off.

"Sorry for shouting at her."

You switched the kettle on and got a tea bag out of the cupboard.

"She was so mean," I said.

Then, without turning around, you said, "Shouldn't you be at school?"

I swallowed, afraid again suddenly, wondering what I was even doing there, why I hadn't just told DI Burke about you and let the police come and search your house. I said, "They sent us home. A girl's gone missing."

You turned around then. You leaned against the countertop and folded your arms. "Oh, right," you said. You scratched the side of your head above your ear. "Do you know her?"

I shook my head and shrugged as if it wasn't really anything to do with me, but your eyes on me were making me really nervous. "No," I said.

You nodded slowly. You didn't ask when she'd gone missing or say *How terrible* or anything like that. You just kept watching me, and then after a few seconds you said, "I expect she'll turn up."

"Yeah, probably," I said and then I got this funny sense as

the kettle got louder and louder that you were watching me and I was watching you and you knew I was watching you and I knew you were watching me. I don't know if that makes any sense, but it was like that mirror thing, when there's one mirror in front of you and one behind and it looks like you go on forever and ever.

"Anyway," I said, looking away and shrugging like it was no big deal, "it's good for me because I get the day off."

The kettle switch popped and you turned to stir in the water.

"I thought I could maybe take Bea for a walk," I said. I didn't want to take Bea for a walk obviously. I wanted to get upstairs and look in that back room. But I didn't know how I was going to do it, so I just kept talking. I said, "So when are you going to start redecorating?"

"Oh," you said, "soon," half turning away to make a roll-up on the countertop. Then I suddenly thought if I told you my ideas for redecorating your house, I could maybe get upstairs.

I said, "Only I'm good at design. I mean, I'm not bragging or anything. I just mean I like it."

"Oh, right," you said and ran your tongue along the Rizla and sealed it. "As in interior design."

"Yeah," I said.

You picked your tea up and started going through to the front room.

"So can I tell you what I was thinking?" I said, follow-ing you and then suddenly I really *did* want to tell you my ideas, and not just to get upstairs, because I'd thought a lot about how brilliant your house could look. I waited for you to sit down, but you just put your tea and your roll-up on the little round table by the chair and went out again, into the bathroom.

I stood there waiting for you, hoping you'd love what I was going to say, and then my brain actually started working because I realized I didn't have to try to talk my way into getting upstairs now that you were in the bathroom—I could just *go*—so I went into the hall and called, "Just going to wash my hands," then started up the stairs quick.

Halfway up, though, I stopped. I must be completely thick, I thought. Like mega-thick. Because if Alice is up here, in about thirty seconds' time, *you'll* be up here, too... I peered up through the banisters. There were three rooms—a bathroom at the top of the stairs, a bedroom back along the landing above the front room, and the room that overlooks the garden. And that door was shut. I listened. Nothing. Nothing from upstairs or down, only the cuckoo clock and the faint sound of the fan from the bathroom. I couldn't even hear Bea. It was like I was completely alone, the only soul in the house. I thought I should maybe go back down before you came out, but then I thought of Alice and I knew I couldn't. *I have to look*, I told myself and ran up the rest of the stairs, pushing open the bathroom door. I washed my hands quick, rinsing the bar of soap because my gravelly hands had made it all dirty. Then I went along the landing, checking the front bedroom to make sure Alice wasn't there, checking the ceilings in case there was a hatch to a loft or anything. Then I was outside the door to the back room. My heart was thumping in my ears so loud I couldn't hear anything else—like if you were coming out of the bathroom—but I had to look and I knew the quicker I did it the better, so I held my breath and turned the handle.

One of the curtains was pulled open a bit so that the room was bathed in dark pink light and, as I went in, there was that same warm, clinging smell of sweat I'd smelled on you outside, mixed with smoke. The duvet on the bed was tangled, the pillow pushed in where your head had been and, on the other side, on a bedside table, a lamp, a black-and-white photo of someone in an old silver frame and bits of paper, keys and coins. I went to pick the pillow up to smell it, but let go quick because I heard the stairs creak.

You were coming.

It's okay, I told myself, Alice isn't here. I looked at the pink rosebud wallpaper so I could pretend I was thinking about the decorating, then when you got to the landing, I called, "It could be great when you do it up. The rooms are really nice."

"What you doing in here?" you said, standing in the doorway, and even though you weren't very happy at all, I couldn't help looking at your chest again.

"I came up to wash my hands," I said. "I did tell you." And I smiled at you, trying to ignore the look on your face. When you didn't say anything, I looked away, down at your duvet, but then I realized that where I was staring there was a wet stain. "Oh, sorry," I said, embarrassed because I knew you'd seen me looking at it. "I just wanted to see." And I went out, past you.

There was a really awkward silence as we went down the stairs and I wished I could think of something to say. Then I remembered I hadn't told you my ideas for doing the house up and, as well as wanting to move away from the wet-stain moment, I really did want you to hear them, so I said, "I thought a minimalist look would be good, especially as the rooms aren't that big." You still didn't say anything, so I went on. "I was thinking white walls. Or off-white…" I thought even though you weren't happy about me being in your room, you probably believed I'd gone in there to look at how you could do it up. "Then if it's floorboards under-neath," I said, glancing back up at you, "we could take the carpet up and varnish them and in the front room we could buy a black leather sofa and chair, and a glass coffee table and a shaggy white rug."

Then, when I was in the hallway, I realized you weren't behind me anymore, so I turned around. You were standing at the bottom of the stairs watching me, your hand on the banister post. For a horrible second I thought you knew what I was doing. I thought you were going to say, *We both know why you're really here, don't we, Yasmin?* You didn't, though. You scratched the side of your head, held the banister post again and said, "We?" I felt my face go red. Had I said "we"?

"Well, only because I'd help," I said quickly. Then when you didn't say anything, I said, "What do you think?"

You just stood looking at me. Then you said, "I think you probably shouldn't come around here anymore."

I felt the blood drain out of my face. "Why?" I said. I hadn't expected that at all. I didn't understand. And you were being so calm about it, like you were talking about something that didn't matter. Like you were talking about the weather or something.

You said, "I don't think it's a good idea."

"Why?" I said again.

You shrugged, all casual, like it was no big deal. Then you said, "People might get ideas."

"What people?" I said, and then I knew. "You mean your neighbor."

"Yes," you said, "my neighbor," as if your neighbor was just one person who might get ideas.

"But that's their problem," I said, because I didn't understand why you were saying any of it. Because who cared what your horrid neighbor thought? Who cared what *anyone* thought? "It's not like there's anything going on," I said. "I'm only taking Bea for walks. I'm only helping you out. We're friends."

You took your hand off the post and started smoothing your hair down at the back. Then you did the same silent laugh that you'd done when you were doing the trick with the glass, shaking your head and looking at the ground. "You don't want to be friends with me," you said, and you sounded so sad, I swear I forgot for a second who you really were and why I was really there, because all I wanted to do was go to you and hug you like I had the night before, to tell you that I knew why you were saying I shouldn't be your friend and that you didn't have to, because I knew what you'd done and I didn't care.

Instead, I just said, "Why not?" and then, because I was scared you'd answer, I said, "I *do* want to be your friend." But you'd turned away and were going to the front door. "I'm sixteen," I said, even though I'm not yet.

"Exactly," you said and opened it.

I said, "It's old enough to know who I want to be friends with," but you weren't listening. You wanted me to go.

My head was all over the place walking home. I didn't know what was going on, why I felt so upset about you saying I shouldn't be friends with you when it was Alice I should be upset about. And I *was* upset about Alice. I kept whispering, "You took Alice, you took Alice," over and over and telling myself that you were totally 100 percent right—that I *didn't* want to be friends with you, that being friends with you was the last thing I wanted. But even though I told myself that, I knew it wasn't true, because, if I didn't want to be your friend, why hadn't I told the police about you? I'd even thought about hugging you and telling you it didn't matter that you'd taken Alice, when of course it did. Of course it matters! I thought. What's wrong with me?

Then when I got to our road and saw all the black trash bins out along the pavement, I panicked. I started running past them all to Gary's house, going "Oh my God, oh my God, oh my God," and jabbing my key at the lock to get it in because it was garbage day and I'd put Alice's things in the bin and I wanted them back. Even though I hadn't told the police about you, and even though I liked you, I still wanted Alice's things. It was different now that she'd gone. I didn't have to grow up or stop thinking about her. I think part of me also thought that if I got her things out again and taped her box back together and put it all like it was before, maybe none of this would be happening—that maybe I'd go to school tomorrow and she'd be there and the whole thing would've just been in my head.

The kitchen bin was empty. There was a new bag in it. I put my hands over my mouth. I ran back outside and looked in the trash bin, but the garbage men had been there.

It was nearly 3:00 p.m. Of course they'd been there.

I got the phone off the table and took it down the hallway and sat on the stairs. *Do it*, I told myself. *Do it now.* I even dialed emergency dispatch, but then I hung up because I remembered your face and how sad it'd looked when you'd said, "You don't want to be friends with me," and all of a sudden I realized why you'd said it. You'd said it to protect me, because of who you were, because you didn't want me getting mixed up with someone like you, because you knew you were no good. Because if you'd meant it, you'd have said, *I don't want to be friends with you*, wouldn't you? Not the other way around. Not, *You don't want to be friends with me.* Not looking so sad. And I knew then that you did like me—that you cared. That you cared so much you were willing to lose me rather than put me in danger.

And then I remembered the wet patch on your duvet and how you'd seen me looking at it, and I laughed out loud and had to bury my face in my hands thinking how embarrassing it was—for both of us, but especially for you. You must've died! That was probably another reason why you'd said I shouldn't go back, because you were so mortified about me seeing it, and I sat there on the stairs with my head in my hands, squirming more and more every time I thought about it, and going "Awww, poor Samuel! Poor Sammy!"

By midnight the *Help Find Alice Taylor* page had more than five hundred hits, with comments from people all over the country and uploaded pictures of her—family ones, school ones, one from a wedding or something like that, with her beaming at the camera in a bright green dress and a ring of white flowers on her head. There were loads of prayers, too, with suggestions like, was she hiding at a friend's house, had they checked with the trains, were the police looking at CCTV, had they contacted Missing Persons? It said there'd been a search at seven o'clock across the football field that runs alongside Rectory Road. At the top, it said: *Still no Alice. No sightings. No signs. Police-coordinated search goes out again at 9:00 a.m. Please help. Meeting at The Bell on the High Street. 9:00 a.m.*

I looked at the status bar at the top of the screen. It said *Write something.* I wrote *I know who took her.* Then I got scared I'd post it without meaning to and deleted it. I wrote *I hope ur ok Alice* instead and stared at it for ages, chewing my cheek and wondering if I should delete that, too. In the end I posted it and shut my laptop down.

I turned my bedside light off, too, and lay in bed staring at the red light from my bubble lamp moving slowly over the walls and across the galaxy on the ceiling. I remembered DI Burke's big eyes at school that morning and wondered why I hadn't told her about you, why I hadn't done what I'd been planning to do since I'd first seen you watching Alice from the wooded path. I thought it was probably shock—discovering that something that'd existed only in my head was suddenly happening for real. Because deep down I don't think I'd believed you'd take Alice—not for real—so it turning out that I was right wouldn't compute. Because I'm never right about anything ever. You know, like, *Here lies Yasmin Laksaris: never right about anything, but loved a jammy doughnut.*

The other thing that was so weird was that, even though it *was* happening for real, it wasn't anything like it'd been in my head. It's a bit like when someone tells you about someone and you get this vivid picture of them and then you meet them and they're nothing remotely like that picture.

I wondered if there was another reason I hadn't said anything, though—if part of me didn't really believe you'd taken her, and that like all those people were saying on her Facebook page, she might be hiding out somewhere—that she'd just turn up, like you said. I mean, she definitely wasn't in your house. I thought maybe she was somewhere with Darren— that they'd planned her vanishing together and he was outside the chippy that night only to get himself an alibi, then, later on, in a week or something, he'd join her wherever she was. Maybe she was pregnant...

I didn't really believe that, though. I knew Alice wouldn't get pregnant or run off. And I kept remembering you with that tool bag and your eyes avoiding mine when you handed me Bea's lead.

Then I realized something that made me sit up, made shivers run down my arms and up my neck into my hair. "Oh my God!" I breathed, going over the thought again, realizing it had been sitting there in my head all day, only I hadn't noticed it till now. I realized if I *had* called the police—if I'd said about you—they might not believe that I'd got to know you just so I could protect Alice—especially as I'd taken so long to tell them. They might think I'd known you for ages. And then, once they found out I was looking after Bea when you took her, they'd think *I was in on it*—as in really in on it—that I'd planned it with you…

It was on the local news the next morning. When I went into the kitchen, Mum was standing staring at the television even though the toast had popped, a butter knife in her hand.

A woman in a beige mac was talking into a microphone outside our school gates, then the man in the news studio was saying Alice's name and showing the picture of her that was on the *Help Find Alice Taylor* page and saying she'd failed to arrive home on Sunday evening. He said her phone had been recovered from the grass shoulder on Rectory Lane— the lane where she was last seen by witnesses.

Even though I'd thought it might be on television, actually seeing it—seeing the presenter I'd watched for years suddenly saying Alice's name and the name of our school—was frightening. It was like in horror films when you realize the creepy person on the television isn't talking to everyone—just you.

"Oh my God," Mum said. I wasn't sure if she'd heard me come in, but then she turned to me. "That's the Taylors," she said. "That girl goes to your school."

"She's in my class," I said. I got a bowl and spoon and the Crunchy Nut Clusters, remembering Alice showing Katy the HTC smartphone she'd got for Christmas at the start of term.

Mum turned back to the TV. "Gary did a job for them only a few weeks ago."

I sat down and shook some Clusters into the bowl, shocked that Mum was being so dramatic. She was making me feel even more freaked out than I already was, and it wasn't as if she even knew them. She'd seen them at parents' evenings, that's all.

She lowered herself onto the chair next to me, gripping the edge of the table. "Did you know?" she asked.

I poured milk on my Clusters, trying to keep my hand steady. "The police were at school yesterday," I said. "They told me."

"They *spoke* to you?"

"It's all right, Mum, they spoke to everyone." I started shoveling in the Clusters so I could finish quick and get away from her.

"Why didn't you say something?"

My mouth was full. I held my hands out to say, *I'm telling you now, aren't I?*

"I'm taking you to school from now on," she said decisively. "And you mustn't go anywhere after on your own. You come straight home."

"She probably just ran off somewhere," I said.

"They said on the report it was totally out of character," Mum said. "And her phone…"

"Parents don't know anything about their kids," I said. Then the doorbell rang. Mum got up to answer it.

I thought it was the postman, then heard voices and Mum saying, "Come in," and a second later the kitchen door was opening and Mum was looking at me all worried, and DI Burke was coming in behind her, with a man who wasn't the one at school. This one was older, tall and skinny, with a pointy face. He was wearing a dark gray suit and tie.

DI Burke said, "Hello again, Yasmin. Sorry to barge in on your breakfast."

"No, not at all," Mum said. She was being all smiley and false, but threw me a meaningful look. "Please, sit down," she said. "Can I get you a coffee? Tea?"

"Tea would be great," DI Burke said, "just milk," and the tall one nodded like he'd have the same.

They sat on the other side of the table. I could smell the cold morning air on them.

"This is DI Grayson," DI Burke said. "We just need to go over a few things with Yasmin. It shouldn't take too long."

I saw Mum behind them glance at her reflection in the oven door and plump her hair up. Then she turned the television off. "Do you want a tea, love?" she said.

I said, "No, thanks," and pushed my bowl away, even though there was still some left. It's not nice eating with two police officers ogling you. I didn't think it was very considerate of them to just come barging in. I mean, they could've phoned. And Mum was embarrassed because she was still in her old sweatpants she wears for making breakfast and her face wasn't on. I thought she might go up to get ready after giving them their drinks, but she said, "I'd like to stay, if that's all right?" and sat at the end of the table.

DI Burke smiled and said, "We'll need you to stay in any case, Mrs. Thornton."

I was glad. I didn't want to be left on my own with them.

Then DI Burke turned her smile on me, only now it was a kind of *Okay, we're about to press you for information* sort of smile. "Sunday," she said and wrapped her hands around her mug of tea. "The day Alice went missing." She sounded like she was narrating a play or something, setting the scene. "We'd like you to go over what you did that day."

I shrugged. "I was here," I said. "Then at about six I went to the chip shop." I glanced at Mum, wondering if she knew I'd really gone out earlier than that, but if she did, she didn't say anything. She was looking at DI Burke.

"Which chip shop?" DI Grayson said. It was the first time he'd spoken. His voice was hard like his pointy face and his lip had a curl to it like he could be really mean if he wanted to.

"The one on Belmont Road."

"Walk there?" he asked. I didn't like him. He looked like a crow.

"Yes."

"See anyone on the way?"

"No." I glanced at DI Burke. "Not till I got there. Then I saw that boy, Darren."

"Oh yes, that's right," he said casually, as if he'd heard somewhere that I'd said that. "Can you take us through that again?"

I shrugged. I said, "I walked there, then saw him standing outside with his bike. He was talking to three other boys."

DI Grayson nodded along as I talked, then narrowed his eyes. "You went straight there?" he said.

I hesitated. I could feel he was trying to trick me. "Yeah."

"From here."

"Yeah."

He looked up, pushing his tongue against the inside of his cheek and thinking. "Hmm," he said, "that's odd…"

Mum cleared her throat and said, "I don't really see how—"

But DI Burke cut her off. "Please," she said. "This is just police procedure, Mrs. Thornton. In the circumstances, I'm sure you understand."

Then DI Grayson leaned forward. "We spoke to Darren," he said and instantly I felt my face burn, even though it was obvious they'd have spoken to him. "And he said he saw you, too."

A high-pitched ringing started in my ears. I knew any second he was going to say something about Bea, about Darren saying I'd been there with a dog. That's why they'd come to the house, wasn't it? Why else would they have come?

"Only he said you were coming from the direction of the park."

I swallowed. Mum was looking at me. "I went around the back way," I said. DI Burke started twisting one of her gold stud earrings, rolling it in her fingertips.

"Up Chancery Lane," I said. "That way."

DI Grayson tilted his head. He narrowed his eyes. "But you said you went directly."

"Will this take long, Officers?" Mum said. "Only Yasmin has to get to school and I've got work. I haven't rung in."

DI Burke said, "No, not long," like she didn't want DI Grayson interrupted.

I wished I'd said yes to tea or asked for a water because I

didn't know what to do with my hands and my face was still burning. "I did go directly," I said. "I just went the long way."

DI Grayson shook his head, wrinkling up his nose and grimacing, acting like he just didn't get the logic of that, like he didn't believe me.

I bit my lip and looked down at my hands. "I'm trying to lose weight," I said. "I wasn't supposed to be eating chips."

Mum leaned across and put her hand on my arm. "I walked that way to burn some calories," I said.

"She's been having a hard time," Mum explained. "We'd had a row about it, hadn't we, Yaz?"

I looked back at her, nodding, but I wasn't thinking about that. I was thinking about Darren. I was thinking, please, Darren, don't have seen Bea…

I could feel DI Grayson's crow eyes on me, studying me. Then he pulled a small black notebook out of his jacket pocket and said, "Mind if I take a look at your phone?" It was on the table. I unlocked it and pushed it across to him. The only messages on it were to Mum—Wen u home? Wat's 4 dinner?— or from Mum—Home by 6. B a luv and get sausages out of freezer. Not exactly incriminating.

"What's your phone number?" he said, pulling a tiny pencil from inside the spine of the notebook.

I told him and he scribbled it down, then looked at Mum, swiveling the book around and pushing it across the table toward her. "Could you note your number in there for me, too, Mrs. Thornton?"

When she was halfway through writing it, he said, "Oh, and your husband's if you could. Plus email accounts."

I don't think Mum liked him either because she stopped writing and gave him a look, but he didn't notice. He was leaning back on two chair legs and squinting at my phone screen, scrolling with his thumbs.

DI Burke waited till Mum had finished. Then she said, "Were you at home Sunday evening, Mrs. Thornton?"

"Yes," Mum said.

"And your husband?"

"Yes."

"He was home the whole evening? You're sure."

I thought Mum might say about me getting in late, but she didn't. She closed the notebook and slid the pencil back into its spine. "Yes, he was. Well, most of it, anyway. He had to go and pick up some piping for a job, but he wasn't long."

"What time was that?" DI Burke asked.

Then Mum suddenly held her hands out, like to stop them. "Look, hang on," she spluttered. "Really. I'm not sure I like this. You've come to my home without any warning, frightening my child and asking about Gary as if he could know—"

"We have good reason," DI Grayson interrupted lazily, still rocking on our chair like she was boring him or something, like it was his chair to break.

Mum's mouth fell open.

His eyes flicked to mine. He set the chair legs down and put my phone on the table. "We spoke to Beth Porter," he said. His face was slack, like this was the deadly serious bit, the bit they'd really come to see me about. "She told us about an argument you had with Katy last Monday. In the lunch break. She said Alice was there, too."

I shifted in my seat. I knew exactly what argument he meant and I didn't want to talk about it, not with Mum there, and I couldn't see why he'd want to know about it anyway. "It was nothing," I said.

"That's not what Beth said. She said it got quite nasty."

I shrugged.

"I'd like you to tell us about it."

I glanced at Mum. There wasn't any way DI Grayson was going to drop it. I had to tell them. "They came out of lunch behind me," I said. "Like, on purpose."

"Who was there, do you remember?"

"Katy, Sophie, Beth and Alice," I said. "They were saying I'd followed them in town."

DI Grayson raised an eyebrow and leaned on his elbows. I wished DI Burke had been on her own or with the officer at school who just wrote things down and didn't say anything. I wished Mum would go away, too—go and get dressed, so at least it looked like we *could* leave for school.

"Beth seemed to think it was Alice you were following," he said.

"I wasn't following anyone," I said. "I was just in town."

"She said Katy spat in your face," he said.

"Yaz, is that true?" Mum said, horrified, looking from me to the officers, then back at me.

"That was a spiteful thing to do," DI Burke said. "I told Katy as much when we spoke to her and her parents got to hear about it." She was saying that only because Mum was there—trying to make out like she cared, but I knew it was an act. She hadn't cared about my bruised arm.

"Just before that happened," DI Grayson said, his voice quieter, "Beth said you mentioned a man. She said you told Katy you were trying to protect Alice from a man." I felt the blood drain out of my face. I didn't think any of them had heard me say that. I'd forgotten I'd even said it.

I shook my head, pulling the corners of my mouth down too far and my shoulders right up around my ears like I had no idea what they were talking about, even though I knew they could see I did. "No," I said.

DI Grayson looked at DI Burke, then back at me. "So… you *didn't* say anything about a man?"

I struggled to swallow, shrugging again. "No." I could feel Mum staring, too, now.

Then he reached out a bony hand and held it over his mug like one of those metal claws in arcades that drop down and close around a prize. He picked the mug up by the rim and turned it a bit, let go, then did it again. "Well, that's odd," he said and he stuck his tongue in his cheek again, moving it around so it looked like an alien trying to push its way out. "Because when we asked Sophie Albright and Katy Ellis to tell us about it, they said you'd said that, too—that there was a man and that you were trying to protect Alice."

I felt paralyzed. I couldn't move a muscle. I couldn't breathe.

"Yaz?" Mum said, only she didn't sound like normal.

She sounded dazed.

There was a long silence.

DI Burke twisted her earring again. "Look," she said eventually, "even if this man you mentioned is just an idea you have, a person you're not sure about but maybe suspect, you must tell us, Yasmin. If he's innocent, you have my word he'll be cleared." She paused to see if I was going to say anything, then when I didn't, she went on. "But you should know that we have to follow this up."

Then DI Grayson pinned me with his crow eyes. "Because if we feel you're perverting the course of justice," he said, "we'll get written statements from these girls. Girls who say they're happy to swear by what they heard, if need be, in a court of law."

I didn't get into school till halfway through History. Everyone kept looking at me. I suppose they'd heard Sophie and Katy and Beth's story about what I'd said and wanted to know all the details. I'd had enough of the whole man-thing already. Mum'd been at me the whole way to school, asking me over and over, "What man? What man?"

And I'd told her over and over, "There *is* no man," and "I never *said* there was any man," till I was shouting it.

I watched Mr. Caplin's mouth as he read from the textbook. I thought, so what if they're saying I said something about a man? What can anyone do about it if I say I didn't? And if I have to, I'll say okay, I *did* say it, but I made it up. I started to feel better then, because I knew no one could prove anything even if they didn't believe me. And the police hadn't mentioned Bea. That was the most important thing. Darren hadn't seen her. The second the lesson finished, Chelsea came over. "Why were you so late?" she said, like she had a right to know. Avril and Laura and a few other girls came over, too, and they all stood looking at me.

I wasn't going to tell them anything. It was none of their business anyway. They can all just pee off, I thought. But when Laura said, "Did the police speak to you again?" I looked down, pulling at my cardigan cuff, and then I nodded. Don't ask me why. I'm weird like that. Sometimes I do things when I've decided I'm definitely not going to do them—like going back to see you after I had more than enough on you to tell the police.

"God," Chelsea said, looking around to check everyone had seen me nod. "Is it about the man? D'you know who's got Alice?"

"She doesn't know anything," Avril cut in nastily, as if I was an idiot. As if I wasn't even there. "You know what she's like."

Laura ignored her, though. She said, "Oh my God," in a half whisper, her eyes going wider and wider. "It's Mr. Faraday, isn't it?"

They all went quiet then, waiting for my answer—even Avril—and I suddenly felt like I was going to cry. I think it was the stress of the police and Mum and now everyone's eyes on me. A tear went down my cheek.

"Oh my God, it *is*!" Chelsea said, and because more people had come over now, she looked around at them all, saying, "Mr. Faraday took Alice."

Everyone started gasping, saying it was so obvious it was him and how he was always lusting after her, then asking why he was still in school teaching...

Laura bent down to look me in the face, her hand resting

lightly on my arm. "Are we right?" she said. "Aren't you al-lowed to say?"

I stared at my cardigan sleeve and shook my head and thought about Alice's hair that day in the drama studio, slip-ping like water through my fingers and then, before I even knew what I was doing, I was saying, "We were really close."

There was a sudden silence. Laura took her hand off my arm.

Then Avril said, "What, you and *Alice*?" like it wasn't even possible that we could've been close. Like it was more likely I was close to Mr. Faraday than to Alice.

When I burst into tears, though, and said, "I was the last person to see her," Laura reached out again—put her hand on my shoulder.

"God," she breathed, "poor you."

And Chelsea said, "Jeeesus."

It didn't take long for that to reach Katy. She marched into the art room after break with Sophie and Beth behind her, even though none of them do Art, and said, "What the fuck?"

I knew she'd find me the second she heard. I was expect-ing her. What I wasn't expecting was how she looked—so tired—the skin around her eyes red and dark, and there was a weakness in her voice. She'd have to have looked a whole lot worse for me to feel sorry for her, though. She'd have to have been dead. I carried on bulldog-clipping my sheet of paper to the board underneath and said, "Can I help you?"

She gripped her books tighter to her chest. "What the hell are you doing?"

"I didn't say anything about it being Mr. Faraday," I said, knowing that it wasn't Mr. Faraday she'd come about.

"I'm not talking about that," she spat. Then, when I didn't say anything, she did a nasty voice: "'I'm protecting Alice...'" she said. "'We were really close...'"

I looked at her as calmly as I could, aware that people were coming in after break and watching us, hoping something big was about to kick off. I waited. I wanted as many of them as possible to hear. Then I said, "Well, maybe there're some things you didn't know about Alice," and I bit my lip and lifted my eyebrows. "Things she never told you."

There were a few gasps and shocked laughs around us while Katy blinked helplessly, speechless as she tried to compute the idea that Alice could have had anything to do with me—and maybe a whole lot more than just anything. It was priceless. Worth it even though I knew she'd tell the police or Alice's parents what I'd said and I'd have to admit later that I made it up—the bit about being the last person to see her, anyway. There was no one to say the rest wasn't true.

She got herself together enough to splutter, "The only way that you were the last one to see Alice, Doner, was if you were the one who *took* her," but she was too late. Everyone had seen her falter.

"*Yasmin* took Alice?" Robert said. He'd arrived only in time to catch Katy's last comment. "I can't keep up. I thought it was meant to be Mr. Faraday?"

"Shut up, Rob," Katy snapped.

"So, how'd she do it?" he said, laughing as she pushed past him. "Eat her?"

★ ★ ★

It was on the main news at six o'clock. The senior investigating officer—a man with a big bulbous nose and red cheeks—was on, surrounded by loads of hands pointing microphones at him. He said all leads were being followed, CCTV being gathered. He said he was appealing for anyone who saw Alice on her route home between 6:15 and 7:20 p.m.—particularly on or around Rectory Road, where two witnesses had already come forward to say they'd seen a girl matching Alice's description, and where Alice's phone had been found. Gary and Mum were glued to it. Gary was hunched forward in his armchair, shaking his head and stating the obvious, like, "The poor kid," and, "You don't expect it, do you?" I went up to my room before the report finished. I knew if I stayed Gary would start asking me all sorts of questions, like how was everyone coping and did any of us kids have any ideas at all about where she could've gone. Like *he* was a cop.

He came up anyway, knocking and waiting for me to say he could come in. "The reporter said there're searches going on for her," he said. "Something about a web page." I was looking at it. I turned my laptop around on the bed for him to see and he came and sat next to it, pulling it onto his knees. It was weird, his sitting on my bed, because he never comes into my room.

"Christ," he said, looking at all the photos and shaking his head. "Poor kid."

"There's a search at seven," I said, "meeting at the Bull's Head."

He looked at his watch. "Right," he said, "I'm going."

"Should I go, too?" I said, faltering a bit because I didn't want to, because I knew Katy and Sophie and a whole load of others would be there and that they'd round on me, telling everyone what I'd said at school.

He looked at me for a second like he was thinking about it, then he said, "It's not really the place for a teenager, love. And it'll be getting dark soon."

A few minutes later I heard him go out of the front door and helicopters going overhead.

I didn't know where I was when I woke up. It was pitch-dark and I could hear rain whipping in waves at the window. Maybe that was why it took a few seconds to figure out what was real and what wasn't, because it'd been raining in my dream. I'd been stumbling through woods in the dark, holding up the sodden skirts of my long crimson dress, crying and calling out for you, even though I couldn't see you. Then I was turning, looking into an endless maze of tree trunks, till I caught sight of your white shirtsleeve. You were digging with a spade and spattered with soil. You looked up only when I got close. I was crying and laughing at the same time, going "You're okay, thank God you're okay," my hands reaching out to you, but then you weren't there anymore. I swung around, blinded by the rain, but you'd disappeared. "Where are you?" I was calling over and over and then I looked down and Alice was there in the ground, half-buried, rain filling her open mouth, her hair all splayed about and sinking into the black, liquid mud.

★ ★ ★

There was a strange atmosphere those last days of term. People were talking and being almost normal, but not quite. They talked a bit quieter, they sat a bit stiller. I think Alice was on everyone's mind, and because term was ending it felt like if she didn't come back now, before we broke up, she never would.

I kept seeing her. I'd catch her out the corner of my eye, then look to see some other girl there, and the seat she should've been in for morning register was so empty it was like it was shimmering with her goneness. When I stared at it, a faint outline of her face appeared, then a bit of pastel blue cardigan, hovering in the air till I blinked.

Words kept drifting into my head, too; weird phrases that seemed like they didn't come from me but from Alice. Things like "Don't worry about it, Yaz" and "There's nothing you can do now." Then I'd hear your voice going "Steady," and I'd get this rush as if I was with you in your front room again, swaying to the music and looking into your shining black-hole eyes.

Usually there're awards for commendations and sport announcements and that kind of stuff at the end of term assembly, but there was none of that this time. Miss Ward said that Easter was a time of suffering what with Jesus on the Cross, and that this year his suffering had come into our lives—to Alice's family, to our school and to the community as a whole.

She told us she was going to say a prayer for Alice that would be followed by two minutes' silence and that in that time we should think our own thoughts about Alice and say a personal prayer for her safe return. We all stood up. She said:

Dear Lord,

We ask of you,

Keep Alice safe and sound,

Let no harm come to her before she is found.

She is lost from her family,

From the ones she loves,

Return her home,

And protect her from above. Amen.

I don't *remember* the prayer, obviously, but because it was so good and I wondered if Miss Ward had written it herself, I did a *Missing person prayer* search on Google and found it.

Anyway, I did think about Alice in the two-minute silence. I thought about how she'd looked that day you were watching her from the path, walking backward across the tennis court with her light, bouncing steps. I thought about her pale cheeks turning pink and her green eyes watching me. Then I looked along the row in front and saw Katy. Her eyes were screwed shut and tears were rolling down her cheeks.

Mum was waiting outside school in the car. I lobbed my bag on the backseat.

"Hi, love," she said, but I could see straight away something was up. She pulled out into the road before she told me. "The police took Gary in."

I got a nasty acidy taste in the back of my mouth. "What?" I said. "Why?"

"They asked to have his van, too." She glanced across at me. "They said CCTV showed a Ford Transit on Rectory

Road when Alice disappeared. They said they only got a part index on camera, but it's the same as Gary's."

"What's a part index?" I said.

"Just part of the license plate. The last two letters, I think Gary said. That's all they could see on the CCTV, but they match Gary's."

I was stunned. I didn't really know what that meant, how unlikely it'd be for a van to have the same last letters as another van.

"They can't say how long they'll have it, either. He's furious, Yaz. They told him about what those girls are saying you said. I think he thinks that's the real reason they pulled him in. I told him you didn't say it, but he's not listening. It's shaken him, that's why. It's being questioned. It's not nice."

I tried to swallow the acid. "Is he still there?"

"No, he's at home."

"So he's okay, then? I mean, they let him go. They don't think he did anything?"

She took her hands off the wheel to shrug. "Well, I don't *think* so. But they kept his van. He won't be able to work."

"But you said he went to pick up piping. The police can check it, can't they?"

"He said the bloke he got it off wasn't there. He'd left the pipes out for him."

We pulled onto our drive. Mum switched the engine off, undid her seat belt and turned to me. "Are *you* okay?" she said. "You're not getting any trouble off those girls?"

"Yeah," I said, "I'm fine."

Her eyes were searching mine, full of worry. I flipped the door handle. "I'm *fine*," I said.

Gary was standing in the living-room doorway when we came in, leaning against the frame with his arms folded like he'd been waiting there for us.

I didn't like the way he was looking at me, his face set like he hated me, so I just said, "Hi," then started up the stairs, even though I knew I wouldn't get very far.

"Yaz," Mum said, putting the keys on the hall table. "Come back down."

"Why?" I said, even though it was obvious.

"We need to talk."

Gary turned and went into the living room. Mum waited for me, then followed me in. The TV wasn't on and there was a bottle of whiskey on the table next to a full glass and his phone. Gary was standing in front of the fireplace, his arms still folded, watching me.

Mum sat on the sofa and patted the cushion next to her. I sat down.

"Feeling guilty, are we?" Gary said. His voice was tense, like he was trying to control it.

"What d'you mean?" I said.

"Sloping off to your room, when, because of one of your elaborate little fantasies, the police have taken my van."

"We don't know that, Gary," Mum said, shooting him a look like she didn't think he was being fair. She put her hand on my knee. "It's not your fault, love," she said. "It's just we can't understand why the police asked Gary to go with them to the station like that, in the middle of a job."

"You said it was because of the van," I said. "The part index thing."

"There're probably a hundred vans around here with those same letters," Gary said, throwing his arm out. "It's because of what you told those girls."

I looked at Mum. "I didn't say *anything* about a man."

"You didn't say anything about a man?" Gary repeated, nodding and pulling a face like he didn't believe me.

"I didn't!" I said.

"Right," Gary said. "So you didn't say anything, but suddenly I'm a murder suspect. One minute I'm under a sink, the next I'm in the back of a fucking police car…"

"*Gary!*" Mum said, "that's…"

"…my van hauled off to be—Christ knows what—torn apart!"

"You said you wouldn't do this," Mum said.

"Oh, well, excuse me," Gary said, sarcastic. "But I've had enough of this. She must've said something, Jen. They pulled me off a *job*!" He said it as if the job was the Holy Grail or something—the be-all and end-all of the universe—his voice going hysterical. "Mr. Cummings has a bunch of pipes unscrewed and no water!"

"Don't be ridiculous," Mum said.

"Okay, then," Gary said. He unfolded his arms and held them out like a preacher calling on God. "Tell me why those girls would say she told them that."

"Well, clearly," Mum said, moving to the edge of her seat, her voice like *Let's all stay nice and calm now*, "there's been a misunderstanding, hasn't there?"

Gary threw his arms up.

"She doesn't know," Mum went on. "The police asked her about that in front of me. She says she never said anything like that."

"Three girls heard her," Gary said, karate-chopping the air. He ran the tip of his tongue backward and forward along his bottom lip. "Not one. *Three*, Jen."

"That could just be…"

"They all said the same thing! Exactly the same thing!" His fingers etched quote marks in the air. "That she was 'protecting' Alice from 'a man.'"

When neither of us said anything, he started to shake his head, squinting at us like *What's wrong with you people?* Like he couldn't figure out how it was possible for people to be as thick as us.

"Look," Mum said. "Maybe she made a mistake…"

"A mistake?"

"Yes, Gary," Mum said firmly, "a mistake. She's a kid, for God's sake."

He turned away from us then, then back again, laughing in that horrid way when it's not laughing at all. "A kid?" he repeated. "A kid?"

Mum stood up.

His teeth were pulling on his bottom lip so hard the skin kept turning white, and he was shaking his head. "She's fifteen," he said. "*Fifteen.* I was working when I was fifteen, so don't give me that shit, Jen. When's it gonna stop, eh?" He was still shaking his head, but even more nastily now, his neck craned at Mum's face. "I mean, come *on*. She can't be getting over Terry forever."

Then suddenly Mum lost it. "That's *enough*," she bellowed. "No more! You hear me?" She waved her hand behind her back at me. "Go upstairs, Yaz! Pay no attention to him! He's drunk!"

I went. I wasn't going to argue, either.

I'd never seen Gary like that and it scared me.

As I went up, I heard him say, "You only have to *look* at her to know things aren't right." I imagined him screwing his finger into the side of his head.

I closed my door. I sat on my bed and stared out the window.

The sky was gray with a heaviness that meant it was going to get dark any minute. I thought about going downstairs and out of the house, closing the front door quietly behind me. I imagined myself walking up the road, then along Highfield Road to a bus that was waiting just for me. I get off in town and walk up the empty precinct to Cromwell Road, over the pedestrian crossing and up the steps to the police station.

In my mind, the man behind the desk isn't too bothered about dealing with me until I say *I know who's got Alice Taylor*. He eyes me then, unconvinced, but calls over his shoulder through an open door to someone out the back.

DI Burke appears, saying *Yasmin*, like she's been expecting me, like she's relieved to see me, and I let her lead me along a corridor and sit me down in one of those police rooms with a one-way mirror that looks into it. Then the young officer that was at school—DC Hill—comes in with a hot chocolate and puts a blanket around my shoulders. He asks if I'd like something to eat as well, and I nod and he brings a plate of assorted biscuits like from those fancy tins people get at Christmas. I tell them both I'm sorry, and I break down and cry.

I say, *I hope I'm not too late*, and I tell them about you. I tell them how you've got a dog called Bea and how you said she was grieving because Mrs. E. Caldwell died, which is why I kept going around—because I felt sorry for her. I tell them I didn't mean to make friends with you, that it just happened. I tell them, even though you've taken Alice, you were always nice to me. I open my hand and show them China Bea.

But I don't tell the police everything, even though they're only listening in my imagination. I don't tell them about your dark, dark eyes or how, when you look down and smile your sad smile, it makes me want to kiss you.

CURRY FOR TWO

I WAS IN MY ROOM when the doorbell rang the next evening. I heard Mum come out of the living room and open the front door, a man's voice, then DI Burke's.

I recognized it straight away.

They've come for me, I thought. Darren's remembered about me having a dog and now they know about you and me and everything...

Then I heard Gary shout, "This is crazy!"

Someone was coming up the stairs. I grabbed my inhaler and sucked on it, looking around my room. I thought about trying to escape through the window, but that wasn't going to happen. That happens only in films. I thought if I tried, I'd just fall and break my legs on the decking. I'd probably go through the decking. So I opened my door.

An officer in uniform was standing there. I think she'd been about to open it because her hand was out. "Hello, love," she said. "Are you Yasmin Laksaris?"

I nodded.

"I'm DC Edwards. DI Burke and DC Henderson are downstairs with your parents. We need you to come with us to the station."

"Why?" I said.

"We have a warrant for a house search. You need to come immediately."

I turned around, looking back at my room. I saw Alice's Manga girl on the wall over my desk where I'd tacked her.

"You can't bring anything, I'm afraid," the officer said, "only prescribed medication. Do you take any medication?"

I could hear DI Burke downstairs in the living room talking in a low voice, like she was reading something, but I couldn't hear what because Mum kept saying things loudly over the top of her. Things like, "You can't do this!" and "This is wrong. You've got it wrong!"

I opened my hand to show the officer my inhaler. "What's happening?" I said.

"Is it just the inhaler?"

Then I was nodding dumbly and she was standing to one side to let me go past her and down the stairs.

DI Burke came out of the living room, looking up at me, and it was like it is in films when it all goes slow motion—Gary coming out behind her, holding his arms in front of him, me seeing that he was holding them like that because his wrists were handcuffed. Me saying, "What's happening?" again. Then another officer—a man in uniform—coming out behind Gary, a hand on his arm, and Mum behind him, her face all screwed up and wet with tears, going "Nooo, you can't dooo this!"

There were two police cars on the road across the top of our driveway, a dark gray car and a van and people everywhere—people in white overalls with hoods putting on blue gloves, people in suits, police officers in uniform. I saw one officer stop Mr. Henshaw from next door coming onto our driveway, and the old couple from the next house along standing and watching everything. Gary was put in the back of one of the police cars and Mum and me were told to get in the other one. The woman who had come to get me, DC Edwards, sat between us. "Gary!" Mum was calling even when the car he was in had driven off. Then two policemen got in the front seats and we were driving, too, making our way slowly through all the people. I turned to see two men in white overalls going in through our front door.

I didn't know where we were. I hadn't been paying attention and it was dark. But we were on a motorway. The M1, I think. Mum was ranting, saying how they were wrong, that Gary was innocent, that she wanted a lawyer, that it was barbaric how we'd all just been chucked out of our own home.

I looked out past my reflection in the window. Nothing made any sense. I thought, how could Gary have taken Alice? How could he, if you were the one who took her? Then I thought, does Gary know you? Did Gary and you take her *together*?

I turned my head away more so DC Edwards wouldn't see me whispering. I imagined the people in white overalls going into my bedroom and opening my cupboards and drawers. Then I thought of Alice's Box and *thank God* how it wasn't sitting there in my cupboard, because if they found that and figured out it was Alice's stuff, they'd think I was a freak. They'd think *I'd* taken her, because even though it isn't really that weird keeping a box of someone's things, the police would think it was, wouldn't they? And with Katy and everyone telling them I was stalking her, the police would say Alice's Box proved it.

We parked and got out in front of a modern, low building with a lit-up entrance and sign over the door that said Bricket Wood Police Headquarters. I remembered I had a friend at junior school who lived in Bricket Wood. I think I went to a party at her house.

Mum had been quiet for the last part of the journey, but she started up again as we were led across the tarmac. "Where's Gary?" she kept saying, and when one of the policemen took her by the arm, she snatched it away, going "Get *off* me!"

It was bright with strip lighting inside. We were taken down a corridor. A man in a suit came out of a door and told Mum, "You'll be free to leave the station once we've questioned each of you separately. Do you give your permission for us to interview Yasmin? She'll be in the room right next to you. There'll be a social worker present."

Mum nodded. "Yes," she said. "Yes, all right. Whatever. Whatever you need..." Then, when they led me farther down the corridor, she called out, "Just tell them the truth, Yaz!" There was a table in the room with a recording machine on it and four chairs tucked in, two on each side. That was it. Nothing else. Not even a one-way mirror.

"Someone will be right with you," DC Edwards said. I sat down and waited for a minute, then DI Burke came in with a clipboard and a man in a brown suit.

"Have you found Alice?" I said. "Did Alice say Gary'd done something?"

She didn't answer. She just sat down, waited for the man to sit next to her, then turned the recorder on. He smelled of BO mixed with cigarette smoke and I glanced at DI Burke to see if she could smell it, too. She must have because it was disgusting and she was nearer him than I was, but she didn't wrinkle her nose up or anything. She said, "Interview with minor, Yasmin Laksaris. DI Burke and social worker Mr. Derek Jeffries in attendance. Bricket Wood station, April 8..." She pushed up the cuff of her suit jacket, looked at her watch and said the time. Then she crossed her legs and put the clipboard on the table. She looked exactly as she had every time I'd seen her—same suit, same hair scraped off her face, same gold stud earrings. The only thing that was different was her shirt, blue this time. And, like every other time, she was watching me steadily. "Yasmin, this is Mr. Jeffries," she said.

The man put his hand out, looking at me over his glasses. I think he wanted me to shake it but I didn't. I didn't want to touch him.

"Why've you arrested Gary?" I said.

She looked at me a bit longer. I think she was deciding whether or not she was going to tell me. Then she said,

"We've found some evidence that indicates that Alice may have been in Gary's van."

"What d'you mean?" I said.

"We're waiting on forensics for confirmation." She rolled her earring between her finger and thumb and looked at me for a second. Then she said, "Yasmin, has Alice ever been in Gary's van?"

I pulled a face. "No."

"Has he ever given you and Alice a lift anywhere, into town maybe or home after school?"

"No."

"Did Alice ever talk about your stepdad? Did she know him at all?"

"No," I said, but I remembered Mum saying he'd done a job at Alice's house.

"You're certain of that."

I shrugged. "Yeah."

She glanced down at the clipboard, looked up at me again and licked her lips. "You and your mum moved into Gary's house the year before last, is that right?"

"Yeah," I said.

"How's that been, living there?" Her voice was softer than usual, like she was concerned about me, except I knew it was only for show because the social worker was there.

I shrugged. "All right," I said.

"Do you like him?"

I thought that was a bit of a weird question, because if Gary took Alice, why did it make any difference if I liked him or not? "He's okay."

"How would you describe your mum and Gary's relationship? Do they get along well?" I thought about Mum rubbing her hands all over the bronzed six-pack on the Adonis cooking apron she got him for his birthday and going "Oooh, Gary, I never knew you had such a body!"

"Yeah," I said. "I suppose."

"Do they ever argue?"

"Not really."

"Has he ever lost his temper?"

I looked at the social worker. He was picking at a thread in the knee of his trousers. "Sometimes," I said. "Sometimes he shouts, like if I'm late and he's giving me a lift. He doesn't like waiting."

She was looking at me like she wanted me to go on, so I said, "He wasn't very happy after you'd questioned him."

"You mean yesterday afternoon?" I nodded.

"What did he say?"

"That it's my fault he got taken in because of what Katy and the others said."

"And what do you think?"

I shrugged.

"Do you think it's your fault?"

I looked at her. I wasn't sure what she meant, but because she was staring intently at me, I said, "No, not really."

She didn't say anything for a few seconds. Then she said, "Has Gary ever struck out at you or your mum? Hit either of you?"

I shook my head.

"For the recording, please, Yasmin."

"No."

"Your mum works, doesn't she?"

"She's a mystery shopper," I said.

"Does that mean you're sometimes alone in the house with Gary?"

"Yeah, sometimes," I said. I could guess where this was going.

"Has he ever done anything that's made you feel uncomfortable in any way? Made any sexual advances?"

"No," I said. "Gary's not like that." I couldn't even picture it. But an image did jump into my head. It was Gary in Alice's kitchen, lying under the sink with a wrench in his hand and looking at Alice's legs disappearing up into the darkness of her short school skirt as she reached into a cupboard.

DI Burke was looking at me like she was still waiting for an answer.

"No," I said again.

Then she leaned forward, pushing the clipboard to one side and interlocking her fingers. "Yasmin, you can tell me the truth." Her lips were pressed together and she was frowning, like she was all heart. "It can feel very frightening to tell someone if a person—especially a person who lives in the same house as you—is behaving inappropriately, doing things they shouldn't. But you have my word that you would be looked after, get the best support there is."

I thought about playing along—saying, *Okay, Gary has been doing things he shouldn't. He's been coming into my room when Mum's out, telling me if I tell anyone I'll be sorry*...but I didn't. I said, "I am telling you the truth."

She kept on staring at me. Then she said, "Is Gary the man you were talking about when you told the girls at school you were trying to protect Alice?"

"No," I said. "I never even said that."

She was looking right into my eyes. "Yasmin, I'm trying to help you here, but one way or another it's clear you're not telling the truth. We know, for example, that you said in front of a number of your classmates that you were the last person to see Alice before she disappeared on Sunday." She waited to see if I was going to say anything, then went on. "And if that's true, then both you and your mother must have been lying when you told DI Grayson and myself that you were home all day Sunday and only went out to go to the fish and chip shop on Belmont Road."

I thought it was obvious I'd made that up. Alice'd been with her singing teacher and the police had CCTV of her walking home on her own, so I couldn't have been the last person to see her. DI Burke just wanted to make me say I'd lied out loud for the recording. "Okay," I said, "that wasn't true."

"What wasn't?"

"I wasn't the last person to see Alice. I said it to get back at Katy. I never said anything about Mr. Faraday, though. That's what *they* said—Laura and Chelsea."

"You also said you and Alice were close," DI Burke said, ignoring what I'd just told her about Mr. Faraday. "You implied the two of you had some kind of secret relationship. Was that also untrue?"

I looked at her big brown eyes. I didn't want to say I'd made that up. I wanted to say it was true, that Alice and I *were* close, that once we'd even gone into town after school and eaten strawberry tarts in the John Lewis café. But I knew if I did, she'd make me give all kinds of details and she'd find out I was lying, so I shook my head. I looked down at my hands. "No," I said, "we weren't friends."

She sat back in her chair. "And are you telling me absolutely everything you know regarding Alice?"

"Yes," I said.

"You and Alice were not friends?"

"No."

"Alice has, to the best of your knowledge, never been in Gary's van?"

"No."

"You never said that you were trying to protect Alice from a man?"

"No."

Then suddenly, out of nowhere, she got up and banged her hand down flat on the table. It made me jump. Then she dropped forward so she was right over me, staring down on me, her nostrils flared. "We have three witnesses," she said. "*Three* witnesses who all say you clearly told them that you were protecting Alice from a man. And *still* you deny it?"

She was scaring me. I started to panic. "No," I said. "I didn't think it mattered…"

"A girl has been taken," she shouted, bits of her spit hitting my face. "A girl who might be somewhere at this very second having God knows what done to her, and you think it doesn't *matter*?"

"I didn't mean that!" I said. Tears were filling my eyes. "I'm sorry..."

She slammed her hand down again. "Did you say it? Did you?"

"Yes!" I said. "I said it! I did! I'm sorry, I—"

Then she was level with me, squatting next to me, one hand holding the edge of the table, the other on my leg. "And who is he?" she said, her voice intense and low, like she'd never shouted, like she didn't want even the social worker to hear her now. "Who is he, Yasmin?" she said. "Tell me. Is it Gary?"

I realized then what she thought—that because I'd said about there being a man, it must be true.

"No," I said, "no," wiping the tears off my cheeks and looking into her eyes. "I'm sorry," I said. "There isn't a man."

She gave a tight shake of her head, like that wasn't possible.

"I did say it," I said, "but I made it up. I'm sorry." She didn't move. She just stared at me. Then slowly, she stood up. She walked in a circle around the table, around me and Mr. Jeffries, her palm pressed to her forehead. Then she stopped behind her chair and turned to me. "Why?" she said, as if it made no sense. "Why would you say that?"

"I don't know," I said. "They were saying I was stalking Alice. I made it up so they wouldn't say it anymore."

There was a long silence.

I looked at the social worker. He was frowning at me over his glasses, a grim expression on his face.

"So there's no man?" DI Burke said.

I shook my head. "No," I said. "There's no man."

★ ★ ★

When I came out, I could see Mum through the swing doors at the end of the corridor. She was at the front desk, taking some papers from a policeman in uniform. She looked like she was arguing with him.

When I came through the door with DI Burke, she rushed over and grabbed my arm. "Yaz, love, are you all right?" Her face was puffy, her makeup all washed away.

"Yeah," I said. "I'm okay."

"Let's get out of here." She threw DI Burke a dirty look.

"Where're we going?" I said when we were outside. I didn't think we'd be able to go home with all those police people there.

"They called a cab," she said, hugging herself because it was cold and we hadn't got our coats. "They've arranged for us to stay at the Premier Inn."

"Did they tell you why they got Gary?"

"No," she said. "Reasonable cause was all they said. How can they arrest someone on reasonable cause when they won't even say what reasonable cause it is they've got? It's despicable!"

I thought she was going to carry on once we'd got in the cab, but she went quiet and stared out the window, her fingers pinching and twisting her bottom lip.

Except for the purple carpet, the Premier Inn wasn't anything like it is in the TV commercial with people bursting through the doors laughing, their arms full of shopping bags. The girl behind the counter wasn't smiling like the one in the ad either.

The room was nice, though—really smart—everything white and purple. The beds had purple silk runners going across the white duvets and the window had a white sort of see-through curtain all across it—probably because the parking lot wasn't a very nice view—and purple curtains to pull in front. The bathroom was nice, too, all clean with fluffy white towels folded neatly on a shelf over the toilet and a bath with a glass panel for when the shower was on. There was a television, too, on a chest of drawers. I thought maybe we'd watch a film later on, when Mum had calmed down a bit, snuggled up in our beds with hot chocolate.

She sat on the bed nearest the window and stared into space.

I closed the curtains and sat on the other bed so I was facing her. "It'll be okay, Mum," I said.

"Gary's a good man," she whispered.

I put my hand on her leg, and she gripped it and looked up at me. "He's a good man," she said again.

I nodded, feeling a bit awkward. "I know."

Then her face crumpled, like now she didn't know anymore if he was good or not. "Isn't he?" she said. I thought the police probably asked her the same questions they'd asked me about Gary making me do things I didn't want to.

"Mum, it's okay," I said. "Gary's never hurt me. He's never touched me. I told them that."

She nodded. She was still gripping me just as tight, though. "Oh, good," she said, sniffing and nodding, trying to smile. "That's good."

I said she should have a nice bath, and went to run her

one. It took me ages to work out how to get the plug to go down because it wasn't one on a chain or one where you pull up a lever, but in the end I figured it out. You had to turn the big silver shower dial the other way from if you wanted a shower. Anyway, I ran the bath, squeezing in the little sachet of shower gel that came for free with the room. It didn't really foam up much but it smelled nice.

When it was full and I'd turned off the taps, I went back into the room and took a ten-pound note out of Mum's purse in her handbag. I said I was going to walk over to the big Tesco that's open twenty-four hours and get us some toothbrushes and stuff. I wasn't sure she heard me because she was staring into space again. "Mum," I said, so she looked at me. "I won't be long. Get in the bath."

When I got back, Mum was lying down, curled away from me. She hadn't got in the bath. She was still in her clothes, the bedspread half over her.

"Mum?" I said quietly, but she didn't answer. I went over, around the end of her bed. Her eyes were open. "Hi, Mum," I said.

She lifted her head off her hands. "Oh, hi, love."

"Are you hungry?" I said. "I got some sandwiches."

She shook her head. "No, I'm okay," she said. "You carry on."

"Okay," I said. It was obvious we weren't going to watch television, so I said, "I'll be back in a bit. I'm just going down the hall."

She put her head back down and closed her eyes.

I took the hoisin duck wrap and sweet 'n' salty popcorn I'd bought out of the Tesco bag and went into the corridor, closing the door quietly behind me. Then I went to reception. I'd seen a waiting area around the corner from the desk when I came back from the shop and heard a TV there.

It was on the wall—a big flat-screen—already on *BBC News 24*. The newscaster was laughing, having some joke with the weatherman. I sat in one of the purple tub chairs and chewed my duck wrap slowly. I got an uneasy feeling waiting for the report, like I didn't really want to know what they were going to say in case they said Gary's name or showed our house, but at the same time I wanted to know if they were going to say anything about the reasonable cause they had. It had to be something to do with Gary's van, because that's what DI Burke kept asking about.

When it came on, I stopped eating and listened. The reporter said that a man, the owner of a Ford Transit similar to one captured on CCTV and believed to have been known to the missing teenager, was assisting police with their inquiries. My heart banged in my chest. "Believed to have been known to the missing teenager." Alice knew Gary? There was no way Alice knew Gary! Unless "believed to have been known" to her meant something like she just knew who he was because she'd seen him picking me up outside school, or something like that, or because of the work he'd done at their house.

No one was around, so I said, "Alice was in Gary's van," to test how it sounded—to see if it sounded any more possible out loud than it did in my head. It didn't. It sounded even crazier. It was *all* crazy. I mean, why was everything that was happening so close to me? It was so confusing, I couldn't even think—like there was so much stuff it wouldn't fit in my head. And the more I tried to think, to make any sense of it, the more tangled up it all got.

When I looked back up at the TV, Alice's parents were on. They were sitting at a long table behind microphones, police in uniform standing behind them on each side. DI Grayson was there in his dark gray suit. Her mum looked different to how I remembered her. I'd seen her only a few times through the windshield of her silver Audi. She was always smart, with perfect makeup and orange waves of hair sprayed into place, looking out at the world like she knew her daughter was better than anyone else's. Maybe that's mean of me, but that's how she looked—sort of *through* people. On the television, though, her hair was flat with dark roots showing, her face pasty without makeup. She was clenching a tissue in her fist and kept dabbing at her eyes with it.

I'd never seen Alice's dad before. He was tall and had silver hair and his face was gray and papery like he'd had no sleep, his jaw muscles tensing as the cameras started to flash. "Alice is our angel," he said. "She loves to sing. She always sings when I play the guitar, even if she's somewhere else in the house." He started to smile thinking about that, but couldn't hold it together, and then he clamped his hands to his face, pressing his fingers into his eye sockets. Her mum huddled against him. Then he took his hands away, sniffing, and said, "She's a happy kid. She'd never run away." I could see the effort it took for him to look into the cameras. "Please…if you know something, *please* come forward."

I closed my eyes. My chest ached and I got a massive lump in my throat seeing Alice's dad like that, because it made me think about my dad and how the last time I ever saw him he'd held the tips of my fingers in his and looked at me like he'd give anything to be able to stay with me, only he didn't have anything left to give. I used to imagine that instead of going to school the next day like I did, I'd gone to the hospice and climbed into bed with him and held him so tight that when his heart stopped beating, mine stopped, too, and that together our bodies just vanished into thin air, so we were nothing and nowhere, just gone.

I felt dizzy going back to the room. Colored blobs were swimming in front of my eyes like the stuff in my lava lamp. I realized I'd left the popcorn back by the TV on the little table next to the chair. I didn't go back for it, though. I didn't want it.

It was dark in the room. There was just the yellow light from the bathroom. I could tell from Mum's breathing that she was asleep. I got the new toothbrushes and toothpaste, brushed my teeth and washed my face, then took my jeans off and got into bed. I left the bathroom light on because the sound of the fan was nice. I didn't want to be in silence. With the fan, I thought I'd be able to imagine I was in a spaceship in some galaxy far away, cruising through space. I closed my eyes and tried to picture myself sitting on the *Enterprise*, not doing anything much, just putting in coordinates to alter course slightly and looking out at the vast blackness. What kept coming into my head, though, was that policeman's hand gripping Gary's arm as he led him out through the front door.

I wondered how many other neighbors had seen us being taken away. I thought, I bet they all rushed indoors to write about it on the *Help Find Alice Taylor* Facebook page. It'd be all over that by now, wouldn't it? Then I took off my fleece because I was hot and felt something hard in the pocket.

It was little Bea. China Bea.

I took her out and held her, kissing her and whispering to her till she was warm. I was so happy I had her with me. It meant that all the time DI Burke had been leaning over me and shouting, raining her spit on me, little Bea had been there, secretly helping, giving me the courage not to break down and tell her about you. Realizing I had China Bea with me felt like an omen, or at least like a message from you.

I wished I could talk to you. I wished I could pick up the phone and say *How are you? What you doing?* and *Did you see the news?* I imagined you saying *Yeah* and how sad it was seeing Alice's parents and then asking me if I was okay because you'd guessed how seeing Alice's dad like that would've made me think about my dad. We'd talk about decorating your house again then, and I tell you my idea for the kitchen— shiny white cupboard doors with a black floor and red blind, with black-and-white-checkered tiles and red accessories like jars and a kettle. I can feel you smiling at the other end of the phone, your eyes shining because secretly you think it's cute when I talk about the two of us decorating your house, even though you have to pretend it's not appropriate for us to be friends. And then I say, *I'll come and see you soon* and *Give Bea a kiss from me,* and when you say 'bye, I say, *Samuel, you know you asked me if I believe in fate? Oh, right,* you say, *Yeah, I remember,* and I say, *Well, I do—I do believe in it.*

Obviously I couldn't phone you because I didn't have my phone or even your number. So I did a Vulcan mind-meld with you instead. I closed my eyes and whispered the words over and over, thinking of you lying in that warm tangled bedding surrounded by pink flowers, your hair all messy and your shirt done up wrong, whispering with me...

Your mind to my mind
Your thoughts to my thoughts
Your mind to my mind
Your thoughts to my thoughts...

And the more I whispered the words—over and over, around and around—the more weightless I got till I was floating in neither my mind nor yours. Then I saw my hand reach out in front of me, except it wasn't my hand—it was yours—moving the pink curtain in your mum's back bedroom to one side and looking past the reflection of you in the glass, down over the black garden.

Breakfast was amazing. It was laid out all along this sort of bar that was in a semicircle, and there were booths to sit in around the edge of the room and tables in the middle with nice purple chairs the same color as the carpet.

I was glad Mum hadn't come, even though I knew I shouldn't be. She'd said she couldn't face it. I'm not sure whether she meant she couldn't face eating or seeing other people. Both, probably. But if she'd been there, she would've looked at all the things I was putting on my plate and thought it was disrespectful or something, as if enjoying a free breakfast meant I didn't care about Gary. She'd have tutted and gone, *I don't know how you can eat at a time like this, Yaz.* I answered her in my head as I trapped a chocolate croissant in the silver tongs: *Actually, quite easily, Mum. I'm starving.*

I took anything I liked the look of as I went along with my tray, adding two normal croissants and a white crispy roll with four sachets of apricot jam and some mini butters, a peach yogurt, a bowl of fresh tinned peaches, a boiled egg and some cake, then carried it over to one of the booths. Breakfast got even better when I saw the Hot & Tasty Breakfast Menu propped between the salt and pepper and a girl in the Premier Inn outfit coming toward me with a notepad and pen. I ordered a full English with fried eggs, chips and tea.

It was *so* nice sitting there on my own, eating that fry-up, I can't tell you. The eggs were perfect—runny and warm, but not so runny that any of the white was like ectoplasmic goo— the sausages were the fat juicy kind, and they had bottles of ketchup and brown sauce, so you could have as much as you wanted without having to mess with those stupid sachets that have only enough sauce in them for one chip.

I think it was finding China Bea and doing the mind-meld that'd cheered me up. It felt like everything was going to be okay, and I remembered Dr. Bhatt's words: "Because it will feel like the sun is coming out…" I know he meant it'd feel like that when I got thinner, but the sun didn't have to come out *just* because of getting thinner, did it? It could come out for lots of reasons. For example, if Alice was at that second walking through her front door. I thought if that happened, Gary'd probably get compensation for everything he'd been put through—maybe enough even for me to get my own flat somewhere. And he'd definitely give me money for that. And then I could buy somewhere near your house and get my Havanese puppy and meet up with you in the park and tell you how, when I first saw you, I thought you were this bad man who was going to take Alice and we laugh about it and you say something like, *You've got one hell of an imagination, Yaz,* and then we catch each other's eyes. You look away, of course, all shy, but I put my hand on yours and then, without even turning back, you close your fingers around mine and our dogs start barking because they're so happy we're together at last.

I made a butter and apricot jam croissant for Mum, wrapped it in a napkin and took it back to the room. She'd opened the curtains and was sitting on her bed, looking out through the white net curtain at the parking lot.

"I got you this," I said.

"Thanks, love," she said, taking it, but she didn't eat it. She put it on the bedside table.

I sat down next to her. "What you going to do?" I said.

She sighed and looked down at the tissue in her hands. "Go to Watford police station," she said. "That's where he is. Maybe they'll let me see him. I don't know." She looked out the window again. "But I'll tell them we need some things from the house. They can't expect us to live in the same clothes day and night."

"I saw the news last night," I said. "They didn't say Gary's name. They didn't even say they'd arrested anyone—just that a man's helping them with their inquiries."

"Oh, that's good," she said, glancing at me, but I could see the corners of her mouth going down like she might get upset again.

I rubbed her back. "It'll be okay," I said.

She nodded.

"I'll come with you."

"No," she said and blew her nose in the tissue. She looked at me again. "I don't want you to. It's been bad enough for you already. And I'll probably end up sitting there having to wait for hours on end anyway. Why don't you go into town or something? Take some money."

"Okay," I said, thinking of you, of course. "If you're sure."

When I got to your house, the windows upstairs were all open. I hadn't seen you for a while and, even though I knew you hadn't meant what you'd said the last time I was there, I wasn't sure how you'd react when you saw me. I thought if you were still pretending you didn't want to see me, I'd say I had to tell you something and I'd tell you about Gary getting arrested. I thought I might even say that I knew it was you who took Alice if the moment was right and that you didn't need to carry on saying I shouldn't be your friend to protect me because I'd made up my mind that I liked you anyway. I thought you'd have to let me in then. Bea started barking in the hallway and you appeared at your mum's bedroom window.

"Hi," I called up.

You didn't say anything. Then you disappeared. I waited ages. I thought you weren't going to come down at all, then finally I heard you saying something to Bea in the hallway and the door latch turned.

You were wearing jeans and a black T-shirt that had Guinness written on it, spattered with white paint, and you were wiping your hands on a rag.

"Oh, you're painting," I said, bending to say hello to Bea.

"I told you not to come back," you said.

I stood up again. "I know," I said, "but I've got something to tell you."

You didn't say anything. You didn't move, either. You were waiting for me to tell you there on the doorstep, I think.

"I can't tell you out here," I said.

"Why not?"

"I just can't," I said. "Can't I come in?"

I followed you with Bea into the kitchen. Everything downstairs looked the same, but I could smell the paint. You filled a glass at the sink and gulped it down. "I should've worn something old," I said, even though I couldn't have anyway because the police weren't letting us into Gary's house, "then I could've helped you."

"What do you want to tell me?" you said, rinsing the glass and putting it on the draining board. You turned to face me, leaning back against the sink.

I chewed my cheek because now that I was in your house I wasn't sure it was such a good idea bringing up Alice again, but you were waiting for me to say something and there wasn't anything else. "It's about that girl," I said slowly, watching you. You scratched at some food stuck to the countertop. "You know, the one who's missing?"

"Oh, right," you said, not looking up.

"Did you see they've arrested someone?"

You stopped scratching and folded your arms. "What about it?"

"Well… I know him."

You didn't say anything. You just kept looking at me and suddenly I didn't have the balls to say about it being Gary, so I said, "I mean, I don't know him well or anything—he's our plumber. It's just…he was at our house the other day and he kept looking at me in this creepy way, so when I heard it was him, it really freaked me out."

You scratched the side of your head. "So you thought you'd come around here and tell me?" you said.

I shrugged. "I know it sounds stupid," I said. "I just got scared. I didn't want to be on my own."

You looked at me for a bit longer, then put the milk that was on the counter in the fridge. "Well, you've got nothing to worry about now, then, have you? If the police have arrested him."

I shrugged again and looked down. "I know," I said. Bea was sitting at my feet, looking up at me like she wanted attention. "I just got scared." I chewed my lip and wished I was wearing clean clothes, because even though I'd had a shower after Mum left, I felt dirty. I stroked Bea's head and thought about saying how I hadn't got anywhere else to go, but I thought that might sound a bit desperate so I said, "I wanted to see Bea."

You didn't say anything. You were wiping the counter with a tea towel.

"I won't get in your way," I said. "I promise. And I could help. I could take Bea out."

And then I knew what I'd said had worked because you shook the tea towel out and hung it over the back of one of the chairs without saying anything, and then you sighed and ran your fingers through your hair. "Well, you're persistent," you said. "I'll give you that."

I smiled at you. I said, "Can I see what you've done?"

On the way upstairs, I said, "It's good the police have caught him, though."

"He might not have done it," you said, half over your shoulder.

"What d'you mean?" I said. I thought it was an odd thing for you to say because surely you wanted everyone to think he had? And then I got a funny feeling that maybe you weren't just taking me upstairs to look at the redecorating—that you were taking me up to tell me something like, *As it happens, Yasmin, I* know *he didn't do it because I did and now I've told you, I'm going to have to kill you, too.*

You didn't say that, though. You said, "I mean, it's possible he's innocent. The police do this all the time—get the wrong guys. 'Specially when they don't have any idea. They haul in every Tom, Dick and Harry just to make it look like they're getting somewhere."

You went into the back bedroom. It was empty except for long shreds of wallpaper all over the floor, a stepladder, paint can and paint roller in a tray and an old radio that was on the windowsill next to your Drum. You'd done one wall and half the one opposite the window.

"How d'you know?" I said.

You went over to the tray and picked up the roller. "I've just been around," you said, "that's all."

I watched you roll the roller up and down in the paint tray a few times. Then I said, "You went for white, then?"

"Stone, actually," you said. "Shouldn't have bothered stripping the paper, though."

"Why?"

You looked at it all around our feet. "Because it didn't want to come off. Took me all bloody day yesterday."

Bea waddled into the room and stood looking at me. I went over to the open window, remembering how I'd looked out the same window the night before, only through your eyes. It'd been dark then, but now in the daylight, I could see for miles. Between the bushes and trees at the bottom of the gardens I could see bits of the railway line that goes to Euston, and beyond that fields, some with horses in them.

"Nice view," I said and then my heart suddenly stopped because they're always saying that on those house programs, aren't they, when people are looking to buy or sell? They always say paint in neutral colors, too. Colors like "Stone." I hadn't thought of that before, but it was obvious, wasn't it? Especially as you'd been living somewhere else before your mum died. Somewhere farther north. You might want to go back there.

I picked a bit of fluff off the windowsill and rolled it under my nail, and in the silence watched the cat that'd jumped up on your fence when you'd caught me in your driveway. It was making its way gingerly over the pile of ash and charred wood near the barbecue. I watched your reflection in the window, too, painting the wall, your T-shirt going up every time you reached up with the roller, showing your back.

I said, "There's something else I need to tell you." You carried on painting.

"I do know that girl—Alice."

You turned and looked at me, and I turned around, too. "I know I said I didn't," I said, "but I do. She's in my class."

You rolled the brush in the paint tray but I could tell you were listening carefully.

"I dunno why I told you I didn't," I said. "I felt bad, I suppose. Because I'm sort of pleased she's gone."

You kept rolling the brush, but you still didn't say anything.

"I know that's a horrible thing to say," I went on, "but she wasn't very nice. She used to bully me. She was always calling me names, like 'saddo' and 'freak.' She even spat at me once."

Then you looked at me, and at that moment the sun came out from behind the clouds and shone through the window on the back of my neck and on your face, making everything orange, and you looked so nice I wanted to walk through the flowery paper and slide my arms around you and press my face against your chest. I wanted to close my eyes and listen to your heart beating, and to tell you I didn't care if you'd taken a *hundred* girls because just being with you was all I ever wanted.

"Samuel..." I said.

You let go of the roller and shielded your eyes against the

light so you could see me. I bit my lip and hoped you thought I looked nice.

"...do you think she's dead?"

You didn't move. You just kept looking at me, your hand above your eyes. Then you cleared your throat, looked down at the floor, then back at me. You said, "I think it's likely, don't you?"

I got a weird feeling then, deep inside—like nothing anywhere in the whole universe mattered except you and me—like we belonged, in some preordained, destined way, to each other. Like fate.

And then you turned away and started painting again and, after a bit, you said, "Well, I could murder a sandwich."

I was so happy, I couldn't answer right away. I was smiling too much, my heart going too fast. I clicked my fingers for Bea to come over and bent down and gave her a big fuss. "Okay," I said.

"There's some money on the microwave. They do sandwiches at the convenience store just there."

Bea sat at the top of the stairs and just looked at me as I went down, but when I called her, she came. She followed me into the kitchen, watching me as I got the tenner and three pound coins off the microwave and pushed them into the pocket of my jeans. I looked around to see what you had already, because I wasn't going to get you a prepacked sandwich. I was going to make you one. There was some bread in its bag on the counter but it wasn't nice bread, just Hovis, and quarter of a tub of Stork margarine that was green in one corner.

"That's not nice, is it?" I said to Bea, which made her bark.

Then I looked in the fridge and nearly died, because the only thing in there apart from milk, right in the middle, was half a family bar of Cadbury's Dairy Milk Turkish Delight! I couldn't believe it. You had my favorite chocolate in your fridge! I don't know why it was in the fridge, because that's a weird place for chocolate, but that didn't matter. What mattered was that my favorite chocolate was your favorite chocolate, too! It was something else we had in common—another omen telling me everything was going to be okay. I told myself it meant you weren't going to sell your house. And then I remembered something from *CSI: Miami*—something completely brilliant. The police always watch out for anyone looking to move away after a murder's happened, so you *couldn't* sell. Putting the house on the market would be like telling the police it was you. I was so happy then—knowing you'd have to stay, knowing I could be your friend forever—that I took Bea out without even asking you. It felt like I lived there, doing that—like you and me and Bea were a proper family that could just come and go without having to ask each other.

I went to the convenience store first, where you'd said, but they didn't have much and it wouldn't give Bea enough exercise anyway, so I carried on to the co-op on the other side of the estate. I was thinking about sandwiches all the way because I didn't want to make you any old sandwich. I wanted to make you the best sandwich you'd ever had.

I don't think I've ever felt nervous in a food shop before, but I did then, standing by the fridge section with my empty basket. I stared at all the ham and pâté and cheeses in the

fridge and then stared at them all again. I couldn't decide
whether to buy ham or get cheese and do like a ploughman's.
Then I saw some slices of beef and I knew I'd get them, so it
was easier after that. I got two Little Gem lettuces, two big
tomatoes, mayonnaise, crusty white bread, mustard (in case
you didn't have any) and Worcester sauce potato chips, because I thought they'd go well with it. I got two small bottles
of Diet Coke to drink and a bar of Cadbury's Turkish Delight for after. I thought maybe I'd pretend I hadn't seen the
one in your fridge so it'd be like an incredible coincidence
and you'd be as surprised as I was. Then, on the way to the
till, I passed the pet food and got Bea a tin of Cesar so she
wouldn't be left out.

I deliberately didn't look at the newspaper stand near the
checkout, but somehow I saw the headline anyway: LOCAL
MAN ARRESTED OVER MISSING SCHOOLGIRL. I
turned away and, at the exact same moment, through the
window, I saw Alice.

I held the money out, even though the man behind the
till was still ringing up the things in my basket and putting
them in the bag.

She was on the other side of the road, walking away so I
could see only the back of her head. Then a bus came, block-
ing my view of her, and the man was putting change in my
hand. I raced outside with the bag and, leaving Bea tied up,
ran across the road.

She wasn't there. I turned around on the spot, thinking,
how could she have disappeared like that? There wasn't anywhere she could've gone. I went back and got Bea, then

crossed the road again. She hadn't gone into the hairdressers or the nail salon. Then, a bit farther on, just past the shops, I saw there was a cut-through, a narrow footpath overgrown with ivy all around the entrance.

"Up here, Bea," I said, pulling her off a half-eaten chicken leg.

The path was quite long with a curve in it that led to a road I'd never been on before. The houses were new, all detached and quite posh, set back from the road with tidy green lawns in front of them. I didn't see her for a second because she'd turned onto a street on the other side and was hidden by a hedge, but then I did.

"Alice?" I called, crossing over. "Alice!" She kept going. "'Scuse me!"

She stopped then, but the second she turned around I could see it wasn't her. She wasn't really anything like Alice, apart from her hair and the way she walked. She was younger, too—maybe only twelve or thirteen—and the face plumper, not as nice.

"Oh, sorry," I called and I held up my bag of shopping in a sort of wave.

She stood for a second, looking, then turned back and carried on. I put the bag on the ground and puffed on my inhaler, holding my breath and counting slowly to five as I watched her disappear around the corner. When I got back to your house, I called up like Mum does when she gets home. I could hear music upstairs on the radio. Then I went into the kitchen and cleared a bunch of paperwork and a dirty mug off the table and wiped it with dish soap because there wasn't anything like Cif or Mr Muscle. Then I washed the stuff in the sink and Bea's bowl that looked like it hadn't been washed since Mrs. E. Caldwell had died, and after that I found a plastic chopping board in one of the cupboards and got to work on the lunch.

When you came down, it looked the business. I'd put potato chips on the side of the plate, the sandwiches were bulging and the Cokes were fizzing with ice in them.

"Blimey," you said, going over to the sink, because you were really impressed, I think, and you washed your hands while I gave Bea her special lunch.

"I didn't put any mustard on in case you don't like it," I said.

You sat down and picked up the bottle. "Love a bit of mustard," you said and after you'd opened your sandwich up and squeezed some on, you ate the lot—the potato chips and everything.

I can't tell you how brilliant it was, watching you eat the sandwich I'd made for you, especially when you went "Mmm" with your mouth full. It made me want to cook every meal for you every day and I made a mental note to look up recipes online so I could impress you with something one evening like I'd just made it up myself. Then I got the Cadbury's Turkish Delight out of the plastic bag and held it up, grinning. I couldn't be bothered to pretend I hadn't seen the bar in the fridge. "I got us some of this," I said. "It's my favorite chocolate, too!"

You didn't seem as amazed as I was that we both liked the same chocolate, but I guess that's because you're older and older people don't get amazed very easily. You said you'd have some later on.

Then you went back upstairs to carry on painting. I closed the kitchen door. I didn't want you to know what I was going to do, which was to clean the whole kitchen till it sparkled. I thought doing that would definitely amaze you.

Bea got in her basket in the corner and I stood in the middle of the floor, looking around. I felt like Julie Andrews in that bit in *The Sound of Music* when she looks at all the kids lined up and smacks her hand down on top of her head, like, where do I start? (I know I shouldn't admit to knowing *any* bits from *The Sound of Music*, but hey, who says Trekkies can't like sappy stuff, too?) I was acting it up a bit to be honest, because it wasn't like it was a complete mess in there, but it was pretty dirty. There was mud all around the door and bits of Bea's food stuck to the lino, and the windowsill was covered in a sticky sort of film with dead flies on it.

First of all, I piled up the clean dishes from the draining board on the countertop. Then I emptied the stuff in the washing-up bowl and rinsed it out. The hot water didn't get warm even after ages, so rather than ask you, I boiled the kettle. Then I put a squirt of dish soap in each of the two dirty saucepans and put boiling water on top and left them to soak. Then I boiled some more water for the sink and started on the washing up. I had to stop halfway through to dry because the draining board got full, but it didn't take long to do it all. Then came the best bit—the reorganizing—because once I'd chucked all the out-of-date stuff in the cupboards away, they were pretty empty. I decided to change things around a bit, thinking all the time about where everything would be best for you, like, for example, because you're tall I moved all the small plates from the cupboard under the counter to the one on the other end and above the toaster where they'd be easy for you to get to—especially when you'd just woken up and wanted some toast. It was brilliant putting everything in new places—like it was our place, not just yours, and I could have everything just how I wanted. I even cleaned the cupboards before I put anything in them. I wanted it to be *perfect*.

When I'd finished, I shut Bea in the front room and cleaned the floor, thinking how Gary was actually right about one bottle of soap being all you need to clean a house. "It's all the same stuff," he always says, throwing his arm out at the commercials on television like they can hear him. "Just in different bottles! They must think we're stupid!" Then I went upstairs. You'd nearly finished.

"Smart," I said, looking around the walls.

You stopped painting and wiped your arm across your forehead. Downstairs, Bea scratched at the front-room door. You must've heard because you said, "You all right down there?"

And then I couldn't wait to show you, even though the floor wouldn't be dry yet. "Come and see," I said.

You said you'd just finish up and I went to put the kettle on, listening out for you all the time because I didn't want you to just walk in. I wanted to be with you when you saw it.

When you still hadn't come down and I'd made the tea and broken the Turkish Delight from the fridge up into chunks and arranged them all nicely on one of your mum's old-fashioned saucers, I called up.

"Okay," you said, "just coming," and then as you came downstairs and saw me standing in the hall with Bea in my arms, grinning at you, you said, "What's going on?"

"Close your eyes," I said. Then I put Bea down and because you hadn't closed your eyes and I didn't want to ask again in case it seemed a bit babyish, I went ahead of you and closed the kitchen door instead. "Okay," I said when you got there. "You ready?" I opened it.

You looked around for a few seconds, then you scratched the side of your head. "Oh, right," you said.

"I did all the cupboards, too," I said. "Everything."

You didn't say anything else, so then I went in and got you to come in, too, and opened the cupboards to show you how smart they all were and where I'd moved things to.

You just stood there the whole time, smoothing your hair down at the back like you were too embarrassed to really look—like you didn't think you deserved to have all that done for you or something.

"What d'you think?" I said.

"Oh," you said after a few seconds, "fine."

I laughed, looking up at you, and said, "Fine? Is that all?"

You smiled, but you still looked embarrassed. Then you said, "You're an angel." I was so happy I had to hug you. I couldn't help it. I squeezed you as tight as I could, pressing my head against your chest just like I'd wanted to for ages, then putting your arms around me, one then the other, so that you were hugging me back.

★ ★ ★

Mum wasn't in the room when I got to the hotel, so I didn't have to pretend that this was a terrible day with Gary under arrest when it felt like the most brilliant day ever. And I knew it was pointless telling her what you'd said about how the police arrest the wrong people all the time just so it looks like they're getting somewhere, because she wouldn't believe it.

I believed it, though. I believed everything was going to be okay—better than okay, even. I fiddled about with the remote control till I got the TV working. When *BBC News 24* came on, I did a big groan at the man on the screen and told him, "No news today, thank you, Mr. News Reporter, I'm not in the mood," and I pressed Menu and went through the channels till I got to *4Music*. I turned it up full. Then I closed the curtains, put the bedside lamps on, got a Diet Coke out of the mini fridge in the cupboard and danced around the room. I was thinking about your face when I'd shown you the kitchen, and you going "You're an angel." I thought about you in that dark blue shirt with the sleeves rolled up and about your lovely, lovely eyes, and when I caught sight of myself in the bathroom mirror, I waved at my reflection. "Whoooo!" I called over the music, holding my Coke up and pretending my reflection was you. "Do you love me, Samuel?" Then, because you couldn't hear me, I laughed and called again. "I said, do you love me!?" Then I turned around and Mum was there, standing in the doorway, the key card in her hand.

I grabbed the remote and muted the TV. "Hi," I said.

"What're you doing?" she said.

I sat on the bed, catching my breath, blowing up on my bangs. "I was just, you know, doing a bit of exercise."

"I've been trying to find you for hours," she said. "I've been everywhere."

"Oh, sorry," I said feebly. "I was in town. Why? What is it?"

Then she put the back of her hand under her nose like she was going to cry, so I got up and went over and put my arm around her.

"What's happened?" I said.

"It was a hair elastic," she said, breaking down. "It was a forensic match."

"Oh my God!" I said, because straight away I knew. It was the hairband I'd picked up from the changing-room floor, the one I'd been fiddling with when Gary gave me a lift.

"What is it?" Mum said.

My hands were over my mouth. I stared at her. I took my hands away. "I dropped it there."

"*What?*" she said, and she seized me by the shoulders. "Oh my God, we have to go! We have to tell them!"

A car picked us up. Mum gripped my hand the whole way. She'd already told whoever it was who answered the phone about me dropping Alice's hairband but she couldn't get there fast enough to tell them again.

When we arrived, though, we had to wait for about twenty minutes. Mum was sitting on the edge of her plastic chair, clutching her handbag and watching people going in and out through the swing doors like she couldn't stand waiting for a second longer. Then DI Grayson appeared and she jumped up. "We've come to make a statement," she said.

"We'll need to speak to you separately," he said.

"Okay," Mum said, nodding and putting her hand on my back. "That's fine. You'll tell them, won't you, love?" DI Grayson showed me into the first room along the corridor. It was bigger than the one at the other station.

There was a microphone on the table, and a camera high up in the corner.

"Have a seat," he said, pointing to the one he wanted me in. He dragged one of the chairs on the other side so it was farther away from the table and sat on it, crossing his legs. He held out one arm then the other, brushing his sleeves.

Then DI Burke came through the door and I thought, thank God, because it was better than being alone with the horrible crow. "Hello, Yasmin," she said. She sat down opposite me, glanced at her watch and said the time and date, then put her hands flat on the table, palms down.

"You'd like to tell us about Alice's hair elastic?" she said.

"I dropped it in Gary's van," I said, glancing at DI Grayson. "I was fiddling with it on the way home and must've dropped it."

"Can you describe it?"

"Yeah. It's brown with gold bits in it—like gold thread."

DI Burke nodded. "And when was this? Which day?"

I chewed my cheek because I didn't know. "It was last week," I said, then remembered I'd found it after PE. "On Tuesday. I saw it on the floor in the changing room and picked it up."

DI Burke tilted her head a bit and frowned. "Why did you pick it up?"

I shrugged. "I dunno. Because I saw it."

"Did you know it was Alice's?"

I looked at her. I didn't know whether to say yes or no or even if it mattered.

"Yeah," I said. "Alice always has those ones. And it was where she'd been."

"What d'you mean, *where she'd been*?"

"Where she was changing. We'd had PE."

DI Grayson coughed into his fist. "Where have you been today?" he said.

"In town," I said.

"Shopping?" Sarcastic like always.

"Not really," I said. "Just looking around. Mum said I should go. She was coming here and said I should go into town."

He nodded slowly, like he was deciding if he believed that or not. "And what time did you get back to the hotel?"

"I dunno," I said. "About an hour ago. I was there and then Mum came in saying you'd found Alice's hairband in the van and I realized I'd dropped it there. Then she phoned the station and we came."

"Your mum tell you to say all this?" he said.

"What d'you mean?"

"Well, did she tell you to say it was you who put the hair elastic in Gary's van?"

"No!" I couldn't believe they'd think Mum would do that.

"You're sure about that?"

"Yes."

"Because you've not been the most truthful interviewee, have you?"

I looked at him and chewed my cheek some more. "Have you?" he said again. "In fact, it's pretty lucky Darren and his mates saw you outside that fish and chip shop, or you might be under suspicion yourself."

He stood up then and walked around for a bit with his chin in his hand like he was thinking. Then he stopped and swiveled around on his heels to face me. "Do you know what I think?" he said.

I shook my head. I had a lump in my throat.

"I think you're not nearly as stupid as you let people believe," he said. "I think you knew Gary was going to take Alice…"

I looked at DI Burke but she didn't say anything. She didn't move either. She just kept watching me.

"Because you have to admit," he went on, "it'd be quite some coincidence otherwise, you telling Alice that you're trying to protect her from someone just days before she actually disappears." He put his hands in his trouser pockets and rocked on his heels. "Wouldn't you say so?"

I shrugged. "I don't know," I said. "I suppose."

He watched me for a few seconds, then walked to the table and sat on the edge of it, twisting around so he was facing me. "You see, that's what I don't buy. What I do buy is that you somehow suspected that Gary was going to do something and you tried to warn Alice. Because you liked her, didn't you?"

I felt weird all of a sudden, the way he was talking about

Alice, the way he was so close to being right. I felt like I was floating or melting or something.

"And you tried to warn her, didn't you?"

I couldn't move. I was scared to in case I started nodding my head, even though I didn't want to, and telling them everything right from the beginning, from when I first saw you by the school fence.

Then DI Burke leaned forward. "Yasmin," she said, "we think this whole thing must be a living nightmare for you, caught between doing the right thing and being very afraid. And you've been so brave. Braver than a lot of people would've been."

I looked at her. I wanted to say, *I know I have.* I wanted to tell them how difficult it was answering all their questions so they never found out about you. I wanted to tell them you were nice, too, and that if they knew you they'd see how lovely you really are.

"But Alice is our priority here," she went on. "She may still be alive. We believe there's a chance we could still save her with your help."

I shook my head. "But I don't know anything," I said, whispering, tears filling my eyes. "I swear."

DI Grayson got off the table and DI Burke leaned back in her chair. They looked at each other.

Then DI Grayson sat on his chair again and stared at me, his tongue pushing into his cheek. After I'd wiped my eyes on my sleeve, he said, "We checked your computer. We can see how worried you've been—the sites you've Googled—pedophiles, murderers, missing kids... Are you scared of what

Gary might do to you if you tell us what you know? Are you afraid that, even if he goes to prison, there'll be a day he gets out and comes looking for you?"

I shook my head again. "I don't know anything about Gary."

They looked at each other again. I don't think they knew what to say next.

Then DI Burke opened her jacket, took a card out of her inside pocket and held it out.

It was dark green with a picture of a tree on it, like the one near Dad's grave. It said:

Police.
Child Protection.
Start Talking. Stop Abuse.
0800 460 460. 24hrs.

Out in the corridor, DI Burke said, "Yasmin, a moment." Then she looked at me with her big serious brown eyes. "I understand why you feel unable to speak out." Her eyes were searching mine. "But keep hold of that card, okay? In case you change your mind, in case you feel able to help at any point. I forget who said this but remember it—'Only the truth will set you free.'"

Mum was different after the interview. On the way back to the Premier Inn she kept saying, "Why don't they believe you dropped it? They think I made you say it." Then, later on, when we were back in our room and she was sitting on the end of her bed, she said, "Why did you have Alice's hair elastic, anyway?"

I told her again how I'd just picked it up, but I could see she thought that was weird or not very likely or something. I thought I should've said Alice'd lent it to me for PE. Then she said, "You didn't put it there on purpose, did you?"

I turned around and stared at her, stunned. "How can you say that?"

"I don't know," she said. "It's just none of it makes sense. The way you said there was a man, then Gary's taken in and there's Alice's hair elastic in his van."

"But Alice wasn't even missing then!" I said. She was watching me, though, a funny expression on her face like she didn't trust me or something—like she thought I'd put Alice's hairband there *after* she'd disappeared. "I know you've never liked him."

"What's that supposed to mean?"

She shrugged. "I mean, you never wanted me to meet anyone else after Dad. You never wanted me to get married again."

"I can't believe you think I'd do that!" I said. I was shouting a bit. "That's horrible! I'd never do that! I can't believe you think I would!"

"All right," Mum said like she was too tired to think. She stood up and walked around the other side of her bed. "I'm sorry." She shook her head, ran her fingers through her hair and sat down again, her back to me. "I just don't know *what* to think anymore."

We didn't say anything else, just got ready for bed and

turned the lights off. Because of the hairband, Mum never got to ask about going back to the house to get pajamas and clean underwear, so we had to stay in our old clothes.

I held China Bea in the dark and thought about what Mum'd said again and the more I remembered her looking at me and going "You didn't put it there on purpose, did you?" the more angry I got. She'd basically asked if I'd tried to frame Gary! How could anyone's mum think their daughter would do that? I thought Gary had got to her, made her think that way, because she never would've thought anything like that before.

Anyway, I thought, DI Burke and DI Grayson think he's guilty. I imagined Gary sitting on a bench in a white windowless cell, the peephole thing in the door sliding open and DI Grayson's cold crow eyes looking in, and I thought, good, I hope he never gets out. It wasn't like any of it was even my fault. I mean, I'd tried to tell the truth, hadn't I? It wasn't like I'd made out Gary was guilty, which was something I could've done. Easily. It wasn't my fault if they didn't believe me. I thought, it's fate, that's what it is. It's all happened like it has and nothing anyone says or does can change it.

I was still asleep when the phone rang the next morning. I heard Mum pick it up and go, "Hello?" her voice all flat, but then a second later she was throwing the covers off her and standing up. *"What?"* she said into the phone. Then she laughed, spun around to face me and, covering the mouthpiece, she said, "He's free!"

"Huh?" I said. I still wasn't properly awake.

"Can you send a car?" she said into the phone. "Okay, well, tell him we'll be there as soon as we can." She pressed buttons on the phone, gripping the receiver with both hands as she waited for someone to pick up, then she said, "Yes, I'd like a cab please. Room thirty-two. Straight away." Then she put the phone down and smacked her hands on top of her head. "He's free," she said again, looking from me back to the phone like she couldn't believe it had really rung.

"How?" I said.

"They said they'd got some new CCTV. It clears him. I don't know, but he's free!"

That ringing in my ears started up, and I was wide awake then. I was thinking CCTV of what? CCTV of *you*?

Mum was standing and pulling her boots on. "Well, come on," she said. "What's the matter?"

"Nothing," I said, scrambling out from under the duvet. "I'm coming."

I stayed in the parking lot outside the station while Mum went in to get Gary, but I got out of the cab. I was looking up and down the road, whispering, because I was so afraid I was going to see a police car any second with you in the back of it.

When they finally came out, they were wrapped in each other's arms, Mum smiling up at him with tears on her face. She kept kissing him and saying, "I knew it'd be okay."

"Hi, Gary," I said.

He said, "Hi," but he didn't look at me properly. It was obvious he thought I'd put Alice's hairband there on purpose.

Mum said, "Why don't you sit in the front, Yaz?"

They hugged and kissed each other all the way back to Gary's. It was so embarrassing, and the cab driver was embarrassed, too, because he kept glancing nervously in the rear-view mirror and then at me, like he thought their behavior was a bit inappropriate. Mum didn't care, though. She just laughed and said, "I knew it! I knew they'd find *some*thing..."

And Gary said, "Clear as day, the picture, Jen. Me, singing away as I went up the A41. Twenty blinking miles from the crime scene!"

I closed my eyes. I felt like I could breathe again, because even though I didn't like that Gary was back or how he and Mum were talking as if—now that he'd been released—Alice didn't matter anymore, at least I knew the CCTV the police had found was of Gary and not of me with Bea, or of you.

I thought the police would've tidied our house up, seeing as Gary was innocent, but it was a mess. All the cupboards and furniture had been pulled out of place, the cushions had been taken off the sofa and our DVDs were all over the floor, their cases open. It looked like we'd been burgled.

"Bloody hell, look at it!" Gary said, going from the dining room into the living room, his voice rising. "*Look* at it!"

"Hey, come on," Mum said, putting her arms around him and rubbing his chest, even though she was looking around everywhere, just as shocked. "It doesn't matter. You're home. That's all that matters."

I went up to my room. It was the same there. Everything everywhere. The only thing, ironically, that hadn't been touched was Alice's Manga girl. She was still tacked to the wall, staring out like she was pretty angry at what had gone on there.

I grabbed my laptop the second I saw it on the desk, opened it up and waited for it to connect to the internet. I went on Alice's Facebook page. I suppose it was obvious people would've written stuff about Gary, but I wasn't prepared for how much, or what they'd said. There were nasty posts all over it—pages of it—saying things like how he was so evil he'd even joined one of the searches. There were things about Mum and me, too, like about us being *a peculiar family* and a family that *kept away from the community*. Someone had even put that Mum looked like the serial killer Rose West.

I typed *IT'S OFFICIAL—GARY'S INNOCENT! HA!* and posted it before I could even think about not posting it. Then I went downstairs and into the living room. Gary was in his armchair, his head in his hands like he was exhausted. Mum was kneeling on the floor, putting the DVDs back in their cases and piling them up.

"Hi," I said.

Gary looked up but didn't say anything, just pressed his lips together, like he didn't know if he'd ever be able to say anything to me.

"Do you want a tea?" I said.

"No, you're all right," he said. "Just give us a bit of time. We need to…" He held out his hands. I wasn't sure if he meant they needed time to tidy everything up or to decide whether they were going to forgive me. "I don't know," he said and shook his head at the floor. "We just need time."

I stood there a bit longer, feeling awkward. I wished Mum

would stop doing the DVDs and say something, anything—like *Come on, then, you coming in or what?* But she didn't. She didn't even look up. She'd obviously decided it was all my fault, too.

I went back to my room.

I didn't even flinch when the doorbell rang that evening. I just thought, here they are again, come to arrest me this time, and good, because I don't care anymore. I even got off the bed. I thought, prison can't be any worse than here, and I put China Bea in my pocket and opened my door, ready to go quietly.

It wasn't the police. It was an Indian takeout. I listened to Mum in the kitchen, getting plates and cutlery and the mango chutney out of the cupboard and putting them all on a tray to take into the living room like we always do. I held my breath when she carried the tray down the hall and pushed the living-room door open, but when she didn't call me down and the door closed again, I realized I wasn't invited. It was curry for two.

TURKISH DELIGHT

I SAT STARING AT Alice's Manga girl. It seemed stupid now that I'd given it a name. It was just a drawing.

I got up and pulled it off the wall and sat back down on the bed. And then, as I was looking at it, something happened. The girl seemed to change. The eyes changed. They were still black and gleaming, but after staring at them for a bit they didn't look like they had before—confident and defiant, like they could take on the world. They looked *fearful*— like the eyes of a cat that's been cornered by a ferocious dog. I held the drawing at arm's length, looked away, then back again: the same! How weird was that? In the whole time I'd had it, I'd never seen any fear at all—but now that I had, it was all I could see.

I thought about DI Burke's big eyes and how confused they'd looked when I told her I'd made it up about there being a man. I thought about how much I'd wanted to tell her and DI Grayson about you, and how lucky it was I hadn't.

And that horrible second in the hotel room when Mum said Gary was free because the police had CCTV and I thought it was CCTV of you. My heart started pounding again just thinking of it.

I pressed Alice's drawing to my chest and looked up. I closed my eyes. I thought, thank God for you. Thank God, thank God, thank God for you, and I thought again about how you'd stood looking around your kitchen and saying, "You're an angel." That same word Alice's dad had used to describe her—*angel*.

I started to imagine then that rather than just hugging you and pressing my head against your chest, I'd looked up into your eyes and kissed you and that in that kiss you somehow understood everything I'd done for you, how I hadn't told the police about you when they came to school, how I'd lied to them when they asked me if I said anything about a man, how I'd lied again at the station even when it meant Mum and Gary would hate me, and how I'd go on lying for you forever. You look deep into my eyes and I can feel that you've understood and then I go with you to the countertop and stand right next to you as you pour two rum and Cokes, because now you know what I've done for you, you want me close to you always. Then you turn, though you're too shy to look me in the eyes, and you say there's something you want to tell me. I follow you into the front room, which is done up just like I imagined it, with a black leather sofa and black armchair and a glass coffee table on a shaggy white rug. *Sit down*, you say and then you sit down, too. Then you look at me and your eyes are shining and there's a sort of smile that isn't really a smile on your lips. *What?* I say. *What is it?* You put your drink down and lean forward, holding your hands out for me to take in mine, which I do, thinking, this is really crazy, what's going on? Then you tell me you were planning on leaving—going back to live up north again—but that you're not going to do that anymore. You say you've decided to stay and live in the house. You say it looks too good *not* to live in and I look around and say I have to agree, which makes you laugh. I give your hands a squeeze and say, *I'm so happy.* Then you say, *But that isn't all*, and you're looking so far inside me with your dark eyes that when you say, *Move in with me*, I think my heart is going to burst.

The next morning I got up before Mum and Gary.

Most of my clothes were out of the drawers anyway from when the police had been there, so I just sifted through till I found some old leggings from Primark. Then I tried on about six or seven tops that wouldn't matter if they got paint on, but they were all clingy and showed my fat rolls, so I wore one of my favorites—my red one with a custard tart on the front. Even though I didn't really want to get paint on it, I figured it was a sacrifice I was willing to make to look nice for you.

Then I put on a bit of makeup—not too much because of how you'd been the last time I'd worn some, even though I knew that was probably more because you were nervous about taking Alice than about me wearing makeup—just mascara and a bit of blusher. Then I put my hair in a high ponytail. I thought it'd be good like that for painting and you hadn't ever seen it up. I imagined your face when you did—how when you opened the door, smiling because you'd guessed it was going to be me, your eyes would see my new look and flick away shyly, your hand going up to smooth your hair—and suddenly I couldn't wait another second to see you.

I kept doing little skips down the pavements so I'd get to you faster, thinking how when I got there, I'd do a *da di-di-di da da* knock on your front door, but when I arrived and saw that the side door down the driveway was open, I thought it'd be fun to go in that way and surprise you. I thought I might even be able to make you a tea before you heard me and then, when you came into the kitchen, I could swivel around, holding it out and bowing like you did to me, going "For you, sir."

Of course that didn't happen because I'd forgotten about Bea and she started barking and came running into the kitchen before I'd even stepped inside. "Shh!" I said, holding my finger to my lips and laughing because it's impossible to do anything secretly with her there, and then I walked her through into the hall, bending over and rubbing her sides.

You were in the front room, halfway up the stepladder with a paintbrush in your hand, twisted around to see who it was. "Did you come in the back?" you said. You looked like you couldn't believe I had.

I stood up. "I knocked," I said, going in.

You'd taken the net curtains down, and the sofa and record player were pushed forward and under the ladder and all around it were sheets of newspaper. A picture of Alice was there on one of them, staring up at you. "You can't just wander in," you said.

"Sorry," I said. "I didn't mean—"

But you cut me off. "Why are you here, anyway?"

"I've come to help," I said, and I smiled and held my arms out to show you I'd come dressed for it, but you didn't smile back. You turned away and dipped your brush in the paint can that was standing on the platform bit of the ladder. Then you reached up and started painting a line along the top of the wall.

I chewed my cheek and looked around the room. You'd taken some stuff out—the round side table and the lamp and the plant that stands on the floor. You hadn't painted any of the walls yet, though, only the bit where you were. "And to tell you you were right," I said.

You didn't say, *What about?* You just carried on painting, so I said, "About the police. About what you said about them arresting the wrong people all the time." I realized then it hadn't been on the news that Gary'd been released, but it didn't matter. I still could've heard. I said, "They released that man."

I bent down to give Bea another fuss, but she made a noise deep in her throat. I'd never heard her make a noise like that before and it didn't sound very friendly, so I stood up again. "So, how's it going?" I said, trying to be cheerful, even though it was obvious you were in a mood—you *and* Bea. When you didn't answer, I thought you might snap if I kept on, so I said, "Can I go and see upstairs?"

You'd painted everywhere up there—both bedrooms and the upstairs hall—but even though I was walking around and whispering words like "Nice" and "Smart," I wasn't really even looking. I was trying to figure out why you were being like you were—whether I'd done anything to make you that way. The only thing I could think of, though, was coming in your back door and that wasn't *that* bad, was it? Then I remembered you saying "You're an angel" and I told myself your mood probably wasn't anything to do with me—though it was a pretty stupid thing to tell you about the police releasing Gary, because that wouldn't exactly cheer you up, would it, knowing that the police were out there looking again? Then I remembered the funny mood you'd been in when I came to look after Bea, and how that hadn't been because of me either. And you hadn't even seen me since you'd said "You're an angel," so I told myself to calm down, took two really deep breaths, tightened my ponytail and went back downstairs going "Wow, it looks amazing."

When I went into the front room, I said it again. I was going to say I'd make a tea, too, but you weren't up the ladder anymore. You'd finished painting the alcove and were moving the china dogs onto the hearth, and because I thought that was something I could be doing, I rushed over, going "I can do this," and taking some of the dogs off the mantelpiece, and then I don't know how but I dropped one and it broke on the tiles, its head rolling away from its body. "Oh God," I said, "I'm so sorry! I didn't mean to drop it…" I went to pick it up but you put your hand on my shoulder.

"Leave it," you said.

"No," I said. "Please…" I went to reach for it again, but you kept your hand there so I couldn't. Then suddenly you stepped back, away from me. You ran your fingers through your hair.

"Look, Gemma," you said, "I meant what I said."

I stared at you. I didn't understand. I thought maybe I'd heard you wrong. Because you knew my name. I'd told you my name. "I'm not Gemma," I said. "I'm Yasmin."

"Yasmin," you said, glancing up at me, "sorry. Look, go home. I don't want you coming around."

"But…we're friends," I said.

"No," you said. You rubbed your forehead. "We're not friends."

I knew you didn't mean it—that you were still just trying to protect me—but tears stung my eyes and the corners of my mouth went down like they were being pulled on strings. "But I made you lunch," I said. "We had a nice day."

And then you laughed—a weird laugh like you didn't think it'd been that nice—and turned and picked a rag up off the floor, the same one you'd had when you were painting upstairs. I stood there, blinking the tears back as you wiped your hands, thinking, don't cry because I knew you wouldn't like it if I cried. I said, "Is it because I'm so fat?"

You threw the rag onto one of the ladder steps. Then you said, "I'm not even going to be here much longer."

"What d'you mean?" I said.

"I'm leaving."

I watched the rag slip off the step and fall on top of the picture of Alice. I tried to take in what you were saying. "But… the house?" I said.

"I'm selling it."

And then, before I could think about what I was doing, I

was going "No! You can't!" too fast and too loud. "It'll look too suspicious!"

I realized the second it was out what I'd done, and even though it was too late, I clamped my hands over my mouth.

You were staring at me, your eyes black beneath your frown. "What did you say?" you said.

I stared back at you, my hands still over my mouth. I shook my head. Then I started backing off. "Nothing," I said, and "I've got to go," and I went out quick, stepping over Bea, who was still in the doorway.

"Hold on," you said, coming after me but still unsure, still figuring it out. "What do you mean, *suspicious*?"

I opened the front door. "Nothing," I said. "See you later."

But you were coming up the hall, going "Wait," and then, as I pulled the door behind me, you yanked it back, reached out and caught me by the wrist.

"No!" I said, spinning to face you, my voice high and panicky because I couldn't help it, and then your grip on me locked and I think I must've screamed because suddenly your face was right up in mine, the vein in your temple throbbing as you said, "What you playing at?"

And then Bea was there, barking, and you were pulling me like you wanted to get me back in your house and I was going "Oh God, oh God, oh God," and "Let go! Please let go!"

Then your neighbor's front door opened and that woman was there. "What's going on?" she said, ignoring Bea's barking and coming toward the fence. Her eyes went down to your hand on my wrist. "Is there a problem here?" she said. She was looking at me. "Is this man…"

"No," I said, "it's okay, it's okay," and then your grip loosened. You let go. I looked at her, rubbing where you'd held me because it hurt. I shook my head. "It's my fault," I said, "really," and I smiled to try to convince her, even though she didn't look very convinced at all. She kept looking at my wrist, and because I thought she was going to say *What was your fault?* or worse, something about calling the police, like last time, I held it out to show her and said, "Look—see, it's nothing," and then I turned to you, thinking you'd say something to back me up, but you weren't even looking at me. You were staring down at the path, clutching your cheeks in your hand.

I didn't know what else to say, so I just smiled at her again. I said, "I'd better go," and then I said, "'Bye, Sam," and I walked away and didn't turn back.

I started running as soon as I got around the bend in your road, whispering and looking behind me and wishing I *could* actually run, because I knew you'd come after me as soon as you could—as soon as you could get away from your neighbor, because you'd definitely figured out that I knew about Alice. You wouldn't have grabbed me like that if you hadn't. I thought about how if your neighbor kept you there long enough for me to get away, I'd be able to tell Dr. Bhatt I had a new motivator for my list. I was sure he'd think *Running Away from Murderers* was a good one and I could see him in my head, smiling as he said it in his Indian accent, rolling the *R*. By the end of your road my lungs were like two burning lumps of coal and my throat was so tight it was like you'd grabbed me there instead of my wrist. I had to stop running and walk. You still weren't coming, though. And you *still* weren't when I got to the park.

I leaned on the back of a bench—the one I'd sat on the night you took Alice—gasping for air and sucking on my inhaler till I calmed down a bit. Then I sat down, thinking, where are you? Because now that I was somewhere public, I *wanted* you to come. Out here, with people around, you wouldn't be able to be mad at me and you'd have to listen. And once you'd sat down and heard about how I'd known all along, before you'd even taken Alice—right from when I saw you watching her—you'd realize how it was lucky that it was me who saw you and no one else. You'd realize that if it wasn't for me, you'd probably have been caught and you wouldn't be angry with me anymore.

But you didn't come—even after ages.

I started to think about the things you'd said, like "We're not friends" and "You can't just wander in," and that laugh you'd done when I said we'd had a nice day, and the more I thought about them all, the worse I started to feel—the more unlikely it seemed that you'd ever liked me. Because nobody likes me. Nobody ever likes me, and then I thought, why *would* you come after me? No one ever does—not even when it's to kill me.

I told myself it didn't matter, that once you'd sold the house you'd be gone anyway, one way or the other. You'd either get away with it and move up north or wherever it was you were going, or you'd be arrested and sent to prison, where you'd sit in a cell, hating me for wrecking your life. Either way, we'd never be friends. And you wouldn't *not* sell the house, would you? You wouldn't listen to what I'd said about it looking suspicious. You wouldn't even think about that, because you didn't think about me at all. You didn't even know my name.

I picked a stick off the grass and broke it in half, then broke those bits in half and then just sat there breaking more twigs into smaller and smaller pieces. I thought about going to the police and telling them about you after all. But I knew I wouldn't. I couldn't face it. I never want to speak to another officer as long as I live. And anyway, there was no point in telling them then because, like you'd said, Alice was dead.

Then I thought about going to the graveyard. It was far away, though, and I didn't have any money to get a bus or buy flowers like I'd promised. So I stayed where I was, breaking up sticks and thinking how maybe I didn't need to go there to see Dad because maybe he was here with me—in the trees and the grass and the low blanket of clouds. Maybe he was watching me. I wondered what he'd say if he was. *Go home, love*, that's what—and I would've done that if I had one, but Gary's wasn't home. Our old house was home—the one I'd lived in with Mum and Dad. And then I saw us there—Mum in the kitchen and Dad in the front garden, clipping the roses. I thought about how I used to help him look after them. I wore his big leather gloves and picked up the bits he cut off, putting them all in a bucket, then taking it around the house to the compost heap at the bottom of the garden. There was a rusty gate there and a narrow, overgrown path full of spiders' webs that led to the little green. I wasn't allowed down it on my own, but I went with Dad. We used to take the

snails there because I liked to pretend they were baby drag-
ons and that if we set them free their shells would grow into
wings and they'd fly away. "Don't tell Mum, will you?" he
used to say. "She'll think we're nutters," so I never did, even
though I knew he was just saying it to make it more exciting
and that Mum knew in any case because she always got the
plastic tub out of the top cupboard for me to collect them in.

Then without really knowing I'd been walking at all, let
alone where I'd been going, I was there. I was home.

I hadn't been there for years—not since Mum and I moved
into the flat after Dad died—but it looked the same. There
was a basket hanging next to the front door with a long trail-
ing plant in it and a tricycle on the porch, but apart from that,
it was just like it always was. I could remember it inside, too:
Mum and Dad's big bed with the plum-colored duvet and
matching chair that went with her dressing table, the stairs
that came down into the lounge, which meant I always fell
asleep listening to them watching the TV and saying things to
each other. Then I remembered the bowl of marzipan fruits
Mum always had on the sideboard in the kitchen—small and
perfect, just like the real thing in miniature. I hadn't thought
about them in years. They were her favorites, but she never
had them anymore. I don't know why. I don't know what
happened to their duvet or her matching chair and dressing
table either.

Dad's roses were still there, growing along the front wall.
Mostly they were just leaves and buds, but there were three
yellow ones out. Three, I thought, for Mum, Dad and me.
They had only a very faint rosy smell. I wanted to pick one,

so I could take it home and put it in a glass of water and look at it and try to remember more of the things Dad and I did together. I thought I could take it to the graveyard the next day and put it on his grave as an Easter present. He'd love that, to see how his roses were still there after all this time, blooming away, spring after spring.

Then I heard knocking and looked up. It was old Mrs. Manners from next door, looking at me through her window. She was smaller than I remembered, like she'd shriveled up, but I could still see it was her. She'd been nice to me when we lived there. She'd taught me how to make a pom-pom— wrapping wool around two cardboard circles, then, after ages and ages, when no more wool could fit around it, cutting through it all with her big old-fashioned scissors with black handles. She disappeared and came out of her front door in fluffy slippers.

"Yasmin?" she said, leaning out and squinting at me. "Is that you, Yasmin?"

I could've waved back and said, *Yes, it's me, Mrs. Manners.* Maybe if I had, she'd have asked me in and made me a sandwich and a hot chocolate and I'd have told her everything. It would've been easy to tell her, to sit quietly in her front room, and I think she'd have listened without interrupting right to the end. But I didn't. I didn't say anything. I just turned and walked away.

"Hi," Mum said, coming into the kitchen a few days later, like she hadn't been practically ignoring me ever since Gary'd been released. I knew already this wasn't just her being nice to make friends again, because her voice was light and high, like it is when she wants to tell me something but doesn't want me getting upset about it (i.e., making things difficult). Like when she told me that we were going to move in with Gary.

I carried on eating my Crunchy Nut Clusters.

She put the kettle on, then opened the dishwasher and started taking stuff out, putting it away in cupboards.

"Want a tea?" she said.

"No."

Then she looked out the window and took a deep breath in through her nose and sighed like she was out enjoying the wilds of the countryside somewhere. "God, it's good that's all over with."

I tipped my spoon and watched the milk dribble off it back into the bowl. "It's not *over with*," I said. "Alice is still missing."

"Oh, I know, love, but after all we've been through."

"What?" I said flatly.

"Oh, come on," she said. "You know what I mean." She took a mug out of the dishwasher and put a tea bag in it. "It's just got me thinking, you know, about the future. Now that we've got one again."

I didn't say anything.

"I was thinking about how you said you wanted to do nursing," she said. "You still want to do that, Yaz? After your GCSEs?"

What do you care? I thought, but I didn't say it. I kept eating.

She poured hot water into her tea and stirred it. She said,

"Only I saw the NHS has got a new work experience scheme. It's in Saint Albans, but you can live in while you're doing it. I thought you'd like that." She glanced at me. Then, pretending that it wasn't blindingly obvious what she was doing, she went on. "You know, spread your wings a bit, have a bit more independence." She raised her eyebrows at me when I looked up, like, *Exciting, hey?* "What do you think?" she said.

I didn't say anything. I didn't even shrug, even though I'd rather live *any*where than there with them. But I wasn't going to make it that easy for her to get rid of me—to turf me out of her brilliant new life with Gary—so I dropped my spoon in the bowl and went back upstairs.

She didn't follow me because she felt guilty. At least I hoped she did. I hoped she felt guilty as hell.

When Gary got back from a job, I went down again. I pushed past them both in the kitchen doorway, saying, "'Scuse me," and went out into the back garden and started picking all the daffodils in the flowerbed, tramping on Gary's plants to reach the ones at the back by the fence. I knew they were both watching, and I knew they wouldn't have the guts to stop me because they'd figure the flowers were for Dad and feel too bad about how horrid they'd been.

There were more people at the graveyard than the last time. I thought it was probably because it was Easter weekend, which, because of Jesus on the Cross, made everyone think about death and how their loved ones weren't with them anymore. I said hello to Annie Stott. I put a daffodil on the graves on each side of her because I thought Sidney Atkins and Rosalind Jones were probably pretty pissed about the amount of flowers Annie always got. I thought they probably wished she was still alive so they could climb out of their coffins and throttle her themselves.

I put the rest of the flowers in the rusty vase on Dad's grave, even though there wasn't any water in it. Half of them fell over because the vase wasn't tall enough. I told him how his roses were still there and how I was going to bring him one but that Mrs. Manners had seen me so I couldn't, but I felt stupid standing there talking to nothing. It wasn't like the time before when it felt like he was listening—maybe because there were more people around, or maybe I just wasn't in the right mood. So I stopped talking and looked at everyone instead standing by graves or walking along the paths slowly, arm in arm, and then I saw the police officer who'd been at school with DI Burke—the one who'd written everything down, DC Hill. He was wearing jeans and a check shirt and standing with his hands in his pockets looking down at a gravestone, but I still recognized him straight off. It was his hair—curly and too long for an officer. I thought the police would've had a rule about their men having long hair, like they do at school—not that some boys take any notice. George O'Malley's hair goes way past his shoulders (which is supposed to be the limit). It makes him look like a girl, but because he so obviously actually wants to *be* a girl, the teachers don't say anything. I thought maybe DC Hill wanted to be a girl, too, so the other police officers kept quiet. Or maybe the police don't have a rule about long hair. Maybe that's just the army. I left then. I didn't have anywhere to go, but I didn't feel like staying. If it'd been any other day,

I'd have hung about till DC Hill left so I could go and see which grave he was looking at, but I couldn't be bothered. I thought, who cares whose grave he's looking at? Not me. I didn't care about anything anymore.

I wandered off toward town, pretending everything was fine and normal, my mind saying stupid things to try to keep it busy—things like, "Oh, look at that bird there hovering over the field," or "I wonder if it's going to rain"—but all the time all I was really thinking about was that laugh you'd done, as if you didn't think we'd had a nice day and you didn't like my lunch, and I thought, you *did* like my lunch. You ate it all. You even went "Mmm." I kept seeing your face when you grabbed me, too—your black eyes and the vein in your temple and the gap in your clenched teeth.

I didn't feel too good. I couldn't breathe properly, but it wasn't like asthma. I wasn't wheezing. It was more like I couldn't get enough air into my lungs, even though I kept breathing in as much as I could. I made myself carry on, though. I puffed on my inhaler and kept walking and then eventually, after ages, I stopped thinking about how I couldn't breathe normally and how angry you'd been, and started thinking instead about how it must've felt for you, finding out that I knew what you'd done. Awful, probably—and frightening. Because even though I hadn't said anything to your neighbor, you'd have thought that I was going to go and tell someone, wouldn't you? Because you didn't know anything about how the police had been questioning me or how I'd protected you. I thought about the eyes on Alice's Manga girl—about how they'd looked angry for so long and then how suddenly they'd looked scared—and I thought maybe it was the same with you, that maybe it was fear more than anger that'd made you grip my wrist so tight like that.

Then I realized something—that even though when you'd grabbed me you would've thought I was going to tell on you, you wouldn't still think that now, would you? Because if I had—if I'd told anyone at all—you'd have been arrested. And realizing that, I started to feel better. I could breathe more easily. Because whatever you'd thought when you grabbed me didn't matter anymore. It was what you thought *now* that mattered—and you'd definitely know by now that your secret was safe—that, against all the odds, you had a friend. A friend who knew the *real* you and *still* loved you! And that would change everything for you, wouldn't it? Everything! I thought you were probably, at that moment, wishing I'd come back so you could tell me how you'd really liked me all along, but how you hadn't been able to tell me because of what you'd done. I thought you're probably waiting for me.

I stopped walking then, because suddenly my heart started beating too fast, and as I stood there on the High Street, catching my breath and looking at all the Easter eggs stacked in the window of Poundland, I suddenly knew what I was going to do.

I love Easter eggs—the colorful boxes and shiny foils and the feeling you get when you unwrap them and see the egg there for the first time, smooth and perfect and just waiting to be smashed into great long shards of melting deliciousness. And even though I thought this would be the first year I wouldn't get one (because Mum and Gary wouldn't get me one, would they? They were so thrilled to be together again, they probably wouldn't even notice it was Easter), it didn't matter—because it'd be the first year I'd get *you* one.

I chewed my cheek, looking at them all and wondering which one you'd like most and thinking I'd better choose quick the way people kept swiping them off the shelves. Then I saw a bin at the end of the aisle—one of those big metal mesh ones—and I went over and fished out one of the sacks of eggs that were in there to have a look. They were Cadbury's Turkish Delight eggs! Mini ones, wrapped in gold foil with Turkish Delight–colored splashes on them. I'd never seen Turkish Delight eggs before. I didn't even know they made them. It was like magic—a massive, flashing neon sign that everything was going to be okay—and I knew my idea to go back to you was a good one.

The next day I got up early, had a shower, put on my peach sweater and jeans, put China Bea in my pocket, got the Poundland bag with the Turkish Delight mini eggs in, and went out before Mum and Gary were up. Because it was still pretty early, I decided to walk a different way to your house, along Rectory Road where Alice disappeared. I thought that, seeing as it was Easter Sunday, I'd look at all the flowers people had put there because I'd seen them only on TV.

The police were there—four of them—standing spread out along the middle of the road. They were wearing those bright yellow see-in-the-dark vests, even though it wasn't dark, stopping cars and bending down to talk to the drivers through their windows. One of them saw me, but I don't know if he knew who I was. Maybe he did, but it's hard to tell because people stare at me anyway. There were signs out on the road, too. They said:

WE ARE APPEALING FOR WITNESSES.
CAN YOU HELP US?

ABDUCTION

ON SUNDAY, APRIL 2
AT APPROXIMATELY 6:45 P.M.
A 15-YEAR-OLD SCHOOLGIRL WAS
ABDUCTED ON RECTORY ROAD

DID YOU SEE OR HEAR ANYTHING?
PLEASE CALL US WITH ANY INFORMATION

There was a phone number at the bottom in red. I realized then that it was two weeks since Alice had disappeared. It didn't feel like two weeks. It felt much longer—as if she'd been gone for months and months, like maybe she'd never really been here at all and had only ever existed in my head.

There were so many flowers, it was crazy—hundreds and hundreds of bunches, all in their plastic or paper wrappers, some of them new, some all wilted and brown. And there were cuddly toys and candles and cards, too. I read some of them. I didn't touch any of it, though. I didn't want to. Then I looked around, thinking how this was the last bit of world she would've seen—at least, the last bit before she'd have been too frightened to look properly. It wasn't a very nice last place to see—just an empty football field, a wire fence and a road.

That policeman was still looking at me. I thought about making my eyes all starey back at him, but then I thought I'd better not. I thought there's probably some law about making starey eyes at policemen, even if they were staring at you first, and I definitely didn't want to get arrested, so I just walked on without looking back till I got to the footpath that leads to your estate.

You weren't in, and you couldn't have been pretending to be out because Bea doesn't do pretending and would've been barking her head off.

I put the Poundland bag on the step, opened the mail slot and looked in at the hall. It was so empty, so still. I couldn't even hear the cuckoo clock. I thought maybe you'd taken it down to paint the wall, and stepped into the nettles by the stone Scottie dog in your flowerbed to look through the window. I had to cup my hands to block out the light so I could see in.

The front room looked exactly like it had when you'd told me to leave, the clock still on the wall, the ladder in the same place in the far corner, half the china dogs on the hearth, and the walls—no more painted than when I'd been in there telling you you couldn't sell the house. And then suddenly I knew why you weren't there.

You weren't there, because you'd gone—because you weren't coming back.

"Are you all right there?"

I turned around. An old man was standing on the pavement with one of those tartan shopping bags on wheels meant for women. He was smiling at me and nodding at the house. "Locked out, are you?"

I couldn't speak. I couldn't breathe. I could only stand and stare at him.

"Oh, right you are," he said after a few seconds, backing off, wagging his finger to show me he understood it was none of his business, that he hadn't meant to pry.

I suppose, any other time I'd have said something or at least smiled at him, but I couldn't move. I could only stand and watch him walking away with his trolley, thinking you've gone, and feeling like the whole world had gone.

I went down the side of the house, leaving your eggs on the doorstep. I thought it didn't really matter if someone took them now. I trailed my hand along the wall and told myself I should be happy that you'd gone, that at least the police would never find you and that even though it meant I'd never find you either, it was a good thing. Even though I'll never see you again, I thought, never cuddle Bea...

I stopped at the side door to the kitchen and looked through the frosted glass. For a second I thought I saw something move behind it, but it was only my shadow. Everything was so still. Even the leaves on the tree that grows over your garage were just hanging there, limp. I leaned my forehead on the cold glass of the door and listened to a bird singing, a motorbike revving its engine somewhere and driving off.

The garden looked the same as it had the last time I'd stood on the patio—overgrown grass, trees and bushes at the bottom, dog poo and roll-up butts everywhere. It didn't feel the same, though. It felt abandoned, empty and forgotten. I didn't look in through the kitchen window on purpose. I wanted to keep it how it was in my mind, with you standing at the counter and pouring Coke from a can into two glasses. I don't know why, but I knew if I saw the kitchen without you in it, I'd start crying. And what was the point in crying?

I picked one of the daisies hidden in the grass and wandered down the flattened grass path, pulling its petals off one by one and rolling them under my fingernails till they turned into a sticky mush. I remembered the cat and whistled for it in case it was somewhere nearby. If it was, it didn't come.

I looked down at the pile of blackened wood and ash and kicked at it, moving a charred branch with the end of my sneaker. It looked like some material had been burned there— a brown rug—maybe something that'd belonged to your mum that you'd cleared out. I stepped forward into the ashes and pulled up the lid of the barbecue. It opened like a bread bin, the front half of the lid going up and over inside the back.

There was another pile of black, burnt stuff inside—paper mostly, in a big wad like it was from a book, the cover all twisted and black like tar that'd melted then gone hard again. I touched it to see if it was warm, even though it was obvious it wasn't, then picked out a bit of the charred paper. It felt nice—sort of silky—and I stood, rubbing it gently in my fingertips till it disintegrated into a gray dust.

I looked across the fences on each side of the garden and called for the cat again. I thought, I bet it can hear me. I thought, if I keep calling, eventually it'll have to come, even if it doesn't want to, just to shut me up. I picked up a twig and poked around in the barbecue—poked at the hard cover. Then I saw a scrap of white paper, caught in the back corner behind the lid. It was only small, a few centimeters across, and it came free easily.

I turned it over.

It was one of the flowers from Alice's sketchbook—one of the flowers she'd drawn in the corners to show the page numbers. The petals were burned on one side, but otherwise it was undamaged. It was page sixty-four, the number in its center drawn in the same fine, flowing lines as the heart I'd kept in Alice's Box.

I think I stood there in your garden for a long time, the trees and sky swimming slowly around me. Then I went back along your driveway to the front of the house and sat on your doorstep. The eggs were still there, but I didn't eat them. I just picked at some moss and then, after a while, because I didn't seem to be thinking about anything, I wondered what I thought about finding Alice's sketchbook. I supposed it wasn't exactly a shock, even though everything looked strange now—the grass too green, the clouds too low—and when I held out my hands, they shook like crazy. I mean, I knew you'd done it, didn't I? From the second I saw you, I thought. I always knew.

I thought maybe I should go back to Gary's, go somewhere, but there was nowhere else to go. Nowhere else I'd rather be. It made me think of Spock, his hand sliding down the glass in the scene where he dies, telling Captain Kirk, "I have been, and always shall be, your friend," and I thought, even if you've gone, I'm still happiest here. I thought I'd just stay on your step and eventually—even if it took days—someone would call the police. It wouldn't matter if they worked out then that it was you who had killed Alice, because you'd be far away, living under some different name, going on morning runs along a beach with Bea, the sun rising over the sea. I don't know why I thought you'd be doing that, because I've never seen you run and you're always smoking. I suppose because that's what it'd be like if it was a film. Anyway, whatever you were doing, you'd be far away, safe. And I wouldn't care about going to prison for perverting the course of justice, because at least then I'd belong somewhere, and the other people in prison couldn't hurt me like Mum and Gary had.

I looked at Alice's burnt flower and thought about how lovely she was, how she'd looked when she laughed in that light, happy way of hers and how, when she was writing in class, her hair always slipped forward and fell around her book. I couldn't help smiling, remembering her, and then an incredible thought popped into my head right out of nowhere—a thought that should've popped into my head before, but hadn't. It was about the moment I'd said I was trying to protect her from a man. I thought if Beth and Sophie and Katy heard me say it, Alice must've heard me say it, too! I thought, she'd have thought about me saying that when you took her, wouldn't she? It would've been the first thing she thought. It might even have been the last. She'd have known I was never stalking her. She'd have known I really *was* trying to protect her, just like I said...

And then suddenly the sun came out, bathing me in orange warmth, and I looked up, closing my eyes against the brightness so that when I opened them again I couldn't tell if it was really you and Bea standing on the pavement across the road, or if it was in my head, like a mirage.

I blinked and looked again, shielding my eyes. You were still there—not walking but standing and looking at me. And Bea was barking.

I couldn't help crying then—crying and laughing because you were there, you hadn't gone—and I stood up, using your door to steady me because my legs were wobbly and my bum was numb from your step. You were crossing over to me, Bea straining on her lead. I saw you glance at the bag with the Easter Eggs in it, then bend down to unclip Bea's lead.

She rushed forward, jumping up on me, nearly knocking me over she was so pleased to see me. I stroked her head and rubbed her sides and said, "Hello, little Bea," and then tears were blurring everything again so I didn't see you walk past me. You unlocked the door and stepped inside.

I turned to face you. I said, "I thought you'd gone." You were looking down at the key in your hand, turning it over and over. Then you looked at me. "You're not selling the house?" I said. I couldn't breathe.

I daren't breathe. Because even though you weren't saying anything, the way you were standing there, looking at your key, looking at me—you were sharing your secret with me—sharing Alice. Not outright. Not openly. You weren't saying, *I killed Alice*, but that's what you were telling me, what your eyes were saying. I'd never imagined this moment, never prepared for it, but it was so beautiful I can't even explain. Before, it was like I knew that you had Alice and everyone else was looking for her. Now, though…now it was like I knew you had Alice and you knew that I knew. It was like *we* had Alice.

"No one knows," I whispered, wiping the tears off my cheeks, and I smiled at you.

You looked down at the key in your hands again, then your eyes flicked up to mine—dark and wonderful—and I felt sick and dizzy. It was like the strands of our auras were reaching out to each other, pulling and twisting and intertwining, locking us together.

"Are you coming in?" you said.

The kitchen was still pretty clean, but there were dirty dishes and pans piled up next to the sink and breadcrumbs and orange stains like tomato soup on the countertop.

You opened the cupboard Bea's food used to be in. There was a new bag of pasta in there and a four-pack of tinned tomatoes. Then you closed it and opened the one I'd moved her food to and took out a tin, smiling because you'd got it wrong, I think—because you still hadn't got used to how I'd rearranged things. You didn't look at me, though.

I felt embarrassed, as well. It was like the first time we'd met, except now my stomach was fluttering about and I kept wanting to laugh. I pulled on my bottom lip with my teeth and watched you open Bea's food and bend to fork some into her bowl. Then you stood up. "Tea?" you said, going to the kettle and picking it up.

"I could make us dinner," I said, chewing my cheek because I knew it was a bit forward suggesting dinner when it wasn't my house. "If you're hungry." I held up the bag with the Easter eggs in it. "We've got dessert."

You put the kettle back on its stand and took the bag, stepping away again once you'd got it and peeking inside. "Turkish Delight," you said, smiling because you remembered that it's our favorite chocolate, but you still didn't look at me.

I said, "They had them in Poundland."

You nodded and put the bag on the table. There was an awkward silence then while you stared at the bag, smoothing your hair down at the back. Then you said, "We could eat."

You went over and got the pasta out of the cupboard—Napolina Penne—then opened another cupboard and got a jar of tomato-with-a-hint-of-chili sauce.

"Have you got any cheese?" I said.

"I have cheese," you said, making eye contact with me for the first time since we'd gone into the house, but only for a second. You opened the fridge door and took out a pack of cheddar, put it on the counter, picked up the pasta again and turned it around, looking for the cooking instructions.

"We need to boil it," I said, wishing I could just take it from you and tell you I knew exactly what to do. I mean, I knew it had to be boiled, but I didn't know how long for. I filled the kettle at the sink and turned it on.

"Ten to twelve minutes," you said.

We were both standing by the counter. I thought, we have a lot of weird silences when the kettle's boiling, and wondered whether to say it out loud, but then you went and washed a saucepan. I thought about telling you my idea about making your kitchen black and white with a red blind and accessories, but it didn't really seem like the right moment, so I got some bowls out of the cupboard. Then I read the instructions on the pasta packet, too, except that I couldn't concentrate on any of the words. You walked around me, drying the pan with a tea towel, and put it on the stove, pressing the button till the burner was on high.

We both stood looking at the empty pan on the stove getting hot and waiting for the kettle to boil. Then I poured the water in. It splashed a bit and got you on the wrist.

"Oh, I'm sorry," I said, putting my hand out, but you pulled your sweater over it and said it was nothing. The pasta bag split when you opened it and a few bits of penne fell on the floor, but I picked them up and put them in the pan. Then you added about half the packet and fiddled about with the timer on the oven while I stirred the pasta and watched it all bubble up.

I got the colander ready and took the forks and ketchup into the front room and put them on the floor. Then I pushed the sofa and chairs back to the edges and, because it was starting to get dark, got the lamp that you'd put out of the way upstairs and stood it on the floor, so it felt nice and cozy.

When I went back into the kitchen, you were getting two wineglasses out of the cupboard. I gave the pasta a stir and tried it and it was soft so I poured it into the colander in the sink, then put the pasta back in the pan. When I turned around, you were pouring Coke into the glasses from a can, carefully adding a bit more to one of the glasses so they were both the same, and you looked exactly how I'd imagined you when I'd been standing in the garden just before I found Alice's sketchbook. It was like a dream or something—a fairy tale. Like you were only here now, pouring us rum and Cokes, because I'd imagined that was where you'd be and that somehow maybe because I hadn't looked through the window my wish had come true.

You looked at me like you were wondering what I was doing, standing there with the pan in my hands, staring at you through the steam, but you didn't look annoyed. You looked lovely. I smiled at you, thinking about your chest under your sweater and your big strong hands. Then, when you looked away again, I put the pan back on the stove and stirred in some of the sauce so it'd get warm. "D'you think I should stir the cheese in?" I said.

"Sure," you said, pushing the Captain Morgan bottle to the back of the counter. "Let's do that."

I took the bowls of pasta and you carried the two rum and Cokes into the front room and we put it all down on the floor. Then you went and closed the curtains and put the TV on. You didn't sit on the velvet chair like normal, though. You walked right past it and came and sat on the sofa next to me. Then Bea came in and, after sniffing at the pasta and getting a tap on the nose from you, lay down on the floor, put her head on her paws, looked up at us both and gave a big happy sigh. It felt a bit weird in there with some of the furniture gone and the stepladder in the corner, but it was nice, too—like we were a proper couple, a family moving into a new home together, which in a way I suppose we were.

"What d'you want to watch?" you said, putting the television onto Guide with the remote.

I leaned forward and got my bowl of pasta. "Don't mind," I said, putting a cushion under it, and really I didn't, because I knew I wouldn't be able to watch anything in any case—that I'd only be able to sit there thinking I must be dreaming, that none of this could really be happening, and listening to the whisper in my head going, over and over: "You're really here. You're really here..."

The pasta was nice with the cheese all melted into the sauce. You scrolled up and down the Guide, then put it on *Top Gear*, which made everything feel even more cozy because the people on the TV kept laughing and you were laughing, too, between forkfuls. I wasn't listening. I was miles away, happy—*blissfully* happy in that way when you don't want to do or say anything, just to be there forever. I thought about Alice's flower, safe in the pocket of my jeans, and wondered if we'd ever talk about her—if I'd ever tell you how I'd really loved her. Still love her, although now I suppose it's just the memory of her.

When we'd finished and my bowl was sitting in yours on the floor, you leaned forward and handed me my drink, then you sat back again with yours and you did something that was so amazing I'd never even imagined it. You put your arm around me—not like before, when you were a bit drunk and had only done it to steer me into the front room—but properly, like a boyfriend—like a proper boyfriend. And then, when I'd had a few sips of my drink and my heart had calmed down a bit and I'd got used to the weight of your arm across my shoulders and your fingertips pulling gently at the mohair of my sweater sleeve, I said, "You know, I thought I saw her the other day, when I took Bea to the shop to get the stuff for sandwiches."

You didn't ask me who, because you knew. You had a sip of your drink, your eyes shining in the dim, orange light as they looked at the TV.

"It looked just like her," I said. "Same long fair hair, same bouncy walk." When you still didn't say anything, I said, "I followed her."

"Oh, right," you said, and your fingers pulling at the wool of my sweater, your voice so close to my ear, made me dizzy, made me want to kiss you. You said, "Which way did she go?"

★ ★ ★ ★ ★

ACKNOWLEDGMENTS

Thank you to my wonderful agent, Sue Armstrong, and to everyone at Conville & Walsh, who signed me with overwhelming enthusiasm last spring. To Canongate—most especially my editor, Louisa Joyner, who guided this story with such skill and unswerving belief—and to the brilliant Liz Stein, my US editor at MIRA/Harlequin/HarperCollins.

To Lou Kuenzler at City Lit, who was there from the first page and who gave me the strength to keep going, and to her entire class, who were so genuinely helpful and supportive.

Enormous thanks to my writing friends Jen, Jo, Alli, Emma and Steve for their honesty and encouragement, and most especially to Bioux, who was with me every step of the way, unsparingly sharing her every idea and cheerleading me to the finish line.

To Richard Henson, who generously gave up an evening and all his inside knowledge on police procedure in exchange for a coffee and a biscuit.

Thank you, too, to all my family: to James and Mackenzie, who have such faith in me; my brother, Alex; and my Mum and Dad, who have shown me that so much is possible if you just get on with it and who are always at the end of the phone, ready to help in any and every way they can.

Without each of these people, this story would not be what it is. I'm so grateful for this one extra thing in the world that we now all have in common.

ABOUT THE AUTHOR

Tasha Kavanagh lives in Hertfordshire with her family and three cats. She has an MA in Creative Writing from the University of East Anglia, has worked as an editor on feature films, including *The Talented Mr. Ripley*, *Twelve Monkeys* and *Seven Years in Tibet*, and is a windsurfing champion, having raced all over the world. She has had ten books for children published under her maiden name, Tasha Pym, and her first adult novel, *Things We Have in Common*, was shortlisted for the Costa First Novel Award and the Desmond Elliott Prize for New Fiction.

A NOTE FROM THE AUTHOR

People say books can get under your skin and shape who you are, but I had no idea to what degree this was true until I wrote *Things We Have in Common*.

Writers often talk about experiencing an existential feeling as they work, of feeling like little more than vessels for the stories they create, and particularly at the initial stages of writing *Things We Have in Common*, I had that experience, too. When I decided to try to write a novel, I didn't know what theme, character, plot or even genre might emerge. The only conscious thought I had was to try writing to a fictional "you" because that felt intimate and seemed to me to perfectly represent a reader's personal relationship with a book.

I began a sentence, "The first time I saw you, you were standing at the far end of the playing field," and felt instantly drawn to the tone of the voice. I knew it was a teenage girl speaking. I knew she was overweight and lonely and that the "you" she was addressing was a sinister older man. I also knew that what she wanted to tell me was going to be dark, secret and deeply delusional, and I wanted to keep going to find out what that was.

It's fairly obvious why I was drawn to such a dark theme, I suppose, since almost all the books I've read and loved, especially as a teenager, are dark, psychologically driven stories— *The Wasp Factory* by Ian Banks, *Don't Look Now* by Daphne du Maurier, *The Tulip Touch* by Anne Fine, *Magic* by William Golding, *This Sweet Sickness* by Patricia Highsmith—but where Yasmin, my protagonist, came from, I really had no idea. She is nothing like me, from background to life experiences, yet there she was driving the narrative of my story.

My teenage years were happy and active, but I was bullied at a young age, between the ages of seven to ten. Like anyone who has been bullied knows, it is something that stays with you. Maybe it explains why I was and still am drawn to fictional characters that are, for whatever reason, pushed to the edges of society. Rejection is a powerful emotion to handle, even if only temporary, and a fear of rejection is something I think humans all have in common. I'm fascinated by what terrible acts any of us might be driven to commit after being subjected to loneliness as a result of rejection over time.

I was more than two-thirds into my book before I remembered, out of the blue, *The Collector* by John Fowles. I had read it when I was fifteen, the same age as Yasmin. Immediately, I bought it and devoured it again and was stunned by how plainly it had influenced me, how whilst I had forgotten it for so long, my subconscious clearly had not. The story that Frederick tells us, like Yasmin's, is secret: only readers, as helpless voyeurs from another world, can hear it. And both Frederick and Yasmin, without access to love, look for what they emotionally need in fantasies of "golden" girls. In both stories, too, the protagonists are delusional. Unaware of where their actions are leading them, this blindness is perhaps the most terrifying aspect of their characters. Cast out by society, they have lost touch with it, instead creating their own, new moral compasses to fit their needs.

Exactly where Yasmin came from and why I felt I knew her so well is still a mystery to me, though. I can only explain her as surfacing from that same subconscious place as Frederick from *The Collector*. Perhaps, before she came to the surface of my mind, she had been living her life down there among the characters from all the books I've read and loved, and that it was they as much as me who created her and her story.

THINGS WE HAVE IN COMMON

TASHA KAVANAGH

Reader's Guide

PARK
ROW
BOOKS

1. The novel is written in the second-person point of view. How did this affect your reading experience? Why do you think the author chose this POV?

2. Do you think the author intends *We* in the title to include you?

3. Yasmin is a very introspective character, often imagining scenarios removed from her daily life. How does this trait shape her as a narrator? Does this make her unreliable? What external factors contribute to her fantasies?

4. Why do you think Yasmin fantasizes about Alice's disappearance? What emotional need, if any, does this fulfill for her?

5. How does Yasmin's life at school affect her life at home? How does her home life affect her behavior at school?

6. What roles does Mr. Caldwell fill in Yasmin's life? What roles does she fill in his?

7. Does this novel challenge our understanding of guilt and innocence? Who is the perpetrator? Who is the victim?

8. In what ways is this novel a search for belonging?

9. What did you think of the ending? What did you make of the very last sentence?

10. Would you befriend Yasmin?

What would you like readers to take away from the story?

I'm drawn to characters who, for whatever reasons, are outcasts of society. I'm interested in what lengths they— and any of us—might go to in order to get what they need emotionally. I never contemplated what I'd like readers to take from Things We Have in Common *when writing it, but now I hope they will empathize with Yasmin, delight in her determination to attain her goal and perhaps consider the part we all play in creating such a character.*

Do you relate to Yasmin in any way—her obsessive nature, wanting to be popular as a teenager, not quite fitting in, anything like that? Did you know anybody like her growing up?

I'm nothing like Yasmin, yet I suppose since I didn't struggle to write her, I must have more elements of her than I imagine! I think, although I love a good party, I'm a bit of a loner, hence the writing. And like Yasmin I can be obsessive—I definitely listen to songs far, far more times than a sensible person would, and for years longer, too! I'm also dogged and don't easily give up. Writing requires these traits just to keep going. And then there's food. Like many millions of teenagers, I was obsessed with food. I would not have been classed as overweight, but was always dieting and fighting a binging disorder. I never knew a Yasmin growing up—other than the girl who intrigued me as an adult in our street—but I knew an Alice at primary school. There's always an Alice, isn't there? The "perfect" one the other girls want to be like or be close to.

You have a teenage daughter. Did she influence Yasmin's character and/or her voice?

My daughter is sixteen but is nothing like Yasmin. Maybe on some level, having a daughter the same age as my protagonist gave me the confidence to write a character of that age, but Yasmin seemed to come from my subconscious, her voice and thoughts very clear to me. I've written a blog about where characters come from because this is such an interesting question for me. It feels as though Yasmin came from somewhere so deep in my subconscious that I didn't create her at all, rather that she "grew up" around all the other characters in books that have had an impact on me.

Have you always wanted to be a writer?

Yes, since I was eight. I wrote story after story then—missed most of Christmas Day one year for The Adventures of Tinkerbell (a cow in my version). I mainly wrote plays as a teenager, then got into the MA creative writing course at the University of East Anglia, where I was lucky enough to be tutored by Malcolm Bradbury and Rose Tremain. But then I went into film editing, which is similar to writing in many ways. I had a wonderful time working on features, including 12 Monkeys, Seven Years in Tibet and The Talented Mr. Ripley, but I craved solitude and wanted to be in charge of everything! And you can do that as a writer— the direction, the editing, the acting, the lighting and the rest of it, too. That's what is so utterly brilliant about writing, and all for the cost of a notebook and pencil.

Is it true that you only wrote one draft of *Things We Have in Common*?

Not really. It's true in the sense that when I wrote the last line, that was it—finished—but my method is different to many writers. Unable to fly through a draft and then go back to edit, I make much slower progress, editing as I go. I find that polishing and reworking the text en route allows me to discover more depth and meaning in each scene and gives me time to get a feel for what needs to come next. Once under the eyes of my agent and editor, there were changes of course. Mainly, I added a few scenes to allow the story to breathe. I think with my previous picture-book writing experience I'd written too economically in places.

What are you working on now?

As mentioned, I'm drawn to stories about people who are, for whatever reason, social misfits. The protagonist of my second novel is one such character. Unbearably lonely, he is caught between a paralyzing fear of his desire and a yearning to express it. When he recognizes his own suffering in another, he knows he is the only one who can help. But his carefully constructed world is tearing at the seams, he is deeply deluded and his actions threaten to destroy far more than just his sanity.